"In the rarified atmosphere of flying, Armstrong's memoir of life as a female pilot gives us a fascinating glimpse into a world where men still rule. But it's her write-from-the-gut style of story-telling and the unexpected turbulence she meets, not just in her career but in her personal life, that will captivate you. A Chick in the Cockpit is at turns riveting, informative, and break-your-heart funny."

~ **Lee Woodruff,** NY Times bestselling author of *In an Instant; Perfectly Imperfect – A Life in Progress;* Those We Love Most; contributing reporter for *CBS This Morning*

"Captain Armstrong writes like she flies, smooth and professionally. She brings to her work originality and humor, which is rare in aviation literature. Her success flying the 'heavy iron' for the airlines is a must read for any woman considering a career in aviation or facing the challenges of balancing work and home."

~ **Darcy Vernier**, 3 Distinguished Flying Crosses, ATP, CFI, CFII, BA

"Captain Armstrong's powerful message of keeping sight of ourselves and our own hopes and dreams is a winner."

~ **Dorothy C. Westby**, Captain, Boeing 727, retired

"Refreshingly smart and funny. Capt. Armstrong isn't afraid to show her humanity and humiliating moments, and demonstrates deep courage and conviction. Figuring out how to 'have it all' is an ongoing question in most women's lives."

~ **Kristen Moeller**, MS, Author of *Waiting for Jack*

"Reading her work reminds you that life is about fun, even though we have to live through some despair. Through tragedy we sometimes find meaning."

~ **David Lazaroff**, Author of *Live It Up!*

A CHICK IN THE COCKPIT

my life up in the air

ERIKA ARMSTRONG

Behler
PUBLICATIONS

USA

Behler Publications

A Chick in the Cockpit – My Life Up in the Air
A Behler Publications Book

Copyright © 2016 by Erika Armstrong
Cover design by Yvonne Parks - www.pearcreative.ca.

Some names have been changed to protect their privacy.

Library of Congress Cataloging-in-Publication Data

Armstrong, Erika, author.
  A chick in the cockpit : my life up in the air / by Erika Armstrong.
    pages cm
  ISBN 978-1-933016-14-6 (pbk.) -- ISBN 1-933016-14-0 (pbk.) 1. Armstrong, Erika. 2. Women air pilots--United States--Biography. 3. Airlines--United States. 4. Women in aeronautics--United States. I. Title.
  TL540.A677A3 2016
  629.13092--dc23
  [B]
                              2015027700

FIRST PRINTING

ISBN 13: 978-1-933016-14-6
e-book ISBN 978-1-933016-20-7

Published by Behler Publications, LLC
USA
www.behlerpublications.com

Manufactured in the United States of America

To my dad, my flight instructor, my life instructor.
"Fix bayonets"
To my little chickies, the reason for everything
To Dave, for following "Man Law"
To my Book Club Warriors...now you know the
whole story

Author's Note

I mean no harm or disrespect to anyone in this story. The only way to tell this story is to tell the story, the way it happened to me. There is enormous public value from this story, so don't judge the individuals; judge the overall story.

It's my opinion of how my life happened, and I am presenting the facts as I know it to be true. In the meantime, I have removed and changed names, dates, and settings to protect the guilty as well as the innocent. I am grateful for every person in this book and because of you; you will be helping others to find their own wings to soar. In this spirit, I honor all of our mistakes, including my own, so that others can learn.

I am a pilot and everything that definition means. I wrote this story the way I experienced it, but my story will prove I am not infallible. I apologize if I misinterpreted the facts, but I agonized in presenting them in context and as close to the truth as possible.

Table of Contents

Welcome Aboard

"Ladies and gentlemen, welcome aboard your flight with multiple destinations. As you step off the jet bridge onto my aircraft, take a quick glance into the cockpit. Yep, that's me sitting in the captain's seat and that's my first officer laughing about how he accidentally locked himself out of his hotel room. Naked. Again.

We're both a little ripe from flying for the last five days, and this is our fourth trip leg today, but you'll also notice that we're still smiling. That's because we have spent years and thousands of hours training and living an uncommon lifestyle to be up here for you. We know what we're doing, so we have time to enjoy the here and now. We hate all the bureaucracy and company politics that go with the job, but we love being in our pilot seats. That smirk you saw on all the pilot's faces as you walked through the terminal is from years of humble arrogance.

As you walk down the aisle and bang the heads of other passengers with your carry-on bags, look for an open bin to stow your bags. You'll be carrying baggage for the rest of your life, so you might as well learn how to stow it properly. Make sure it's small enough to fit and that it's secure because if it falls out when we encounter a little unexpected turbulence, others could get hurt. Turbulence is only dangerous when it's unexpected.

Locate your assigned seat and strap in. You are now our passenger. For the next few hours, you have to turn your life over to us. It's hard to trust others, but it must be done if you want to get somewhere quickly. We will hand over control of our lives many times without giving it much thought because it's what we must do as humans in a complex society. Trust and doubt, give and take are endless cycles that are part of our human experience and there are moments when you don't have a choice about being in control. During those moments, you'll just have to tighten your seatbelt and trust that others will get you through the storm.

Those flight attendants hustling up and down the aisle are part of our crew. You probably ignore their safety briefing, but as always in life, we don't realize what we don't know until there is an emergency. Those emergency exits are actually really heavy and hard to open, and I'll bet most passengers sitting in the exit row couldn't get those emergency exits open. But they won't figure that out until there is an actual emergency, and then it will be the flight attendant, whom they ignored, who will save their life.

Our route today will take you through a segment of my life up in the air, and you will see things you could never imagine. Since I have been locked in the cockpit with men for several thousands of hours over the years, I have been given a perspective few get to experience. To help you see a different perspective, I am giving you a checklist to use as we move along our route. It will take you from gate to gate and when we're done, we will have both learned a little more about what it takes to fly.

Now…just sit back, relax and enjoy the flight. It's going to be a bumpy ride."

1 Preflight Briefing

Copilot checklist:
1. Don't touch anything
2. Keep your mouth shut
3. If a copilot wishes to offer advice as to how this aircraft should be flown, be advised of the mistletoe hanging on the captain's backside

Before a flight crew begins their duties for the day, they perform a Preflight Briefing together to discuss the known variables for that day's flight. The captain will begin by briefing the flight attendants on potential events that are outside of "perfect day" parameters. Maybe there is an air marshal onboard, or it's snowing, so the aircraft will need to be de-iced, or there is a delay at their arrival airport that will hold them on the ground at the departure airport. Since pilots and flight attendants don't get paid unless the cabin doors are closed, they'll collaborate to get the flight started, even though they might have to wait at the end of the runway.

The captain will also brief the flight attendants if there is a forecast for turbulence or bad weather, and discuss any equipment that might not be working. Airplanes are allowed to be dispatched with a variety of non-essential items not working. There is a procedure for everything. They'll also choose a secret code word to indicate a hijacking and, inevitably, talk about what they'll do on the layover at the end of the day. Since crewmembers often don't know each other, the Preflight Briefing sets the stage for teamwork within a group of strangers.

The captain will then discuss with the other pilot(s) what items they have to pay closer attention. As a crew, they'll review the route, weather, rules, and equipment list to find out what isn't working and how to deal with it. If something is broken, they'll check with maintenance to see if it can be fixed or put on the inoperable list. They'll calculate performance based on weather, weight, and inoperative equipment, and as each issue is discussed, pilots have to delve deeper into their knowledge base.

This Preflight Briefing is the first step towards getting your head in the game. The complexity of the discussion pulls a pilot's attention into the cockpit and helps shut out the rest of the world. Always in the back of a pilot's mind is the acknowledgement that if they make a mistake outside the circle of safety, then a couple hundred people will have to pay for it with their lives. They know the potential for death, yet because pilots train and practice for everything, they don't allow that possibility to have reality.

Instead, pilots visualize what the takeoff is going to look like. They plan, anticipate, and calculate, but events happen that no one could ever foresee. It's in those moments of chaos when they are truly *pilots*. To have everything unexpected thrown at them and yet, because they have trained for thousands of hours, their pilot instincts remember how to fly the airplane despite the abnormalities. They pilot the situation.

In the cockpit, as in life, no matter how much you discuss variables during the Preflight Briefing, nothing ever goes as planned. Good pilots plan on that, too. We all have to plan that life won't happen like we visualized it to be. Those who survive and thrive are able to accept the changes and deal with it as it comes along. Those who panic and forget the basics bend metal and/or die. My first real lesson on variables happened when I was a very new chick in the cockpit...

My assigned captain and copilot were both senior captains, and I was the flight engineer who was too new to realize how much I needed to learn. What I did know was that the content of knowledge sitting in the brains of the men at the flight controls intimidated me into silence.

Mick, our mischievous and arrogant training captain, sat in the copilot/first officer seat while giving Captain Steve his flight line check. Mick was peppering Steve with questions about rules, regulations, and which flight attendant was dating which pilot, so I meekly and methodically went about my duties at the flight engineer's station. I prepared under the assumption that this would be one of the safest flights I could ever be on. After all, what could possibly be more invulnerable than two experienced, gray haired, opinionated guys with giant egos trying to show each other who is the better pilot?

The first leg of our journey took us from Minneapolis to Gunnison, Colorado. For this leg, we were only going to be on the ground in Gunnison for an hour, just long enough to unload and reload passengers and replenish our fuel supply. It's called a quick-turn, and most of our flights were on the ground just long enough to get ready for the next flight.

As we touched down in the moonless night, darkness had already enveloped the mountains. Gunnison is a high elevation airport, so the cabin pressure was already at its operating altitude by the time our wheels kissed the runway. Maybe we can blame the thin air that pecked away at our brain cells, making us brush up against the line that keeps death away from life. For me, whatever brain cells that were sleeping that night woke up and have not fallen asleep since.

Captain Steve had a logbook as fat as his wallet. He was a good pilot, but had very little time flying in the Rocky Mountains. Admitting this, Steve was being exceptionally cautious, since he couldn't see the terrain and had visions of towering mountains along our departure route, even though in reality, the terrain is rather benign. As we taxied to the end of the runway, Steve briefed us that he was going to practice a high performance takeoff. Nothing unusual, just setting takeoff power before releasing the brakes, and he said he'd plan a steeper climb after rotation. Steve was focused on getting us above the earth as quickly as possible, but in that focus, he forgot to plan beyond the first few moments after takeoff.

Immediately after departure on a perfectly calm, clear night, Steve began a steep turn while simultaneously calling for the first notch of flaps to be brought up. Mick had his seat in the relaxed position of a senior pilot and complied with the request with the rigidness of routine. When he realized he'd brought the flaps up a bit early, he straightened up in his seat, but not enough to think this combination of minor errors would add up to a major moment of terror. The thought of having to help Steve with this simple departure was completely out of the realm of possibility in both of their pilot minds.

On any other night, this combination of mistakes wasn't an issue, but the gremlins that reside in every airplane snickered and momentarily interrupted the airflow into the center engine. The winds were calm and because we were in a tight turn, there wasn't enough airflow into the center engine, so the result was a quick compressor stall—similar to a car backfiring. It sounds gloriously loud and it's not usually a big deal, but if you are a passenger sitting in the back then, yes, you think you are going to die.

Since the engine thought it failed (it did, but only for a moment), it sent a signal to the cockpit to announce its irrefutable conclusion, "Engine Failure." In this case, the engine didn't fail, but it was interrupted, and since it doesn't know the difference and has a limited vocabulary, it can only sadly admit that it failed at something. Because the engine thinks it failed, it tells the rest of airplane to save itself, so the packs automatically trip off, which stops providing air to pressurize the cabin. The airplane then tries to use that air to keep power to the engines, while the passengers start hyperventilating because they hear and feel that something isn't right.

In less than ten seconds, our flight went from serene to requiring a change of underwear. The flight deck was lit up with emergency lights and everyone could hear the pressurized cabin was doing just the opposite — it was losing cabin pressure. Since we were already at a high elevation and the cabin wasn't pressurizing, an alarm began its deafening wail, and I knew that the oxygen masks would automatically drop if I couldn't get the cabin pressurized in the next few moments.

Just a few heartbeats later, since neither pilot was watching our airspeed, the required airflow under our wings slowed to the point where the difference between being an airplane and a rock is just a few knots. To prevent the aircraft from entering an actual stall, the manufacturer thoughtfully installed a "stick shaker." It literally shakes the yoke (steering wheel) to wake up the idiot pilot to the low airspeed, and all pilots are trained to slam the throttles forward or "balls to the wall" if we ever get a stick shaker.

Even though I was the newbie, I knew what was happening because the flight engineer gets to watch the show. It's easy to sit and judge as a flight engineer. This whole comedy show only took twenty seconds from beginning to panic. I was frantically trying to silence the alarms, reset the packs, and get the pressurization under control, but both captains were looking back at me pleading, "Which engine failed? What the fuck just happened?!" I kept telling them that the engine didn't fail, we still have three good engines, and that if they would just fly the airplane, I'd get everything back to the point where we could run the checklist. To which they both pointed at the big light in front of them that said "Engine Failure" and reiterated that an engine failed. The light said so. They were absolutely certain that I was wrong and sending us all to certain death. We had three engines on this airplane, we only needed *one* to work.

In the meantime, neither of them is flying the perfectly good airplane. One of them has his hand on the yoke, but they're both turned around looking at me and the engineer's panel because they don't believe what I'm telling them. I firmly reiterated that I had the situation under control, but they both kept their attention on me and continued to watch what I was doing, instead of flying the perfectly good airplane. They viewed the situation through their grizzled experience, so the thought that they had made a mistake was not an option.

At this point, they're flying completely off course, still low on airspeed, and still climbing with the flaps not completely retracted. I could hear departure control repeatedly asking them to read back the last instructions given to them, and neither of them was responding. Realizing that this non-emergency was now turning into a real emergency, I took a deep breath, calmly looked them in the eyes and said, "Just turn around and fly the fucking airplane, I have this handled."

Their eyebrows hit their hairlines. I could actually hear their shock as the intake of breath accelerated through their teeth. It's the last thing they expected to hear from the new, tall, quiet, awkward, blue-eyed girl flight engineer, but they turned around and flew the perfectly good airplane. Like a slap to the face, sometimes you need to treat shock with a shock.

Up until this moment, I rarely ever swore. It was one of my many faults that my flight instructors constantly shamed me for. I was just too nice, too prim, and took offense at the swearing. I said please and thank you. "Gear down, please." I was chided that this was a man's world and men swear. I used it sparingly but when I did swear, I found it was effective and empowering.

Once the pilots turned around and started flying the perfectly good airplane, I got the engineer's panel and my nerves settled down and then pulled out the emergency checklist to work on it as a crew. The flying pilot remained the flying pilot so that the copilot/check airman could turn around to work on the checklist with me. My first task was to review the situation. I took a deep breath and then spoke like a true Minnesotan run-on sentence:

"First, Captain Steve turned a bit too early while pulling the flaps up too soon, which caused a momentary interruption of airflow into the number two engine, which caused a compressor stall, which caused an auto pack trip and engine fail lights to come on, which caused the cabin pressure to raise quickly towards ten thousand feet, which made the cabin pressure alarm go off. The stick shaker was simply that we got too low in airspeed. Now, which emergency checklist would you prefer?" (Take a deep breath here) Both captains shrugged and looked at each other for backup. Mick, the check airman who was supposed to be teaching us asked, "Well, what isn't working?"

I glanced back at the engineer panels to make sure all the emergency lights were extinguished and that the cabin was pressurizing before answering. "All systems are back on-line and functioning," I quietly and respectfully replied for fear of retaliation to the abrupt statement a few moments ago. The irony is that the emergency didn't make me nervous; it was my bold statement to the captains that was now frazzling my nerves.

"Well, there really isn't an exact checklist for what just happened. It was completely pilot induced. Let's complete the checklist for each individual emergency to make sure we covered it. Everything is running as it should be so I think we're good to continue. We'll have the mechanics give it a once over back in Minneapolis. I'll make an announcement to the passengers about the big bang, I'm sure they all shit their pants by now."

After we finished the checklists, Mick started to turn around, but he abruptly turned back to me and with a smirk on his face said, "Hey, Erika, by the way, thanks for growing some big hairy balls back there and setting us straight. You did the right thing." Mick then gave me a big grin, went back to his duties, and neither of them ever said anything else about it.

In that moment, two things clicked in my brain: First, I felt like a real pilot. Sure, I'd been a pilot for years, had thousands of hours already, and had been in several emergency situations, but here is where it paid off. Even though I was a novice in this airplane, and I didn't even get to "fly" it, I knew what I was seeing and what to do despite never having trained for anything like it before. We had briefed for a normal departure and everything fell apart, but it was something I could deal with because I used my pilot mindset to keep us flying.

Secondly, I realized I was forceful and spoke my mind for once and the result was okay. I saw the situation would become worse if I stuck to my usual habit of explaining myself and my actions, so I took a giant leap and said what needed to be said. Just fly the fucking airplane, and then run the checklist.

Just being able to get to the emergency checklist often means survival. By the time you reach for this checklist, damage has already been done, so the point is to work on the problem together. This incident began to teach me that life and aircraft are way more complicated than what is neatly laid out on the pages of a checklist. There really wasn't a checklist that conformed to this exact emergency. The aircraft manufacturer hadn't thought about the pilot who is distracted by thinking about mountains so, by accident, he turns too quickly, climbs too quickly, and pulls up the flaps too quickly. The complicated set of emergency checklists that are put in the flight deck sometimes don't get used as intended in the real world. They are a logical starting point but in actuality, it is best to absorb everything that is going on around you and then put it all together before reacting.

Despite the emergency checklists provided for abnormalities, it's the standard checklists that you use before you begin your flight that often determine whether you live or come crashing down in a pile of mistakes.

2 Checklists and Checkpoints

1. Seatbelts – fastened
2. Parking brake – set
3. Head out of ass – check

Checklists and knowing where you are in the aviation world are vital. These "checks" are potentially the difference between life and death if you mess them up or get the items out of order. If, for example, you miss a checkpoint, the side of a mountain might clarify your position for you.

The objective of a standard checklist is to have the pilot complete the task on their own, and then use the checklist to go back and *check* to make sure the lists and points were done correctly. If the pilot screwed up, they should go back to the beginning and run the list again.

Every aircraft manufacturer also puts together emergency checklists to guide pilots through a variety of nonstandard situations. Ask any pilot and they'll tell you that actual emergencies never happen like the script of the emergency checklist. I can almost guarantee that the cockpit flight recorder listening in on any emergency checklist conversation has one of the pilots whining, "Well, shit, that's not what it says here...why is it doing that?" There are also two lines of thought on dealing with emergencies and the associated checklists.

The first philosophy is that you should memorize at least the first ten to fifteen items on any major emergency checklist. However, I found that no matter how many times you train for each emergency, you still pee your pants when those piercing

alarms and blinding warning lights make you earn your salary. I
have witnessed pilots who shed all information from their brain
at the first scream of an alarm, so memorizing a checklist is
lovely in theory, but the reality is that the memorizing
philosophy is just another accident waiting to happen.

The second line of thought, which I prefer, is to start by
simply remembering one thing: just fly the airplane. After the
non-flying pilot has silenced the bells and whistles, then you can
grab the checklist and figure out, generally, what is going on.
Look around first and take in all the information before deciding
which checklist is appropriate and be prepared that it still isn't
going to work out perfectly.

A palpable example of things not working out perfectly was
during my practice student solo cross country flights in a beat up
old Beechcraft Sport. The plan was to fly from my home airport
to two other airports, about 75 miles apart, and then head back
home. Before departure, I'd spent hours on the ground planning
the trip. I had visual ground checkpoints between the airports
that I would be looking for, along with an estimated time
between each to verify I was progressing like my flight plan
predicted.

I made it to the first airport easily. My flight time was
exactly what I had planned for, and the weather had been
perfect. On the ground, I chatted up a group of old timers who
had their lawn chairs in front of a hangar that contained an
ancient Ercoupe that had recently met its demise from a ground
loop incident, and the owner's friends were still teasing the pilot
about it.

After the usual Midwest conversation about the weather
and where I was headed, I paid for my fuel and started out on
the second leg of my trip. I'd only been on the ground for an
hour, but in that time the wind had picked up a little, but
nothing to give cause for alarm.

Once airborne, my VOR, which is what I was using as part
of my navigation, started swinging from side to side and

wouldn't lock in on a radial. No big deal, I was flying Visual Flight Rules (VFR), so I would just navigate with my sectional map.

I noticed that I should have reached my first checkpoint, but I couldn't see the little river that I'd marked as a waypoint on my map. Minnesota is covered in lakes and streams, so I found a river that kind of looked like the river I was supposed to be over, and started looking for the next checkpoint.

I tuned in the next frequency in my VOR and my ADF (navigation equipment) and watched as the needles swung around, never quite finding their bearing to the station. Meanwhile, my next checkpoint came up faster than I planned. I still assumed it had to be right, so I marked it off and checked my time. Way ahead of flight plan! I must have a tailwind that I hadn't planned on.

I couldn't find my next checkpoint, so I skipped it and planned on finding the next one. It was a town I was supposed to fly over. Who could miss a town? But as I flew over one town and then the next one that wasn't on the map, I had the beginnings of a low level fear that I wasn't where I thought I should be.

Fear turned into panic when I saw another town coming up that wasn't on the map. But then I realized I had enormous checkpoints all along my route that I had ignored — water towers! The Midwest landscape is dotted with giant water towers with the name of the town emblazoned around the top. Duh, the answers had been reaching up to me all along.

I swooped down and circled over the top of the water tower and read the name. Holy crap, I'd never even heard of it. While I flattened out my sectional map, my eyes strained to read the names of all the little towns along the route where I was supposed to be. I simultaneously rejoiced and freaked out when I realized where I was. I was about thirty miles south of my course, but now that I knew where I was, I could fix it. Talk about failing to take in all the information at hand!

That night, when I had the comfort of earth holding me up, I tried to pinpoint where my flightpath went astray. It was possible that the winds weren't exactly as forecast, and I think my compass might have been just a bit off, but the primary problem was that I was making the things I saw fit into my predefined idea of where I should be. Even though it didn't look right, I made it fit my idea.

Along everyone's flight path, no matter how much you've planned and prepared, it's important to remember to take a closer look at your checkpoints and acknowledge what you actually see, not see what you think. We have checklists we create throughout our lives, but too often, we're checking off the boxes and not taking into account the reality around us.

It wouldn't be the last time my flight path would go astray.

I started making standard checklists to keep my thoughts on a chosen path before I even started school. "When I grow up I'm going to be a mom, and I'm going to have four kids (two girls and two boys, of course), two dogs, and a cat. I'm going to live in a blue house with white shutters in the mountains, on a lake, close to the ocean..."

As I moved through life, I modified my checklists because the world started telling me what to do. Oh, I felt like I was in control because, hey, I have a checklist. But the reality is that I was changing my list to fit what was already happening. I mean, really—who has on their checklist that when they grow up they'll lose their career to a dysfunctional relationship and go through a divorce?

My childhood checklist had no mention of being a pilot. I was going to be a veterinarian. I love animals and all things innocent, so naturally I leaned towards working with animals, without realizing that vet school isn't about cuddling furry creatures; it's about dissections, biology, and chemistry. I was chubby, stuttered, had a lisp, and was intensely quiet as a child, so

I figured working with animals would be the best path through life, since they wouldn't have an opinion about my gawkiness.

My childhood checkpoints included crossings that many kids must navigate through. My parents divorced when I was nine, I grew up with a stressed-out single mom and an absent father, and I found out my sister and I were adopted, which would affect and clarify my future checklists. Finding out I was adopted didn't necessarily change my path, but it made me more observant along the way. It dawned on me that I'd been an off-course checkpoint for someone else, and that they had the choice to fly a different path by giving me up for adoption. My ability to be on earth had been debated, so I thank my birthmother for her choice. It's a harder decision than I've ever had to make, so I've tried to live like this is my second chance at life.

As an adopted child, I was intrigued with the distinguishing characteristics of human nature and what influence family, culture, society, or genetics has on the way people think. Since I have always been a wallflower, my quiet observations gave me the ability to fit in with a variety of personalities in the cockpit, even though I was completely different than most of them—and what better place to observe human nature than being locked in the cockpit with men for thousands of hours.

Since I was quiet and shy, people often assumed I would be less capable, especially in the pilot world, where egos rule. This perceived weakness became a strength, and I led quietly.

Despite the knowledge I gathered throughout all those years, I would completely miss these checkpoints in my own life and relationships because I could only see it from my perspective up above, in the air. Just like on my solo cross country flight, I kept making the checkpoints I saw fit the description on my map, even though it was wrong. I simply forgot to *see* what I saw.

Unlike most of my male cohorts who tell me stories about wanting to fly since they could walk, I never thought about being a pilot while I was growing up. The only female aviation icon I'd grown up with crashed into the Pacific Ocean, so I can't say that the idea of disappearing into the deep blue sea was an added incentive. Most girls don't aspire to be pilots, not because they can't do it, but because moving a piece of machinery through the air at a high rate of speed isn't usually high on their list of wants or desires. There aren't a lot of women pilots because not a lot of women *want* to be pilots. It's really that simple. If you're a woman and you want to be a pilot, you can be a pilot. Thank you, Gloria Steinem. You'll have to attain the pinpoint focus of a Buddhist monk, trade your soul for flight hours, experience a few furloughs, sacrifice everything and everyone around you for your career, but you can be a pilot, too.

3 Before Start Checklist

1. Preflight your life - check
2. Navigation equipment – tuned and identified
3. Cycle switches and knobs to impress passengers – check
4. Attitude – check
5. Parking Brake - set

The sequence of events in my life unwittingly set me up for an aviation career. It's like going to the grocery store for some bread and coming home with a new car...who knew? Except in my case, I accidentally completed a personal Before Start Checklist into aviation and was startled to hear an engine start when I was done. Definitely never intended, but clearly amazed that it happened.

I stumbled into the world of aviation when I was nineteen, thanks to a shitty roommate in college who skipped out on the bills, along with my money. Even though I was working two jobs, I was still coming up short, so I took a third job as a customer service representative position (okay, fancy term for working the front desk) at a small airport southwest of Minneapolis called the Flying Cloud Airport. The Fixed Base Operator (FBO) offered a variety of services to private aircraft, and since it was a reliever airport for Minneapolis containing four different flight schools and four corporate FBO's, it was a very busy airport.

My schedule was second shift at Ethan Aviation, so it worked nicely into my already busy school schedule and it was quiet enough after the "suits" went home in the evening that I could fit in some homework and study time. My shift started at

·2:00 p.m. and this was my first experience with a telephone switchboard and flying a desk.

Within the first fifteen minutes of my on-the-job-training, there was crackle and static popping through the Unicom (private radio frequencies/radio to communicate between pilot and FBO) until I could hear a voice from space: "Ethan Aviation, this is Citation November Three Zero Juliet Delta, I'm on Tango Lane and I need the Jet A truck, and I want a little Prist today. I also need a tug and my catering brought over. How soon can you be here—oh, and can you bring the hangar key?"

What language is he speaking and what in the world does he want me to tug on?! The woman training me was on the phone and gave me a look like, "Well, come on, answer the man." I had no idea where to begin because I didn't understand a thing he'd said, let alone know how to talk on the Unicom radio. After a couple weeks of training, I knew that a call like that meant the pilot needed Jet A fuel with anti-ice additive, he was parked at Tango Lane on the airport, and he needed the tug to pull his aircraft out of the hangar.

My first few weeks of training were overwhelming to the point of nausea but, unknowingly, my addiction had started. Aviation is a secret society that you ooze your way into, and it takes time to learn all the nuances of it. It has its own language, syntax, sounds, and smell. There is no quantum leap into aviation knowledge. It takes duration, but once you get it, you're hooked. Ask any bleary-eyed pilot, and they'll say they're addicted. There is no other explanation for it. It's a high that is attained by swallowing enormous amount of input and having that information travel through your blood to your brain. It releases ego grown by knowledge of a complex society that puts machines into the air and gracefully back onto the ground again. At its core, it is a gang with gang mentality, and once you're in, plan on staying awhile.

My primary job description, customer service representative, involved answering twelve incoming phone lines, taking care of the pilots and passengers, and coordinating all the services with the line crew and maintenance department. When a corporate/private pilot is nearing the airport, they often call ahead to the front desk on the Unicom radio so they can let the line personnel know they'll be there shortly and to advise the customer service rep of what type of services they require.

Ethan Aviation provided full service care, which meant I would arrange everything the rich and famous (at least in their mind) desired: rental cars, catering, ice, hotel arrangements for the flight crew and/or passengers, concert tickets, sporting event tickets, liquor, maintenance, fuel, hangar, aircraft tie down, de-ice service, ramp space, etc. I've even had hooker requests, but couldn't/wouldn't help them there. Sometimes with just twenty minutes notice, I would have all the above arranged for them. Then, the yahoo line guy who'd been sitting on his ass counting the number of runway lights would simply walk up to the newly arrived aircraft, open the door to the airplane and receive a $20 tip while I, on the other hand, would receive a tip that "maybe the line guy should park my aircraft closer to the lobby door next time..."

The flight deck Before Start Checklist is one of the longer checklists. At this point, the crew of a commercial airliner is ready to help each other start the engines. It takes a crew to properly start the engines—although you could do it by yourself if you had to.

Each pilot should have already set up their area of the cockpit, and this checklist is to verify that every switch, button, and circuit is ready for flight. It's during this checklist that I would get a feel for how the crew would work together. When it's done right, this checklist is poetry in motion. If someone interrupts this checklist (ummm, Captain, excuse me, we have a passenger who is drunk and passed out in the lavatory...), the proper procedure is to start over, at the beginning, to make sure it's completed and in the proper sequence. When it's done wrong, people die.

The checklist is read and the responding pilot looks at or touches the item in question and verbally responds to its status. I loved the crew that listened to the words and responded in the present moment, and I'd cringe when I saw and heard a pilot use rote memorization to respond to the checklist questions. If I had a copilot or engineer doing this, I would have them repeat the checklist item, and when they still didn't look at or touch the item in question, I'd say, "I'm sorry, what did you say?" Often, they'd just repeat themselves without looking at the item, so I'd ask it again. "I'm sorry, say that again?" They'd get pissed, look at the item, and then give the proper answer. Then they'd look at me and realize the smirk on my face was there for a reason. I'd repeat the process until they got the idea that I wouldn't move on unless they were actually checking the item. I often heard sentiments of "picky bitch" under their breath, but we're all here to talk about it, so I don't really care. My life meant more than the sting of a few muttered words.

Approximately 15% of all aviation accidents are attributed to improper use of a checklist. In just a two year period (1989-90), there were three major airline accidents in which the misuse of a checklist was determined by the National Transportation Safety Board (NTSB) to be one of the probable causes of the accident. Northwest forgot to set flaps/slats on takeoff in Detroit; Delta forgot to set flaps/slats on takeoff in Dallas; and US Air ran off the runway in LaGuardia and dropped into adjacent waters after a mis-set rudder trim and several other problems. Since pilots in commercial aviation don't just kill themselves if they make a mistake—they get to take a few hundred people with them—the least they can do it *perform* the checklist, not just read it.

The key element of aviation checklists, just like life, is the sequence. If you flip this switch, then this will happen. It has to be in a certain order. If/then. As you move through life, it's unavoidable to not realize all the if/then sequences, but you can only see the sequence backwards. You plan the forward sequence, but you won't see the result of the sequence until it's done. Usually, one "if" covers four or five "then." *If* I work three jobs, *then* I can pay for college, *then* I can get a better job, *then* I can buy a house, *then* I will have a mortgage, *then* I will have to work harder because I also want a horse.

Sometimes, we don't realize when an *if* sequence is going to take us on a completely different *then* path. We can only look back and realize, "Wow, if I hadn't done this, then *that* would have never happened..." It's these unintentional sequences in life that sometimes complete a Before Start Checklist.

After 5:00 p.m., most of the suits went home and the airport was lulled into serenity. It was during these hours that my addiction for aviation was inhaled. Most of the line guys I worked with were also taking flying lessons next door. As the sun dipped below the end of the runway, they'd put their feet up on the line office desk and tell flying stories for hours while we muddled through daily paperwork.

I initially thought these guys must be smarter than they acted until it finally dawned on me that they weren't. They were simply focused and passionate about flying, and once that realization set in, I experienced a warm wave of desire to try it myself. It was daunting to think about how much I needed to learn, but as I watched the line guys try to drive the tug into the lobby one night to take a picture, I said to myself, *Erika, if they can do it, so can you. Really. Look at those guys. This must not be rocket science. The airplane doesn't know who's flying it, and doesn't care, so why should you?*

I signed up for private pilot ground school and to my relief and dismay, there was a woman teaching some of the classes. Kip was a tall, dimpled blond who was excited to be instructing new students. She was a brand new ground and flight instructor, and hadn't had the crap scared out of her yet, so she was naively enthusiastic. Our class started with eight students, but by the third week, we were down to five, and we stuck with it until the end. The irony is that even though Kip would teach me how to fly, nine years later she would walk into my cockpit with me as her captain.

I started with the ground school, and when I got closer to taking the written exam, I started taking the actual flight lessons. My first aircraft was a Beechcraft Sport. A BE-19. It was a piece of junk, but all training aircraft are. That's the point. If you can fly this, you can fly anything. When it comes down to it, it is easier to fly a Boeing 727 than a little training aircraft – but don't tell anyone. To defend the pilots, it is actually the experiences dealing with the inflight emergencies, complicated airspace, weather, airline schedule, mechanical problems, crew scheduling, check rides, medical exams, drug testing, politics, the FAA, the flight attendants, and passengers that demand the high salary, and it is well earned. But pilots don't get the big bucks until they've been flying for many years.

Since airline deregulation in 1978 turned the airlines into a purely market-driven business, airlines have to run lean and mean. They have to fill every seat every time, so they are willing to take delays to get connecting passengers onboard, and overbooking seats to guarantee it. Compounded with high fuel prices, the $63 billion cumulative loss posted by carriers from the 9/11 attacks, and the cost of running the equipment leaves airlines running on a small profit margin. However, pilots are their own worst enemy because they love flying so much, they'll whore themselves out to anyone with a shiny airplane. They'll take the low pay and bad hours because they know there is a pilot standing behind them who will gladly jump in the cockpit for peanuts.

Despite the passion, the pilot pool is getting shallow, while demands for experienced pilots get deeper. Salary isn't an incentive, so airlines are relying on passion. For my first year in the airlines, I made $28,000, and was away from home 215 days, and it wasn't much better for the next four years. The public has an illusion about the salary. Only the top 10% bring in the big bucks. Passion pays the new pilots, but that only goes so far.

Flying in Minnesota required considerable patience. I was ready to solo for weeks but had to wait for the perfect day. It was either snowing, too cold, too windy, or too overcast. Finally, on a cold, high overcast morning, it was good enough to go, and I was good enough to do it.

Kip was my ground instructor as well as my flight instructor and after we did a few touch-and-go landings (which means the aircraft is landed and immediately after wheels touch the runway, the pilot adds power and takes off again), she looked me in the eye and said, "Okay, taxi over to the FBO and let me out." I thought I was mentally prepared, but the shot of acid that blasted through my stomach made me question the sanity of letting me go with just a few hours of instruction. What if, what if, what if?

My nerves were calm as I let her out at the flight school ramp until I was at the position and hold location at the end of runway 28R. That empty seat belt where Kip had been sitting looked back at me and screamed *Ha ha, you're all alone in here, little awkward fat girl with a stutter. Do you really think you can fly an airplane all by yourself? Are you really that smart?*

The voice from the control tower interrupted my meltdown and spoke calmly over the radio. Kip had called the tower and told them it was my first solo, so his instructions were godly and soothing, "N6504R, you are cleared for takeoff. Good luck! We'll all keep an eye on you."

Checklist, checklist. Okay, got it all done. Line up on the centerline, check. Check the windsock. Looks okay, a little crosswind maybe. Turn the yoke a little into the wind. Throttle forward, power set. Woo hoo! As I reached rotation speed, I held my breath and gently pulled back on the yoke and rotated off this earth, on my own. It was just me and this oil dripping machine, and I was looking down on the world. I have never wiped that grin off my face.

Three full stop taxi backs, and my first solo flight was complete. My dad, boyfriend, and all my aviation friends were waiting for me back at the flight school to cut the back off my t-shirt. Okay, weird tradition, right? The story is that back in the days without radios, the instructor would have to tug on the shirttails of the student who would sit in front of the tandem trainer. After the student was good enough to solo, the instructor wouldn't have to tug on the shirttails anymore. So cutting it off was a symbol of a successful first solo flight and my Before Start Checklist in life was complete.

4 Talk to God in the Control Tower

1. Know what you're going to say before you key the mike
2. Don't say "ummm..." or "ahhhh..." at the beginning of every sentence
3. Listen to the guidance instructions
4. Trust, but verify
5. You are still ultimately responsible for your actions

Learning to fly at a tower controlled airport adds an extra burden to student pilots. Before moving anywhere on the airfield, you have to get permission from the Tower Gods. It's important to teach student pilots that the people in the tower are just trying to give you guidance through their airspace, while at the same time you are maintaining control of your own aircraft.

It's sometimes frustrating to have to ask the Tower Gods permission for everything, but it's because they see what you can't. They have the big picture of everything around you, while you can only see out your own small windows. Something as simple as a few feet or a few words that you can't see or hear can change or take away your life. So, even though they are called air traffic "controllers," you have the final authority as to where and how you move your aircraft.

The deadliest accident in aviation history was from a simple misunderstanding of air traffic control instructions. On March 27, 1977, two Boeing 747s slammed into each other on the runway in Tenerife, Spain, killing 583 people. They died because of a few confusing words. One of the captains was certain he had clearance for takeoff and even though the copilot hinted that he was wrong, they put the throttles forward to their death.

After my first solo flight, all rational thought to my future went out the window. I decided not to return to the University of Minnesota, but rather, focus on flight training and getting my pilot's license. I justified it by telling myself that once I got that done, I'd go back to school. Ha. I never looked back. Well, I take that back. I looked back, but about twenty years later.

I kept working my three jobs, and any quiet moment I had was spent studying for my ratings. I never got less than 94% on any of my written exams (damn instrument test), and as soon as I got done with one, I'd start on the next. My pilot's license currently reads like this on the back: "Ratings - Airline Transport Pilot: Airplane Multiengine Land, B-727, CE 500. Commercial Privileges: Airplane Single Engine Land. Private Privileges: Airplane Single Engine Sea."

The sea plane rating was just to show off.

"Flight Engineer Turbojet Powered. No Limitations."

That's right. *No limitations.* This was my ticket to seeing the world and having someone else pay me to do it. Getting that list of ratings required me to work seventy to eighty hours a week for years. That kind of schedule alienated every non-aviation friend I had and, as my mom would say, put all my eggs in one basket. I was one-dimensional and boring. Surprisingly, pilots *are* boring because all they talk about is aviation. It's an immersion into a lifestyle. Everything you do and how you live is guided by it. I was at the mercy of my beeper and I never made plans. I had to live within fifteen minutes of the airport, not do drugs, haul myself out of bed at 0200 when it's -20 degrees F for air ambulance flights, and I had to have the attitude of "Yes please, may I have another?"

Despite the dedication, getting the hours in the logbook to make the leap from private pilot to being a paid pilot is an enormous hurdle, and the dropout rate at the first barrier is alarming. The pilots who manage to leap this hurdle have allowed "controllers" to guide them onto the correct flight path. It's these unintentional mentors that guide pilots through the complicated lessons and challenges in aviation. It's frustrating for the pilot because they think they know it all. But they succeed because the controllers in their lives have a better perspective on their situation and manage to get the pilot to listen to their guidance.

Within weeks of earning my private pilot rating, Clara Johansson blasted into my life, all seventy-something, gray-hair, angry, wrinkly years of her.

Clara walked through the electric sliding doors one night and strode to the front desk before I could hide the books I was studying. She had no filter for her thoughts and she forgot to say hello before demanding, "What are you studying there?" I had been studying for my private pilot written exam, so figured I wouldn't get into too much trouble since we were at an airport. I would never have thought Clara was a pilot. Hunched over with curly gray hair and wrinkles blazing between every muscle, Clara was a longtime pilot and member of the Minnesota 99s, which is part of an international organization for women in aviation. Clara was always on the lookout for women pilots, and their sightings were rare.

Clara was exuberant as we talked about flying. She shook her arthritic finger at me and told me to give her a call the minute I earned my instrument rating. Clara said she'd help me get some hours if I was willing to sacrifice some time. Emphasis on *sacrifice*. Several weeks later, I got the rating and gave her a call.

At the time, the 99s were providing volunteer flights for the Red Cross. The Red Cross would reimburse the pilot for fuel and some expense of the aircraft if, in exchange, the pilot would provide pilot services for free. I would work all day and then, especially in winter, I'd crawl into a snowmobile suit at night, get into an unheated airplane, and fly to remote locations in Minnesota.

In the glory of reverse discrimination, this program was only available for women pilots. There weren't a lot of us, so I could fly as much as my schedule would allow. The guys I worked with were pissed, which made me gloat all the more.

Clara was the most cantankerous, loud (her husband Arnie was practically deaf, and I think she just got tired of repeating herself, so she just yelled all the time to everybody), yet determined woman I'd ever met. She kept checking on me, my progress, and would literally yell at me if I hadn't flown for a week or two.

"You been flying lately, Erika?"

"Nope, the weather has been bad, and I added an extra shift at the airport."

To which Clara would reply, "Oh bullshit! Don't you give me that lame excuse. You are young and have no reason to not get your butt out there and at least do a few touch and goes. Don't let this time just slip by, get the hell out there!"

So, with Clara's voice bouncing around the back of my head, I'd called the Red Cross coordinator and told them I was available for a trip.

My task would be to pick up blood from blood drives (those Iron Range football teams would fill more bags of blood than I had room for!) and get it to the processing blood bank in St. Paul. They were going after the platelets, so we were on a strict time schedule.

It wasn't exactly first class accommodations. It would be twenty below zero outside, and the aircraft had a heater that only warmed the air one inch away from the vent, so my snowmobile suit due was my only source of warmth.

When I look back on my early years of flying and training, I can't believe I survived. It's hard to believe any of us do. In my case, I survived because of the arrogance of being twenty years old, flying when it's twenty below zero in winter or one hundred twenty degrees in July, strapped in a single engine airplane, often at night, in the most remote parts of the region. Add in bad weather, being dead-dog tired with minimal experience, loaded with enough boxes full of blood to satisfy all the mosquitoes in Minnesota, and I had a perfect mixture of sheer will and abject insanity.

With all the crazy things pilots do to earn their flight hours, it's amazing we have airline pilots. Crop dusting, flight instructing, banner towing, airborne traffic reporting, glider towing, air ambulance, cargo flying, and parachute dropping is a short list of all the ways pilots earn their hours. They're all dangerous, yet pilots don't see it as a risk. It's just a necessity and, along the way, they just try to stay out of the way of the FAA. I hate even to think about the weight and balance charts that I was supposed to abide by. Catch me if you can, Mr. FAA Man.

Speaking of which, you can spot an FAA person a mile away. He's the only guy wearing a tie and cheap sport coat, carrying a clipboard. Knowing about the walking cliché was delightfully helpful if I ever saw one walking towards my plane—which I did on several occasions. Each time I was ramp checked, I realized I knew more about what I was doing than the person checking me, which gave me confidence.

Even with confidence, modern technology, and equipment, flight training is still very dangerous, and I lost a few friends during this learning period. The most painful loss of a friend during flight training was my co-worker and friend Sal. He was already a mechanic and flight engineer on the Boeing 727 with me, and he wanted to earn his pilot's license so he could fly the heavy iron, not just flip switches at the engineer's panel. He was over the deserts of Las Vegas with his flight instructor doing some standard training maneuvers and, for reasons we'll never know for sure, accidently spun it into the ground. Sal had just married the love of his life and was in the process of moving from Las Vegas to Minnesota. He had a small zoo of animals and a whole future of aviation ahead of him.

The problem with new or young pilots is that they're optimists and they want to go flying. They justify what they think they see: *Oh, the weather isn't that bad. The crosswind isn't that strong. That thunderstorm looks like it's moving the other way.* We don't think that the worst can ever happen. We're in control and we know what we're doing. And for the most part, it's that overconfidence that pushes you through the scary days of single engine flying. Fear is blinding, so the last thing you want your body and mind to do in a bad situation is seize up with fear and shut down. You strive for just the opposite. You want to say to yourself in a moment's reflex that there isn't a doubt in your mind you're going to get through this temporary emergency. It's temporary because you either fix it or you're dead.

The experienced pilot has the same overconfidence, but it is now due to the fact that they have survived their young pilot self and actually lived through it. Bragging rights accompany all old pilots. They've earned it.

The first five hundred hours for any pilot are the hardest to earn—unless you're wealthy. Since the trend has been away from military flying, most pilots these days pay for their own training and have to find creative ways to get those hours. I was blessed that the Red Cross was paying a portion of my flight time. However, this wonderful and life changing program was about to come to a sad and sudden end.

Clara and her husband Arnie were on their way back from a Red Cross blood pick up and were entering the air traffic pattern at the Downtown St. Paul Airport. At the same time, an instructor and student were entering that exact same airspace. If you think about it, the odds of having two aircraft in exactly the same square footage of airspace at the same time is astronomically small, yet they both defied the odds at the exact same moment.

They collided in mid-air and neither aircraft, nor passengers could sustain the impact. The first responders, unaware that one aircraft was transporting large quantities of blood, could not comprehend the scene they came upon.

The family of the student went for the deep pockets and sued the Red Cross, and won, which meant the end of the program. Litigation wins again, and because of this fluke accident which ended the program, others might have died not getting the necessary blood for transfusions.

Clara's death was the first moment where I questioned my own mortality and the intense realization that I was directly responsible for whether I lived or died in an aircraft. The ebbing realization also spilled over into my reality that no matter how responsible we are as pilots, we still might die. It was a preventable accident, but all accidents are preventable in some way; it's the variables that kill us. Put the phrase "if only" in front of all the variables. *If only* they were eight feet higher or lower, *then* they would not have died, *then* they would not have shut down the program, and other women pilots would've benefited. Just eight feet! *If only* they were one minute later returning to St. Paul. The line between life and death is that small.

At the time of this mid-air collision, I had already earned five hundred single engine flight hours and was begging for right seat time in the light twin engine aircraft that were based out of Ethan Aviation. Clara had pushed me down the first path, and I was ready to take it from there. I wanted to honor her life and push on with mine. I sweet-talked the local pilots for flight time, and I had no qualms about batting an eyelash to get there. Multi-engine time is precious and hard to come by, and trust me; every pilot on the airport was working it any way they could. I might as well use my perceived weakness as my strength.

I inched my way up through the flight hours in my logbook and months passed. I begged, pouted, and strode into the charter department daily telling them I'm available for the right seat. I just wanted to run the radios and get the coffee, just give me a chance. Come on!

The chief pilot was a narrow minded, balding, borderline obese man who I wouldn't allow to fly without a copilot if I were a customer paying big bucks to charter an aircraft. He looked like he could have a heart attack at any moment. Without a doubt, he was very knowledgeable about aviation and he wielded it as his weapon to degrade everyone around him to reinforce his position, but he was not the image of a suave pilot.

After an intense flu outbreak that put half our staff on sick leave, the chief pilot lumbered up to my desk on a bleak Minnesota morning, put his sweaty palms on the edge, and leaned his bald head in my direction. His heavy coffee breath carried his voice to my soul, "Okay, get your ass out here at 3:30 in the a.m. tomorrow for a check ride. Pass it, and I'll assign you to a flight as copilot...yes, that is 3:30 in the A.M." I practically swallowed my tongue I was so happy, and 3:30 in the A.M. didn't sound too early for me. Thank God for the flu.

Every pilot remembers the first day they got paid to fly. It's the monumental day that you take your Before Start Checklist and set it aside so that you can move onto the next checklist; the Start Checklist. My first paid flight was as a copilot in a King Air 90 (twin engine turbo-prop) because I did get my ass to the airport at 3:30 a.m. and flew a check ride in the rain. The chief pilot grilled me on the FAA's Airmen Regulations, weather, flight planning, and weight, and balance. It wasn't perfect, but it was good enough to run the radios and get the captain his coffee. I had triumphed and didn't care whose ass I had to kiss along the way. I kissed ass to kick ass.

Once I was able to start logging multi-engine turbine time, doors started to slowly creak open for me. Once I'd see that crack of daylight through the proverbial door, I'd push it the rest of the way open with all my might. I was twenty-five years old, and had been at Ethan Aviation for five years. I had a good relationship with the clientele, especially in the charter department. It was at this juncture that another strong woman entered my life. She was powerful, starting a new aviation company, and I had something that she wanted. I could help complete her Start Checklist, and she could complete my checklist by giving me a pilot position. Ironically enough, she was the one controller who put up the biggest barriers to my aviation career. But while she was controlling the airspace around me to keep me on the ground, I was busy rearranging her barriers to build a new runway.

5 Cleared to Start Engines

1. Situational awareness – packed
2. Make sure area is clear – check
3. Shout CLEAR! Wait one second. Start engines
4. Stay where you are until you are cleared to taxi

Now that the Before Start Checklist is complete, we're cleared to start our engines. There is just one final task a pilot must do before hitting the starter, which mixes the volatile solution of fuel and fire. The pilot must take one last focused look outside the aircraft to verify that no one is near the propeller when it starts to turn. Gory stories abound of decapitations and lost arms because pilots are so excited to get the engine started that they forget to look up and out the window before they start the propeller turning. It's an element of situational awareness, and having it keeps everyone safe. It should begin before you walk out to your aircraft and remain on until you lay your head on the pillow when you go to bed.

Situational awareness is required of everyone in, on, and around aircraft. There are daily stories of losing situational awareness: Air India taxiing into JetBlue while JetBlue was waiting to be hooked up to a tug. Asiana getting too low on airspeed during a routine landing at San Francisco and crashing a Boeing 777 on a beautiful day. A pilot looking out the windshield and wondering what a mountain goat is doing at his flight level.

Sometimes you get so wrapped up in your routine that you forget to pay imminent attention. The sights and sounds coming in fit your routine and, even though something is out of the ordinary, you see and hear what you think you should.

A great example is the Boeing 727 captain who had his onboard auxiliary power unit (APU) fail while at the gate in Minneapolis. The external power at the gate was not functioning either, and there was no power cart available, so the captain logically figured he'd start the number one engine to provide power. He properly informed the ground crew and advised them he was starting an engine, but the captain didn't know that the caterer was still stocking the back galley from the lift in his truck, right outside the #1 engine.

The caterer, so accustomed to hearing the roar of jet engines, didn't realize that the roaring jet noise was actually coming from the aircraft he was standing on. He simply took one step out of the aircraft, onto to his catering truck lift, and got sucked into the engine. It's okay. He was quick enough to grab onto the outside of the nacelle and hold on for dear life as someone immediately notified the captain to shut it down. The caterer wasn't permanently hurt. He received frostbite from the cold air being pushed across his skin at an exponential rate and he probably needed to change his underwear. You can be certain his situational awareness would be forever changed.

The problem with my situational awareness at this point was that I had to filter it through my own internal committee, and they decided how I saw the world. All I could see was climbing into bigger, faster, and higher jets. I lost myself and became nothing but a pilot. I knew I wasn't performing the necessary weight and balance calculations to create a work/life balance, but I didn't care. Before I started the engines, I forgot to look around and contemplate my situation. I was a woman in my twenties and never bothered to wonder what life would look like in ten years. I didn't care. My situational awareness told me nothing mattered except getting in front of two jet engines.

Without looking out the window, I started my engines. I put the throttles full forward and at a certain point during the takeoff roll, I was committed to my takeoff path. About halfway through the flight, I began to wonder if I had packed my situational awareness.

~~~

Pilots sometimes learn about thunderstorms by accidentally entering them. Thunderstorms are often surrounded by benign clouds that look soft and fluffy, but in reality are hiding the true power of Mother Nature. Pilots who survive a trip through a thunderstorm will think they're better pilots because they survived. The reality is that they *are* better pilots only because they'll never do it again.

I lost my situational awareness and entered my own thunderstorm as a young pilot because I was lured in by shiny jets across the airfield from my front desk at Ethan Aviation.

Every airport with more than one FBO has what my workmates at Ethan Aviation called the Evil Empire. Their fuel prices are lower than everyone else on the field, their hangar rates are just a tad cheaper, and they have no qualms about actively pursuing other FBOs' clientele and employees. While everyone viewed this company with malevolence, I only saw their shiny jets and opportunity.

Sharon and Ranger Wellner owned the Evil Empire. Ranger was an investment banker worth millions, so as with any aviation investment, they bought the facility to lose money to offset the income. You really can't make long term sustainable income in aviation, but it's a blast while it lasts, or it's a great tax write-off on the way down.

Sharon had invited me out several times for coffee to woo me away from Ethan Aviation, provided I brought my database of clients with me. I resisted because the group mentality where I worked had predefined my thought process and clogged my filters. All my co-workers had been brainwashed to banish the thought of working on the dark side. They questioned my loyalty, but I secretly kept wondering why. The Evil Empire was thriving; they had four times the charter aircraft Ethan had, ran a twenty-four hour air ambulance service that kept those pilots busy, and the best part was that they had a shiny new Citation, and I wanted those jet engines plowing me through blue skies. Loyalty? Where was loyalty going to get me at Ethan? I'd been there six years and they would never let me transition into their flight department full time. I was a habit for them and no way would they break it. I was enthusiastic and cheap.

Finally, one day after I booked a charter in one of the jets from the Evil Empire, Sharon crooned the shocking words (equivalent to: *Luke, I am your father...*), "Erika, if you bring me your clients, I'll get you in the charter department as a pilot. You'll also have to work in the flight scheduling department, front desk, and accounting, but I'll get you more flight time than what you're flying now." My eyes rolled to the back of my head with pleasure.

I never knew that Darth Vader was a woman.

The next day I took my rolodex (yep, no Blackberry) and turned in my notice. At this point, I was cross-trained in all of Ethan Aviation's departments. On any given day, I could do payroll, avionics maintenance work orders, standard maintenance work orders, front desk customer service, and flight scheduling. I was making slightly above minimum wage and had begged for raises for years, which had always been denied. They knew I needed the experience and wanted flight time, so I had stayed all those years. When I turned in my notice, all of a sudden they realized what a bargain I was. They started negotiating to get me more flight time, but my mind was already in the right seat of that shiny jet across the field at the Evil Empire.

From the moment I walked in the door of The Evil Empire, I could see that appearance was paramount. Everything was placed with purpose to give the air of professionalism. The facility had a sterile, cavernous open lobby with modern art deco hanging from pure white walls, and the lousy acoustics made it noisy even though there were just a few people there at any given time. Sharon wanted it to look modern and stately, but her failure was that she didn't think like a pilot. Pilots want their mothers when they're traveling on the road, which means that warm, soothing, and comforting should be the atmosphere of any FBO. This was not it. But I didn't care. I watched the line guys pull those shiny jets and turbo-props out to the flight line each day, and I wanted in.

I expected that I would have to work multiple desk jobs for a few months before I stepped foot into the airplanes, but after six hair-pulling months, I was at my wit's end. My coworkers from Ethan were right. I'd been lured to the dark side, and it was all a mirage. Sharon had no intentions of letting me fly. I had asked weekly when I would get checked out in one of their King Airs, but Sharon was quick to retort that the office couldn't function with me gone flying. I kept reminding her that flight time was why I came to work for her. What a conundrum! In trying to do such a good job, I was working myself away from my true goal. I wanted to do a good job and increase her charter business, but the result was she started hiring more pilots.

When I realized she was setting up pilot interviews, I sat down with her in her office and asked if I could get on the list. She knew she had put me off long enough and had to just say it. "Erika, look, I'm sorry. I just don't think our executive clientele would be comfortable with a *woman* pilot, no matter how good you are…"

My vision began to tunnel as the reality set in. I was blinded by not realizing I was a *woman* pilot. I'd never thought about it. I was just a pilot, as good as any on the upcoming interview list, and I just wanted a chance. She lured me by that chance, but she had never intended to do anything more than lure. *A woman!* How could a woman discriminate against another woman for being a woman? All she'd wanted were my office skills and client list. I walked out of her office and felt like crying, but didn't want to act like a girl, so I called her a "bitch" in my head and grew more determined to find a way to get my butt in one of her pilot seats…despite her. My fortitude was tested as each new male pilot walked in the door for their interview. Latently, I realized that I had been cleared to start my engines, but forgot that I needed someone else to put gas in the tank.

Sharon proved she could discriminate with as much bravado as any man as I began to see a visual trend of the new pilots being hired. She hired pilots based on what they looked like, how slick they were, and if there was a tuft of gray at the ears—no more, no less. She hired the image, not the skill or ability to keep passengers alive, and it exasperated the chief pilot. I could see him hold his breath as Sharon walked handsome new pilots into his office, without bothering to do a background check, stating that she had just hired him. Her formula appeared to be that if they *looked* like a debonair pilot, they must *be* a debonair pilot. Instead of affirming that the most important element of being a pilot was the ability to fly the airplane, her filter was clogged and she believed the airplane knew the difference between a male and female pilot. I was increasingly frustrated in being able to figure out how to unclog that filter.

Part of my job was to screen pilot resumes, which came in like the daily tide. The chief pilot wanted the list whittled down by a cursory review of the resume. There were so many good pilots, so it was easy to reject a resume that had any kind of black mark. The chief pilot was trying to abide by the book and hire only the best, but his boss made it hard for him.

It didn't matter how minor the offense was on an application or resume. Even a speeding ticket ejected the application into the circular file because competition was that fierce in the pilot world—and still is today.

The first page of the pilot application asked, "Have you ever been arrested?" It didn't matter if you were completely innocent or cleared of all charges. You could be walking by a PETA convention, get arrested accidentally, and the Evil Empire would absolutely not hire you. Why would they when there were hundreds of other applicants standing in line without anything to research or investigate? This is the policy of all flight departments. Where there is a ding, there is a flaw, even if it was fixed.

The battle for pilot jobs is cutthroat and this is the same at all charter and commercial aviation departments. Why take a chance of a scandal when the next pilot has a perfectly clean slate? We've all read the headlines. Anytime there is an aircraft accident, the media looks for any reason to blame the pilot. If a potential new hire pilot has been arrested, even if cleared of all charges, it will be brought up and the company will be blamed for hiring the pilot with a character flaw—at least that's how the media will see it, and that's what I was told to look for when pilots turned in their resumes.

Against the recommendation of the chief pilot and a few senior pilots flying the line, Sharon happened to hire one of those suave pilots without bothering to do a full background check simply because he had the right look. A few months after he was hired, he flew Senator Paul Wellstone, along with seven other people, four feet into the ground. The utter irony is that he had, indeed, been arrested, and it was discovered only after the accident. Not only arrested, but had a felony record. He had served time at a federal prison camp in South Dakota for fraud, and Sharon had not bothered to check because he fit the physical parameters of her cookie cutter image of what a pilot should look like. I did not fit her image, but he did.

It's something women have been fighting against for years, and now here was a woman doing exactly what we fought men against doing. More nauseating was how that pilot became a different person in her presence. He crooned to her, complimented what a wonderful charter operation she ran, all the while running his fingers through his blond hair.

On that fateful day when the handsome, qualified pilot accidentally chose to no longer exist, he lost his situational awareness and let the airspeed get too low due to a quick build-up of ice on his wings. It accumulated fast enough to disrupt the airflow over the wings, and his airspeed got so low that he eventually stalled and spun into the October ground of northern Minnesota. Classic icing crash, and even a low time King Air captain should have been able to prevent it, but we'll never know for sure what happened.

There are conspiracy theorists who say that it must've been a bomb because the accident was just too unexplainably simple. It's agonizingly simple...freezing rain in Minnesota can build up preposterously fast. When you're on approach, you're busy, and in this case, too busy, to check the ice forming on the wings. Or maybe it is not that simple. Maybe they did see it but misjudged how much ice a King Air 100 could carry before it stalled. Pilots are supposed to let ice collect on the wings of these King Airs because the airplane has a pneumatic (air) boot system that blows up a boot along the leading edge to break up and shed the ice. But if you break if off too early, you will make a false leading edge and you won't be able to get it to break off. You have to let a sufficient amount of ice to build up and then blow the boot.

But icing isn't generic and it is not something you practice: it's something you avoid. Yes, the airplane could handle it, but maybe not by a timid pilot who had been out of the industry because he'd been cooling his heels in the slammer. Throw in the classic cliché of the copilot relying on the expertise of the captain (without realizing the captain didn't have any expertise), and you've got a lovely formula for disaster. If that wasn't enough, and to add to the equation, the captain had already flown a flight from 3:00 a.m. to 9:30 a.m. the day before and then worked a nursing shift (he was a nurse, too) from 6:00 p.m. to 10:00 p.m. He was up by 7:15 a.m. the morning of the crash. I'll let you draw your own further conclusions from here.

The moment I heard about the crash, I remembered the last day I saw Senator Wellstone. At the time, I was a captain on one of the corporate jets and Senator Wellstone was going out on a different flight. I was standing at the front counter waiting for my passengers to arrive and Senator Wellstone was waiting for the rest of his party as well. While we were both waiting, we were laughing at his fear of flying.

Senator Wellstone had walked into the lobby before his flight and realized that since he was the first to arrive, he had time to stop in the restroom and get ready for the flight. He had apparently tried to splash water on his face to calm his nerves, but managed to get the front of his shirt wet. He had crazy, curly, thinning hair and I couldn't help but smile as he walked out of the bathroom with his shirt un-tucked, his zipper down, and water dripping down his face and the front of his shirt. He was laughing at himself as he tried to straighten up his wet and disheveled clothes while I was trying to lighten the atmosphere. Every time I saw him I would give him a statistic about flying, and I always had a new one in mind, just in case I saw him.

"So, what do you know today?" he laughed when he saw me.

"Well, Senator Wellstone, at any given moment there are about six hundred thousand people in the air and they'll all arrive safely."

"Ha, they haven't all arrived yet, so how can you say that?" he asked as he forced his zipper to rip through the caught material.

"Well, I'm so sure of it, I'll bet you if you want." He stopped his personal repairs and replayed the statistic in his head. "Wait. Really? Are there really are that many people flying right now?"

"Yep. More or less." I could see him running that number through his head, and it seemed to put his flight into perspective. The final passenger joining his flight walked in the door and as he turned towards the ramp, he tilted his head and closed his eyes for a moment. "Six hundred thousand. That's a lot of people off the earth right now. Yah know what? I love my job and I love doing what I do. Even though this constant campaigning is exhausting, it's all this air travel that's killin' me! I can't stand it. I just don't like someone else controlling my fate. Six hundred thousand? Wow." He started talking to his fellow travelers and clicked into campaign mode and that's the last moment I shared with him.

Yes, indeed. Six hundred thousand, more or less.

~~~

After seven months of working the office in the Evil Empire without a flight, I was kicking myself for believing I'd get to waltz across the airfield into a pilot's seat. During those long grounding months, I'd seriously considered getting out of aviation. I had interviewed for a few other jobs, but I couldn't bear the thought of working in a cubicle without being able to at least see the airplanes I was jonesing to fly. My fervent desire to fly blinded my situational awareness. All I could see was that I wanted to fly so badly and I wanted it *now*. I couldn't stand the reality of being duped into an office job, so I thought maybe it would be better to just get out.

In the meantime, I'd been talking with Joe, the new assistant chief pilot, and he treated me as a pilot, not just a woman pilot. We traded flying stories and challenged each other on aviation rules and regulations. He saw that I was qualified, patient, and ready to go.

After I'd hinted a thousand times that I was ready to get my name on the pilot list, Joe explained that because they'd just hired a few pilots, they currently had enough pilots to cover the schedule.

"Really, is that what's holding me back?"

Joe nodded. Well hell, I could fix that by creating a need for more pilots. Meanwhile, Joe quietly worked at convincing the owner that I was just as good as any other pilot, despite my gender.

I started to hustle my former customers at Ethan Aviation, and after two weeks I was able to bring in and schedule a sudden and significant influx of business from my former employer (sorry about that)—so much so that they started running short on pilots again. Everyone in the office could see it begin to happen by looking at the scheduling board. We suddenly didn't have enough crew. Since the head honcho pilots had already put in a good word for me, strictly out of desperation, Sharon finally said I could fly. All it took was that one moment of desperation for Sharon to clean out her clogged filter and discover that I could actually fly an airplane—just like a handsome man—and just like my resume said I could. It just took a tipping point and after that first flight, my name remained on the pilot list.

After a year of being assigned the worst schedule and all night air ambulance flights, Joe, the assistant chief pilot, became the chief pilot. This kind, quiet, and dignified man became my biggest advocate. He didn't care if I was man or woman, yellow or green, he just knew I could fly and he knew how long I'd been waiting to just be given the chance.

Joe watched as I cut my hair shorter and shorter each time I flew a bigger airplane. I felt I needed to look manlier each time I took a step up the aviation ladder. After I got my type rating in the Citation (jet), Joe and I were crewed together and I relished in the lessons learned from the chief pilot. We were having lunch at a dive café in the middle of Mississippi in the middle of a five day trip and I was sporting my latest butch haircut. He kindly and without malice looked at me, tilted his head and said, "Ya know, Erika, we all know that you're a girl, so you don't have to keep cutting your hair. It's okay to be a girl *and* fly an airplane…" Those simple words punched holes in the barrier I had built. I had been working so hard on blending in with men that I forgot how fabulous it was that I was a women doing this dirty, gritty job. Why wasn't I representing the feminine as long as I was already here? I've never had manicures or spent more than a few minutes putting on makeup, but from that day on, I grew my hair long to honor being female, and I still wear it past my shoulders.

I now had fuel in my tank, guidance to get me to my destination, and I had started my engines.

6 Before Taxi Checklist

1. Brief the passengers – explain engine out procedure (If you have only one engine, never mind)
2. Position lights – on
3. Taxi clearance - request
4. Look both ways when crossing an active runway
5. Hold short at the end of the runway

Before you make another move, take a deep breath and begin the Before Taxi Checklist. You are now locked in your cockpit with the engine(s) running, and the noise around you can be deafening. If you are in a single engine propeller plane and if you don't have headsets on, you'll just have to yell if you want to talk to your passengers. Your lips might be moving, but no one can hear what you're saying. If you're with your copilot in an airliner, the engine noise is tolerable—it's when the engines don't make noise that you're in trouble.

At this threshold on our journey, we've got the engine(s) started, the navigation equipment tuned and identified, radios and frequencies are checked and set, en route charts are out, and airport information is verified. You're ready to move. Depending on which airport you are departing from, or what type of flight plan you are on, you'll probably have to call someone to get a clearance to move, so make sure you have completed the Before Taxi Checklist *before* keying the microphone and asking for your clearance to taxi to the runway.

If at an uncontrolled airport flying visually (in good weather), pilots announce "in the blind" to other aircraft in the vicinity where they are and which way they are landing or taking off. It is every pilot's responsibility to continuously announce to others their position on, in, and around the airport's airspace. Pilots must also remember to listen very carefully to the other aircraft giving their position reports, on the ground as well as their approach, into your airport's airspace.

If you are on an instrument flight plan, especially at an airport with a control tower, your every move is commanded by someone else. It's often easier to let someone else decide when and where you should move. Even though you are the final authority on keeping your aircraft safe, to delegate some responsibility to someone else shifts your attention to complying with commands rather than taking on the full responsibility of deciding what you are doing and where you are going.

Before calling for the Taxi Checklist, the captain or first officer is supposed to brief the passengers about the upcoming flight—en route information and destination weather. I had just completed my upgrade training from flight engineer to first officer and was so excited to be in the first officer seat that I had forgotten part of my new job was performing the passenger announcement. I'd heard it hundreds of times, but I hadn't given it much thought, or realized I had to do it until my training captain took a sip of coffee and said, "Okay, Erika, give the passengers their briefing and let's get this day underway."

Gulp. I hate public speaking.

I grabbed the flight plan and rapidly put a speech together in my head. I rehearsed it in my mind, and just as I was bringing the handheld microphone up to my mouth, my training captain reached over and put his hand on my shoulder. He had such a serious look on his face, I completely dropped what I was doing for fear I was about to do something wrong. He leaned towards me, looked me deeply in the eyes, and with a conspirator's voice loudly whispered, "Oh, I forgot to tell you…just make sure you don't say 'fuck' during your announcement over the PA system."

"Oh, my gosh, okay. I don't think I would have ever said that anyway, but thanks for reminding me." I innocently replied.

And with that, this farm boy captain from Minnesota threw his head back and gave such a hearty and sinister laugh that I started laughing, too, and couldn't stop. All of a sudden, I couldn't stop thinking about not saying "fuck." As soon as I put the microphone to my mouth, I started laughing. It took all my focus and concentration to not say "fuck." From that day on, anytime I needed to do a passenger announcement, or any type of public speaking for that matter, that darn training captain's face comes into my vision and I laugh inside as I remind myself to not say "fuck."

Secretly, each time I began my Before Taxi Checklist, I would have a moment of giddiness mixed with amazement that my hands were going to command a multi-million dollar aircraft across the country. I knew how to do this. I was going to insert my aircraft into this gigantic cog of an aviation system and get us there safely. I was far from perfect and far from knowing everything, but I knew I could handle whatever variety of challenges that were going to be thrown my way. My excitement paralleled my exhaustion. I was quietly putting in eighty hour work weeks at the charter company. Yep, absolutely illegal according to crew duty times, but this was the deal I'd worked with the devil. I kept the office and invoices churning out nicely and in return I flew every air ambulance and charter flight I could get my hands on.

As a consequence of building those flight hours, I was continuously fatigued and I looked like shit. I'd put on makeup, but then I looked like shit covered in makeup. Nothing can mask exhaustion. I didn't have time to pay attention to my health, my hair, or my social life. I justified it with the basic excuses, but I look back and know exactly how I earned these wrinkles. Just like handing over my every move of my aircraft over to the control tower, I had handed control of my life over to aviation, and I obeyed every request that was asked of me.

Each flight physical to renew my medical certificate announced a new, elevated level of blood pressure bordering on the upper limit of normal. I just laughed it off, told the doctor he made me nervous, and off I went with medical certificate in hand. I was only twenty-six, but I had turned into a one-dimensional person. The one dimension was incredible and yes, a Weeble-Wobble will always stand back up if you push it over, but no one wants to play with one for very long.

Now that I had been flying with the Evil Empire long enough to break away from the office chains, I was a "real" pilot living the dream, and now my obsession was earning pilot in command time (PIC). The confident, skilled pilots would let me fly and log captain time on the empty flight legs, of which there were many because the rich and famous don't fret about being efficient.

The marginal pilots, or the pilots who had egos so big they had to stand next to them, would rarely let me do much more than run the radios and perform the flight attendant duties. I had the most fun proving to those pilots that I was just as good as they were and sometimes, even better. I had to prove to them that I had value beyond reading the Before Taxi Checklist to them.

A perfect case in point happened when I flew with Geoffrey. The Evil Empire had a client who required a two pilot crew for their flight operations (even though it was a single pilot aircraft, their insurance required two pilots), so their pilot would call the Evil Empire and pay for a pilot to serve as their copilot. The client was a local large real estate company who had one full time pilot by the name of Geoffrey. He was one of those pilots who had to include their ego in the weight and balance calculations.

I was the only pilot he would request, and I was so honored that I accepted all the flights, but I absolutely dreaded flying with him. He was such a conceited, dogmatic bore that the hours went by reluctantly on our flights together. He spent most of our flight time complaining about the other pilots and how badly everything was being managed, yet never offering up a solution. He would drone on about how everyone else around him was always wrong. Of course, the other pilots thought I was sleeping with him, but I think his ego made flying with other men extremely agonistic.

Part of my job description as woman pilot was the task of being accused of sleeping with every pilot I ever flew with. It was a perpetual joke, and the only way to deal with it was to just join in. If another pilot thought I was getting more flights than the next guy, they just wrote it off to the fact that I must be sleeping with someone. Line guys said it. Front office girls said it. The owner even alluded to it. I got so used to the taunt and underlying tone, that one day as I was preparing my plane for departure, a group of pilots and line guys were talking smack about which pilot I'd be "flying" with today. I smirked and quietly whispered to the group as I walked by: "Yep, that's right, boys. It's my turn to 'fly' (yes, with air quotes) with *him* this week…" It was particularly funny because the pilot in reference was outlandishly gay. I didn't sleep with him, either. They knew it, but it was their way of dealing with a woman taking their flight hours. However, having Geoffrey constantly request my pilot services definitely stirred the rumor mill.

After a few months, and much to my thrill, they traded in their King Air for a Citation (went from a twin turbo prop to a corporate jet). At this point, I had already earned my type rating in a Citation II (typed for all CE-500 series), so my value was intensified because there were only a few of us typed in this jet.

I flew with Geoffrey off and on for over a year and hundreds of hours, and during all that time, he would *never* let me land the airplane. I'd logged hundreds of landings in corporate aircraft, but all he'd let me do was run the radio and read the checklists. He let me land during repositioning flights, but he wouldn't let me land with passengers on board. It was weird and to the point where it was unsafe because he would

just take control of the airplane away from me without any
notice. I'd be flying on approach, and then all of a sudden he'd
say, "Okay, I'll take it from here." The best part is that I would
fly a perfect approach, perfectly configured, perfect airspeed,
and at five hundred feet he would take over and land.

Finally, one afternoon we were flying into the airport at
Napa Valley with Geoffrey's boss onboard. "Erika," he said, "I
told the boss I was going to let you land the plane today, so
don't screw it up." Geez, no pressure.

I had one chance to get it not just right, but perfect. To date,
it is the best landing I've *ever* made in any aircraft. There was
literally no transition from air to earth. Those wheels kissed the
pavement like the gentlest lover. I acted all cool and nonchalant,
like I always land it like that. When we were parked at the
terminal, the boss came up, slapped Geoffrey on the back and
said, "See, I told you she could land better than you! I win the
bet!" Geoffrey was a lovely shade of crimson.

Of course, on the next landing with the aircraft empty, I
smacked it unceremoniously into the runway, but at least the
boss wasn't on board, and it gave Geoffrey a chance to reset his
ego. After that day, he let me do something other than just
perform the Before Taxi Checklist. He let me fly every other leg.

Building jet time and with even more resolve, *pilot in
command* jet time, had been my new preoccupation, and as any
pilot knows, it is the key to the next level. I was valuable now
because I had a lot of money tied up in my brain, and I was
getting inquiries about a possible switch of employers. Sharon at
the Evil Empire knew the value, too, so she made me sign a
training contract every time I went to flight training schools. She
would get a loan from the bank and make me sign the loan
papers. She'd make payments for me as long as I worked there.
If I quit, I had to pay back the loan myself. Training at Flight
Safety was expensive, so the loans were worth several thousand

dollars, which meant I'd have to pay thousands of dollars to quit. I'll let that sink in for a moment.

After six years at the Evil Empire, I did finally get an offer that was worth paying to quit. There was a company at the St. Paul Downtown Airport, Jetways, Inc., that was entering into the new idea of quarter share ownership of corporate jets. They had a hulky old Falcon 20 that needed a crew. They also had a Citation, which I was captain qualified for, so that was my foot in the door, and the Falcon 20 was my bonus. The best part: this time, I didn't have to spend time in the office.

The Falcon 20 is a French business jet built by Dassault, and a beast. The French have a different perspective on engineering designs, so this aircraft was a definite challenge to learn. It's loud, comfortable, and as maneuverable as a camel. But oh, it was gorgeous, and I was going to fly it. I bounced between logging time in the Falcon and the Citation, from seat to seat, and my logbook grew with valuable hours.

However, after a year had passed, I heeded that the time between scheduled flights was getting longer. I also began to notice that maintenance items weren't getting fixed, new business was slowing down, and the business travelers we had were checking out new flight departments. A general desperation of the owners was seeping into the office staff, and it trickled down to the flight line. They were asking the pilots to come in when they weren't flying and clean the aircraft, and do some office duties. That was fine with me, but those requests spoke volumes about the condition of the company. Competition was tough, and we were up against other flight departments with newer, more efficient aircraft that passengers preferred. The death knell of the company had been rung.

At the same time I felt my job slipping away, I had been following the local news that Northwest Airlines had launched a side arm to their company called Main Line Travel (MLT). It was a separate entity from its own aircraft and travel services, but it was quietly owned by Northwest Airlines, and the rumor was they were hiring. They had a non-union division of pilots who flew sports teams, Department of Defense contracts, vacation package flights, and any other executive charter you can think of. It was contract flying, which would be a roller coaster ride on the schedule, but they had a growing fleet of Boeing 727-200s, and every big flight department that has government contracts needs a token female. I could complete that company's Before Taxi Checklist by being their "Token Female." Since they bid for government contracts, they had to have a minimum of diversity to win them. By hiring me, they could check off the minority box to fulfill a quota. If they would let me fly a three-engine jet, I didn't care what they called me. Being the token female worked for me.

7 Taxi Into Position and Hold

1. Runway – clear
2. Instruments – green
3. Remember that runway behind you is useless
4. Hurry up and wait
5. Be ready to go immediately

At airports with an operating control tower, the instructions "Taxi into position and hold" or "line up and wait" are common. The translation is to get your aircraft lined up on the runway and be ready to go, but stay there until the tower says you are cleared for takeoff. It is often assigned because a heavy or jet aircraft just departed off the same runway you are departing from and you don't want to hit their wake turbulence. The other common possibility is that there is traffic crossing your runway or flight path ahead.

"Cleared into position and hold" was always a sublime moment for me. I relished having a few extra moments lined up at the end of the runway where I could see all the rubber skid marks from thousands of tires transitioning from flight to earth. I could see bad landing marks and wondered how many other pilots have looked down this same runway. It also put into perspective the awe of taking the metal below me and putting it gloriously into the sky.

Most people think the landing portion of the flight is the most dangerous segment of the flight, but it's actually the takeoff and departure sequence. It's when the aircraft is at its heaviest and least maneuverable that if an engine failed, the pilot would have to perform perfectly to keep the aircraft where it needs to be—in the air.

There is a moment during the roll down the runway that is the deadliest. It's the transition between being committed to the takeoff or choosing to keep the aircraft on the ground. When the non-flying pilot calls out "V1," the flying pilot takes their hand off the throttle and puts both hands on the yoke. At this point, the pilot has committed to taking off, even if an engine blows up. There isn't room on the runway to stop at this point, because you're going so fast and the momentum of all that weight would careen the aircraft off the end of the runway. However, even though you can't stop, you can't take off, either. The aircraft is still not going fast enough to get it in the air safely—especially if you lost power. The pilot has to wait until the airspeed hits a previously calculated speed, at which point the non-flying pilot calls out "rotate!" It is Pilot Purgatory in those moments, and the implications of the wrong decision between V1 and rotate are disastrous.

You'll have these moments in your life without realizing it—moments of choice where it could go either way. If you've done a good job of being prepared for an emergency, you'll reflexively make the right choice. It you're not ready, the moment between "V1" and "rotate" could be a catastrophe. You'll spend a lot of your time in purgatory, waiting for what comes next, whichever way it goes. Could be Heaven or it could be Hell. It's stressful waiting for the right moment, but remember that you've already calculated the safe takeoff speed. Wait for it. If you pull back too early on the yoke, when you're not ready to fly, you could end up a pile of mistakes at the end of the runway. Sometimes it's best to just keep it on the ground.

This happened to me when I was seven months pregnant, I was flying one of the last trips before going out on maternity leave. It was supposed to be an easy turn from Denver to Mazatlán, Mexico. I was trying to hide my pregnancy with a big blue aviator's sweater that had the epaulet holders on the shoulders, but I wasn't fooling anyone.

The flight down was uneventful. We unloaded our passengers and took on a new load of fuel and passengers. We would be departing hot and heavy for our flight back to Denver, and since I'd flown down, my copilot would be flying us back.

We waited at the end of the runway for two aircraft to land before being given the order to taxi into position and hold. Once the runway was clear, we were cleared for takeoff. My copilot smoothly brought the power up and released the brakes. As the nonflying pilot and captain, my job is to call out the airspeeds, set the power, and keep my hands on the throttles, especially after V1 is called out. Once I call out V1, the flying pilot then takes both hands and puts them on the yoke. At that point, we are committed to the takeoff, no matter what happens.

I called out "80 knots, cross checked" which verified we both had matching instruments that were functioning. In the time it took to take a breath, there was a low level vibration that I could feel in my butt. Engine indications on our instrument panel were normal, but in the instant before I was going to say V1, we all felt and heard an enormous "CABOOM!" I immediately yelled "Abort!" and put my hands over his on the throttles. My copilot didn't need me to say anything, as he'd already come back on the throttles while trying to brake and slow down an incredibly heavy and fast moving aircraft. Since a Boeing is capable of most anything, we got it stopped in plenty of time and immediately shutdown the #2 engine after verifying it was the source of the abnormality. We then told tower we had a mechanical issue and needed to taxi back to the terminal.

Turns out, we had shed a fan blade on one of the high compression turbine fans in the #2 (center) engine. The piece that broke off was only the size of a finger, but for the passengers sitting in the back of the airplane, they're lucky that engineers had invented a shroud to contain shrapnel should this unlikely scenario ever happen. It was like containing a bomb.

Since our company didn't have a bunch of airplanes just lying around, they estimated an eight-hour delay before they could get another aircraft down to rescue our passengers in Mexico. Crew scheduling decided to just get us to a hotel and start crew rest, so we could fly the rescue airplane and our passengers back to Denver.

I sweltered in my sweater, but I refused to take off the sweater until we got to the hotel because I was adamant about downplaying how pregnant I was. My crew was thrilled that we'd been put in an all-inclusive luxury resort, since it was the only vacancy nearby. We relaxed and waited for the rescue airplane, while most of our passenger were in "position and hold" at the airport.

The rescue aircraft finally arrived—later than expected—and as my crew and I came on board, the station manager pulled me aside. He mentioned that we "had a slight problem" with this aircraft. I raised an eyebrow as he told me there had been a bomb threat associated with this airplane.

Since my Spanish was limited and his English was broken, I asked again what he'd said. He verified there was a bomb threat. "A bomb threat?! Are you sure? Are you sure it was a bomb threat?" He looked me gravely in the eye and said, "Yes, a bomb threat."

I went into overdrive. "Okay, *Jesus!* Get all the aircraft groomers and my crew off this airplane now. Tell the baggage handler to stop loading bags and get the damn fuel truck far away from here. Have security pull all the passengers away from this side of the terminal and then tell me what the heck is going on! And why the hell are you letting everyone on this airplane if you've had a bomb threat?!" The station manager shrugged and said he'd never had one before and wasn't sure what to do.

I quietly walked past the passengers in the terminal and pulled a security officer aside and explained our situation. Within minutes, the Mexican security forces had shown up in their Jeeps, fully armed with automatic weapons and attitude. Of course, since Murphy's Law rules, it was Sunday night and I couldn't get hold of anyone at my company. Everyone at our company knew to not answer their phones on their time off. There were only a couple of crew schedulers at the office, and they couldn't get hold of any of our operations people, either. We didn't have an international cell phone, so I had to borrow the one and only phone that everyone in the office used. And at that, I'd had to call collect.

Once everyone was away from the aircraft except the armed security team that was going through every inch of the airplane, I went down to the station manager's office, carrying my seven months of pregnancy and the weight of being pissed off at the entire scene. I got as many people who could translate for us into the office and started trying to sort this out. I asked for a detailed sequence of how this information came to the station manager. With the help of several of us trying to translate, he explained that a passenger on another aircraft had mentioned that the rescue airplane would never make it to Mexico. Okay, well, that's different than a bomb threat! He said the passenger who'd said it just got through customs and was waiting for a hotel bus. I ran (well, waddled really fast) out to where passengers were getting on hotel buses and started trying to locate this woman who'd been identified as making the "threat." I literally stepped in front of a bus that was about to depart and got on and asked if this women was onboard. I must've been quite a sight, pissed off, pregnant, and sweating profusely in my sweater.

The woman was, indeed, onboard. I pulled her off and asked what the heck was going on. She said all she did was tell one of our passengers, who had been waiting for about fourteen hours in the airport, that she doubted they'd get out of there today. Our passenger had been sitting at the bar during this exchange and it appeared that she had been extending her vacation alcohol as long as possible. Now I was even angrier because the station manager had completely blown this thing out of proportion and the wheels were already in motion to treat this like a bomb threat.

To add insult to injury, I had to wait in the security line, again, and realized that the security line wasn't moving because our "bomb threat" had shut it down. I walked to the front of the line and explained that I was the captain on the airplane that was having an "issue" and that I had to get back in to talk to the station manager. They wondered why I was outside the front of the airport and they could simply not believe that this crazy pregnant woman was the captain (even though I had all my security and identity tags on and my four bar epaulets on my shoulders) so I had to wait for the station manager to come and get me and escort me through security.

I explained to the station manager that telling anyone that there was a "bomb threat," when there wasn't, was illegal. He just said he didn't understand. It took another three hours to get the aircraft cleared from the Mexican authorities and to finally get our "safety officer" back in Minnesota to release the aircraft back into service. All the while, our passengers had been waiting in position and hold for hours. No one had told them what was going on, and even though they'd been there for fifteen hours, they didn't want to leave for fear of missing their flight.

When I got back to Minnesota, I wrote up a report explaining, in detail, what happened and how the communication with my company completely failed us. In the days after 9/11, our company had touted our new head of security as being the best in the industry, but when we had a chance to show how our system would work, the reality was laughable. So while I'd been hoping for a "Rotate," we ended up staying on the ground.

Meanwhile, my cleared for takeoff report went sailing into the chief pilot's circular file.

8 Final Items

1. This is the last checklist you'll perform on the ground
2. You are committed to what lies ahead
3. Check the windsock
4. Look all the way down the runway and visualize your flight path
5. You are going to get very busy

Upon clearance to take the active runway, the Final Item checklist is performed. It is a reminder and verification of those important items that have to wait until you are cleared for takeoff. For the Boeing 727, one of the items on this checklist is to turn on the remaining position lights. In busy traffic areas, being visible to other aircraft is of vital importance, and the Boeing could announce itself to others with a dazzling display of lights. The secondary and more subtle purpose of the Final Items Checklist is just a polite way of the manufacturer verifying with the crew that their heads are out of their asses and to be absolutely certain that you and your crew are ready to take control of this enormous piece of metal and put it into the air.

When final items are read, it's important to use this moment as an opportunity to gather all your attention and focus on the enormous amount of input that is about to be sent to your eyes and ears. You must open your mind and be ready to receive and react to all of the input. You must listen and understand the verbal callouts, runway cues, signage, and engine/system instrumentation, to name a few. When a seasoned pilot calls for Final Items, they not only take in all this outside information, they also tune into their pilot instinct. It's a feeling, as well as a knowing, that the aircraft is performing as they have asked, and there is confidence that every item on the checklist is complete.

There is just one final item on my "chick pilot" checklist that I am consistently asked about, so I will confirm this systems check for you before we line up for takeoff. This particular malfunction has no standard emergency checklist, but it's something you have to be prepared for before, during, and after takeoff. The malfunction can go one of many ways, but no two are alike so, unfortunately, you'll have to figure it out for yourself. The indicator light says "discrimination," or sometimes, it's labeled "harassment." But unlike other indicators, it's often accompanied by silence instead of a loud alarm bell.

Since there are still very few women in aviation, I am periodically asked about discrimination and sexual harassment. The answer is yes, of course, it is on every female pilot's checklist. It happens so often that it just becomes part of life. You simply cannot come into aviation and expect instant change, so you grow some thick skin, pull out your humor, and use it as an opportunity to show everyone that a woman can handle it. It's the only way to overcome it. You take it so that the women who follow don't have to fight so hard.

My very first trip as a flight engineer with passengers (yes, all you people on Champion Air flight 601 from Minneapolis to Las Vegas, you were my guinea pigs. I got to experiment on you, and you all lived, thank you very much) was under the observation of my Initial Operating Experience training pilot. It's called your IOE flight, and there are actually three of them (if all goes well). It's a check ride, and the FAA can be there if they want to. Of course, they wanted to be there for mine. I was currently the only woman in this division so, like a sideshow freak, people wanted to peek under the curtain.

Every pilot's first few flights are observed check rides. My task was to perform my duties under the supervision of my IOE training pilot and an FAA Flight Standards District Office representative (if they choose to participate) while actually flying passengers. Yes, it's completely unnerving, but don't worry—as a passenger, it's one of the safest flights because everyone is operating by the book.

What I didn't know is that the first officer on this flight just so happened to be the biggest male chauvinist pig that I would ever cross paths with at this airline. He didn't know what misogyny meant, but he practiced it with religious fervor. Of all the flights and all the pilots, why did he have to be on my first flight? Little did he know, Karma would be coming his way.

Generally, the flight engineer is responsible for inspecting and monitoring all the systems on the aircraft. One of the first duties of a flight engineer is to perform the walk around exterior preflight inspection on the aircraft before and between each flight. This entails checking every compartment, flight control, fluid levels, and surface on the aircraft. In the winter, the APU (the auxiliary power unit is an extra engine that runs during ground operations to provide heating or cooling, and electricity) got a really long inspection because it's warm in the compartment where it is mounted.

The disadvantage is that the decibel level is literally off the charts and while you might be warm, your ears are damaged forever. I have permanent hearing loss in my left ear from inserting a molded in-ear headphone that the company required us to wear and standing a few too many minutes next to the APU when it was twenty below zero in Minnesota.

The flight engineer is supposed to arrive at the aircraft ahead of the remaining flight crew. The engineer checks the maintenance log, gets the flight deck ready, starts the APU, checks the fuel load, pre-flights the engineer panel, and then goes outside for the external check. All the logbooks for the aircraft are kept in the engineer's desk, and this is where the preflight begins.

When I opened the desk top at the engineer station, taped to the inside cover was a hardcore pornographic picture. Since I was the first woman working here, I just figured these were probably on all the desks, but not wanting the FAA man to see it, I inconspicuously removed it.

The first officer had been watching me out of the corner of his eye, and I could see his shoulders jiggling with laughter as he listened to me slowly peel the tape off the picture. I'm also one of those people who doesn't tear gift wrapping, either, so I actually did the courtesy of not destroying the picture. The copilot was now covering his mouth to hide the laughter. Hmmm, so he thinks this is funny? Whatever. Have your little laugh. I thought that one picture was the end of it.

Mr. FAA man told my IOE examiner that he would watch me perform my pre-flight inspection, so he walked down to the tarmac with us. For every inspection compartment I opened, there had been taped a picture of women and men in the act of detailed penetration. If it wasn't a couple going at it, then it was pictures of women making a fashion statement by wearing no clothes at all. I blushed a deep crimson red that stayed with me for the whole inspection as I quietly removed each picture and stuck it behind my preflight checklist. I found page after page from probably ten different magazines. Mr. FAA man had been intently watching and was close enough to realize, after the fourth peeling of paper, what I was removing. I smiled, he blushed, shrugged his shoulders, and I went about my duties. My job was literally on the line. I had to pass this check ride to start getting paid engineer's salary (a whopping $28k the first year!).

I was absolutely unnerved by the end of the pre-flight inspection. I dreaded each compartment I checked. I was trying to deal with my embarrassment and using all my energy to put on a blank face to the FAA inspector, which took away from the concentration required for the true task at hand. The stress was overwhelming enough to be flying the aircraft for the first time, and to remember the millions of details of the job, so this added humiliation was reprehensible. Beyond a practical joke, having paper floating around hot exhaust was dangerous, too, and I was afraid the FAA was going to fine our company for this prank. It would look really bad if I earned a violation for my company on my first flight.

As I plopped into the engineer's seat, I was disheartened to have spent an enormous amount of my life trying to blur the line that I was a pilot who happened to be a woman, and this one prank was ruining everything I'd vanquished. I didn't want anyone to think there was any difference between men and women pilots, but these pictures reminded me of how different we could be. I was infuriated on many levels, and the culprit was sitting inches in front of me.

The Boeing 727 has a huge cockpit (sorry, nothing pornographic meant there), and the ability to carry two extra jump seat passengers, which meant that Mr. FAA man *and* my IOE instructor would be riding in the cockpit with us.

I held my breath during my first takeoff. I was afraid to blink for fear I would miss an indication of anything going awry on my instrument panel. Since every flight in the simulator turned into an emergency, I was astonished that the first takeoff was textbook perfect.

The thrill of this virgin flight muddled my emotions, but also reminded me that I had worked my ass off to get here, and I had the right to be peeved at the pornography that ruined my confidence and first pre-flight inspection. I hadn't said a word about the prank yet, but I had been working the resolution out in my head. I just had to wait for the perfect moment. I waited until we were at cruising altitude.

The captain had the aircraft on autopilot and we were all settling in for a smooth flight. With Mr. FAA man in the cockpit with us, no one was allowed to relax to the level of standard flight crew atmosphere, but there was a shift in mood after transitioning into cruise flight. I reckoned this was a consummate moment to exact my revenge.

I quietly took a deep breath and tapped the first officer on the shoulder and as he twisted his body around to face me, I put on my heaviest Minnesotan accent and feigned innocence as I turned the prank on him.

"Oh, excuse me, Zack? Gosh, I know that you're not married, and I can't even imagine that you would have a girlfriend, so I'm quite certain you'll be wanting – no, needing! - these pictures back. Thank you so much for letting me look at them, that was so thoughtful of you. Oh, and before I forget, that last page there is wet. I'm sure you're not used to anything getting wet around you so I wanted to make sure you're careful with that last page there..." With that, I handed him back the crumpled magazine pages. I had made sure that the raunchiest picture was on the top of the pile for everyone to see. I wanted to turn this into *his* embarrassment, not mine. I tilted my head, sat up straight and gave him a huge smile as I began to turn back to my work station while holding my breath.

I listened. No one moved. Then, there was the sharp intake of breath just before Mr. FAA man exploded with laughter. With his release, the tension broke and everyone laughed so hard that they had to cover their mouths for fear of the passengers hearing this enormous roar of laughter coming from the cockpit. The copilot didn't laugh quite as hard as everyone else, but he acknowledged the touché.

I turned around and laughed with them. I was so relieved that with a simple gesture, I had called him on it and showed the rest that I could handle the "initiation" with finesse. I hoped that no one could see that my hands were shaking so badly I could hardly flip a switch and my stomach was churning so violently I thought I would puke. But it worked. The gauntlet had been thrown and I picked it up and accepted the challenge. I didn't want to whine or tattle to the FAA, captain, or IOE instructor about what was going on. They knew what was going on and they were watching me. Intently.

In the midst of formulating my revenge, It dawned on me that I *was* being treated as an equal — as a man would interpret it. This was an initiation ceremony, and I needed to handle this with my balls rather than my boobs. If I had said nothing or filed a complaint, then it would be calling attention to the fact that I can't handle this myself (Help! I'm weak, save me). Instead, I pushed everything I had into the indignant, righteous side of the brain that every woman has and told myself, *show these sons of bitches some grace under fire.*

The instant Karma that came with this situation was that Mr. FAA man decided to give the copilot a "random" line check on the last leg of our trip. You know what I'm going to say, right? Right. He failed his check ride. You might think that was a good thing, but I thought for sure the copilot would blame me for the failure. It was obvious that Mr. FAA man was trying to do me a favor, but I feared I had made an enemy on my first flight. As it turned out, I had earned enough mutual respect by accepting his challenge that we reached a point where we didn't cringe when we were paired together. Don't get me wrong, we didn't like each other, and he still remained a woman pilot hater (I didn't do much to blunt the sentiment), but we got a kick out of sparring and matching wits, and sometimes that's all you can hope for in this life; mutual respect blended in with distaste.

I realized I'd been discriminated against. I am not naïve. I realized as it was happening, and I purposely gave the appearance that I was not offended. I just kept going like nothing happened because the only way I had a chance was to ignore it and do a damn good job. I lived with the snide remarks, dirty jokes, and pompous attitudes because, in the end, I wasn't the best pilot there was — but I was just as good, and I deserved mutual respect. I didn't always get it, but knowing in my heart that I'd earned it was enough. I was doing what I loved, and my paycheck *was* the same as theirs. One good thing about a unionized industry is that the paychecks are equal—that is if management assigns you to the same amount of flying.

Most importantly, in my twenty-five years in aviation, the percentage of friendly and professional male pilots verses the asshole sexist ones is over ninety percent. Those ten percent of jerks exist no matter what industry or gender. It's easy to remember the misogynist, but the majority of male pilots I flew with were respectful, non-judgmental, and they acknowledged that I was just earning a living like they were. They got used to me being there, and I thank them for that. I set aside femininity to function in the cockpit and, in return, the gents I flew with straightened up their act for me. I know they preferred to tell dirty jokes, describe their latest sexual encounter, and fart at will, but they changed for me, so I did the same for them. Don't forget, this is the first generation of women through the wake of Gloria Steinem. Don't waste your time trying to change a misogynist; give your attention to the good guys, and they'll help you with the rest.

It's simply adhering to the Final Items checklist by making sure your head is out of your ass and to be absolutely certain that you are ready to take control of this enormous piece of thing called Life, and put it into the air.

The Final Item on the checklist is to acknowledge that men and women *are* different. Those pictures prove it. But it's not just the physical, it's the psychological differences, and neither is better or worse. Gloria Steinem had it wrong, but it was a great first step. Martin Luther King was on the right track, but now we need to simply throw away all physical differences and judge someone strictly on "...the content of our character," not our differences, or even our similarities.

That is the next revolution we should all be looking for. Women have proven themselves physically and psychologically. We need to prove that we are, indeed, different, but that we can do similar tasks in different ways and still get the same positive, or negative, result as a man.

Our mistake as feminists is thinking we should be or think more like men. There is nothing feminine about feminism, and that's where we all got it wrong. We should be acknowledging our strengths and weaknesses, not denying them. Women are more able to understand the big picture, lead holistically, and can nurture the positive out of any situation. We've also learned to use kindness while commanding and still get people to follow orders.

I can say that now, but during my years of flight training and obsessive focus on aviation, I unknowingly found myself pulling away from the world of women. I cringed when a girl in my ground school started painting her fingernails during class and the fumes got so bad we had to stop systems training to open a window. She had been failing her tests and cried when she was reprimanded for painting her fingernails. She was an embarrassment to women trying to make it in this man's world. I was ashamed of her, and somewhere along the way I forgot that this was her individual personality, which really didn't have anything to do with being a woman. She was just a bad student, but she told everyone she was being discriminated against, and I didn't want to be in a category with her. I wanted to be a different version of a woman, so I decided to distance myself from *everything* that I thought represented being feminine. I started to only hang out with the guys, which engineered the loss of my own female identity and support group of friends. I slowly started to forget just how great women are because I spent most of my time blending myself into the world of men.

My Final Item Checklist was complete the moment I removed myself from all things that I thought would make me weak. Years later, as I came crashing down into a pile of ashes, I would come to realize that what I thought was weak was actually the strongest bond on earth.

9 Cleared for Takeoff

1. Throttle(s) – push forward smoothly
2. Crosswind – check and controls corrected
3. Last chance to check your instruments
4. Yell "Yee Haw!" at rotation

The work and preparation that makes for a safe flight is done on the ground before the magic words "cleared for takeoff" are spoken by the voice of God in the control tower. Before getting into the airplane, you should have already investigated the current weather for the entire route, weight and balance, weather forecast, fuel requirements, destination airport information, icing levels, charts, notams (notice to airmen info), inoperative aircraft components, alternate destinations, etc. So when you are cleared for takeoff, the only items you are concentrating on are those few moments in the danger zone before rotation.

The indicated airspeed that you rotate at depends primarily on how heavy the aircraft is and the outside temperature. There are other factors, like contaminated runway and crosswind, but predominantly it depends on weight. The heavier the aircraft is, the faster and higher the takeoff speed. Typically, you're traveling at around 145 knots (roughly 167 miles per hour) when you pull back on the yoke of a loaded Boeing 727-200 at rotation.

I mentioned V1 (airspeed/velocity) and rotate, so this is a great juncture to mention the anomaly associated with this moment during takeoff. Despite knowing the difference and implications of those airspeed callouts, the reality is that most pilots will try to abort the takeoff if something happens after V1, but before rotation. Countless accident reports grouse that the pilot should have continued the takeoff, but he instead chose to keep the aircraft on the ground, causing the enormous moving momentum of 197,000 pounds to career off the end of the runway. It's impossible to stop that much moving mass no matter how hard you stomp on the brakes or pull on the thrust reversers. Blame instinct once again. The thought of putting something so large into the air with an unknown malfunction is intuitively unsafe, despite what the performance charts infer. It's hard to stop the momentum, and the thought of departing the surface of the earth with a piece of machinery in trouble overrides training.

Every one of us is going to do something that we know we shouldn't do. We just can't help it. Momentum moves us in a certain direction and it just seems easier to keep traveling in that general direction despite what we've heard to be true. For my own life's accident report, I'm going to blame momentum. In hindsight, I know I should have done it differently but, instead, I kept my life on the ground rather than rotate it into the sky.

On that same fateful day when I found pornography in every orifice an airplane can have, I met the person who would be the reason my life careened off the runway. The irony is that I'm ultimately glad it happened. It's true that if it wasn't for this huge malfunction, I would still be setting those contrails in the sky, but I'm not. I'm here on the ground.

Of course, it begins with, "There was this guy…"

There was this guy named Brad. The first time I saw him, I was in the flight deck looking down the long empty rows of passenger seats. I could see his blue mechanic's uniform as he stood in the middle of the passenger cabin with all the flight attendants gathered around him. I surmised he was telling dirty jokes by the way he tilted his head down and looked at his audience, anticipating their reaction. When he delivered the punch line, the flight attendants blushed and scoffed at his off-color humor, but they still laughed. They walked away chuckling to themselves, and it was nice to have an air of levity because it tends to create collaboration among the entire crew. Happy flight attendants mean happy passengers.

At the time, Brad was a new aircraft mechanic from Colorado, so he worked the night shift, and it was his responsibility to launch the morning departures. Word had spread that the new chick pilot was flying out of Minneapolis, so all the mechanics found time to come up and say hi to the chick working the engineer panel. I thought I had met all the mechanics, but fate saved the best for last.

After the flight attendants had gone back to their duties, Brad had nothing to do. He spied me sitting at the flight engineer's desk in my goofy pilot uniform and clip-on tie. I had just put the menagerie of dirty pictures back into the engineer's desk when a crooked smile spread across his face as he walked into the cockpit to give me some shit.

"*You're* the new flight engineer? Did you know you were a girl? Someone must've forgotten to tell you. Wait, do you really think you know how to do this? Gosh, there are all these funny buttons and switches, and you might break a nail..." he rambled on mischievously while looking directly into my eyes to see how I would react to the jibe.

"Oh, I think I can manage just fine. I actually do know what all these switches do, and look..." I said, holding up my hands, "no fingernails, see?" He accepted my unintended challenge, and gently took my hand into his. He laid my hand on top of his palm and used his other hand to turn it over. He touched what was left of my nervous nails and said, "See, this job *will* break all your nails!" The moment was startling and electrifying. The noise and commotion faded into the background for the moment that he held my hand, which added to the surrealism of the day.

He broke the spell by getting back to business. "So, does the airplane meet Your Majesty's approval? Is the airplane good to go?"

I told him I'd already completed the pre-flight inspection (Omitting the bit about the porn pictures), everything looked good, and we were just waiting for the fuel load.

As he walked away, I shook off the moment by telling myself he was *just another man in the mix*. He was charming and arrogant with his cliché mechanic's persona—being macho and hitting on the flight attendants. I would never date a man like that, a skirt chaser who was just out for a good time. I figured he had similar judgments about me, a nerdy girl who didn't know how to be a woman. We both judged a book by its cover, but then again, some of the most fascinating books have bland covers.

Brad and I saw each other on many of my departures out of Minneapolis, and we'd tease each other incessantly about how incompetent the other was. Mechanics and pilots are always at war. Brad and I would pass many hours before dawn, doling out jabs and pitting each other's intelligence against systems and repairs. It drove me crazy when I wrote up legitimate maintenance problems and he'd go down into the avionics bay with a rubber mallet and "re-rack" the equipment. He would literally just pull the offending item off its connection, shake it, and pound it back into place. It drove me doubly crazy that the majority of the time, it actually fixed the problem.

After three glorious months of flying out of my hometown of Minneapolis, I was rebased and sent to Detroit, and my silly banter with Brad came to a halt.

Hell does exist on earth. Airlines without a contract or union representation (we weren't union at this time) make pilots change their base *and* make them be responsible for getting to their new base *and* provide their own housing. Funny I didn't realize this before I got hired. I willingly went, and so began my introduction to commuting. We all did. We were living the dream.

In the days before 9/11, commuting was relatively easy. Pilots could ride in the cockpit jump seat of other airlines, and if there was a seat in the back with the passengers, they were welcome to sit back there, too. Post 9/11, everything…and I mean everything…changed. The glory and innocence of aviation was gone forever, thanks to a group of men with less than forty dollars in weaponry.

Due to the devastating financial losses to the airlines, they were running lean and mean, and not much has changed in the formula in the years since. Flights were now filled to the brim, which meant flight deck jump seats were full. While earning around two thousand dollars a month as a flight engineer, I couldn't afford to buy a ticket every time I went to work, so it sometimes took me two days to get to my base—especially during the holidays. I'd sit at the airport and work any kind of deal I could. If direct flights were full, I'd jump on any flight headed in my general direction that had connections to my destination. It was stressful, exhausting, and frustrating. By the time I got to my base, I was already burned out and trembling with the adrenaline of possibly not getting to work on time. All of this, we did for free. We didn't get paid to get to our base. I couldn't afford to constantly be moving either, so this was the alternative. Then the really fun part was that after all the joys of commuting, I'd get to my crash pad apartment that I usually shared with six to eight other pilots (yes, male) and had to sleep on the floor or couch if I was one of the last to arrive.

I had several of these apartments over the years and each with its own dynamic of roommates and arrangements. I could write an entire book just about crew crash pad apartments and the drama that is included in the rent. They are a true investigation into human nature and behavior. If you're on a flight right now, just think about where your pilot might have slept last night.

10 Tighten Your Seatbelt, Folks, It's Gonna Be a Bumpy Ride

1. Pilots love turbulence
2. Turbulence will fill the barf bag, but won't harm the aircraft
3. Yes, the aircraft wings are supposed to flex like that
4. You pay money at amusement parks for this, so enjoy

If it wasn't for company policy requiring me to go and find you some smooth air, I'd just tighten my seatbelt, put my arms up in the air and yell, "Yee haw!" I know what these airplanes are capable of, and turbulence, even severe, isn't going to harm the airplane. Yes, we know it spills your coffee, fills the barf bags, and makes you nervous, so you'll hear the engines change power settings as we try to search for a smoother ride.

Big weather systems can dominate an area at all altitudes, so during those minutes that feel like hours when we have to just ride it out, remember that these airplanes are put through wing loading tests that defy reality. New airplanes are required to withstand 150% of the maximum expected load for four seconds. So think of the worst turbulence that's ever been encountered and remember that the airplane can withstand 50% more than that.

The danger of turbulence, of course, are people and things that are not belted in. The flight attendants are most at risk, so pilots inform them if there is forecasted turbulence and ask that they be seated. Not wearing your seatbelt puts you and others around you in danger. Just wear your seatbelt, and you've eliminated the danger of turbulence. You have the power.

Generally, pilots know the area where there is a likelihood of turbulence. It's not an exact science, and that's the problem.

You never know exactly where or when it will happen, so the best you can do it be ready for it. As long as you're in your seat, you might as well just strap in.

I have experienced days of annoyingly constant turbulence, like flying from Denver to Cancun and back, and never having a smooth patch of air. During those flights, you just learn to apologize to the passengers and drink your Coke without spilling it down the front of your white pilot shirt. Contrary to popular belief, it's the calm, smooth days that set you up for danger.

I was flying an empty Citation I from Minneapolis to Vancouver, BC. Since we were flying up to pick up a passenger, the captain let me sit in the left seat and fly the empty leg. It was a crystal clear day and not a bubble of weather anywhere. We had just crossed the intersection of where Montana, Washington, and Canada meet, and were digging into our crew meals.

The mountains were snowcapped and unintimidating from our altitude, and I could see one small line of wispy clouds that were gently rolling in place just ahead and below our altitude. We were just getting a little burble of rough air when suddenly, *WHAM*, we were at a 90 degree angle and the autopilot had instantly given up. We both yelled something to the effect of "Holy Shit!" and I grabbed the yoke and reduced the power as the airplane tried to figure out what end was up. We rocked and rolled for about twenty seconds and then as quickly as we'd entered it, we were in calm air again.

The cockpit had lettuce, Sprite, and ham sandwiches strewn around, and my flight bag had been turned upside down. It happened and ended so quickly, it took us a few moments to react. We just held on wondering if there was more to come and where the hell that came from. I finally looked over at the captain and his saucer eyes blinked once and then he looked at me, and said, "Was that a worm hole in time?"

I finally took a breath and said, "Yeah, it' must've been, because I just saw my whole life flash before my eyes."

He dropped his shoulders and laughed as we got the autopilot back on and began to clean up the mess. I never had anything like that happen again, but when I think back, there were subtle indications of the enormous power rolled up into one little pocket of air. It was a transition between pressure systems combined with an up flow from the mountains. The only outward indication was a small strand of soft white clouds, but inside, it contained an invisible mass of power just waiting for something, or someone, to come inside.

Over a span of my first two years at Champion Air, my bases changed from Detroit to Dallas to Las Vegas to New York to St. Louis to Denver. It was a commuting nightmare. In all that time, I had not seen Brad since the first few months in Minneapolis. We had completely lost touch, and during those years I ended a serious relationship and accepted every upgrade opportunity that was offered, which allowed me to move up from flight engineer, to first officer, to captain in record time. I was now a junior captain and, once again, there was rumor of a new permanent base opening up—this time in Denver. Yee Haw! For me, this was the base I'd been dreaming of; the Rocky Mountains, milder winters (compared to Minnesota), backpacking, hiking, skiing, active lifestyles, and hippies everywhere you looked. I always knew we were in Denver when passengers boarded the airplane wearing wool sweaters, turtlenecks, shorts, and flip flops. I was in my glory thinking about moving to Denver as a thirty year old captain, while everyone else was dreading yet another base change.

Before I could move, I had to make sure this wasn't going to be a temporary base, so I decided to hold off moving for a few months to make sure the company could establish enough business to keep the base open. The company had flown out of

Denver before, but only for contract work, and it lasted just a few months before the base closed. I didn't want that to happen again, especially as a junior captain. Junior captain is an oxymoron.

The bizarre aspect of leadership and being a captain in aviation is that it's based solely on flight hours and flight skill. If you pass your check ride, you can become captain—even if you are completely incapable of being a leader. Generally, I witnessed common elements of the good captains, and it boiled down to integrity, respect, and listening to your crew. All airline pilots are taught crew resource management, but not leadership, specifically. While sitting in the copilot and flight engineer's seat, I hung onto every word of the captains I admired and learned from the captains I detested about what not to do. I watched leadership styles that worked and blended it with my own ideology. I loved being a captain. I loved the personal challenge and found comfort in following the rules.

On my first flight into Denver as a new captain, the ground person guiding my aircraft into its parking spot was none other than Brad. Since Colorado was Brad's home state, I shouldn't have been surprised to see that he got the transfer back home. For the ground crew, it's difficult to see the captain, but if the sun isn't shining against the window, you can see into the cockpit. I still remember the huge smile on Brad's face when he realized who the captain was. He instantly started to over-exaggerate the directions he was giving me with the directional wands. Brad then purposely tried to misguide me, but I kept the nose wheel on the center parking line and stopped when he gave the order.

He came bolting up to the cockpit before the passengers had a chance to deplane and we instantly fell into the old rapport:

"Well Hello Ms. *Captain!*" Brad exclaimed, bowing to me like I was a queen "Oh my God, I can't believe they're letting a woman be in charge of this hunk of crap. What did you break on this aircraft today besides a fingernail?"

"Well, Brad, let's see...if the mechanics had actually done their pre-flight inspection this morning, they would have realized that the generator they signed off as repaired still isn't working properly, the oxygen tanks were so low they were barely able to be dispatched, and the flight engineer found a screwdriver in the wheel well. It doesn't have your name on it, so I assume it's yours. After all, confident mechanics put their initials on their tools."

He responded with a big smile, a few more insults to the pilots' ability to break perfectly good aircraft, and an invitation for the entire flight crew to come to his house for a barbeque picnic the next day. We were all on a two-day layover and just begging for a reason to escape our hotel rooms. His was an offer we couldn't refuse. I rented a car from the hotel and the next afternoon, I loaded up my copilot, flight engineer, and two (of the four) flight attendants, and headed to Brad's house.

Brad's house had white walls, small dark rooms, and beer posters for decoration that screamed "Bachelor!" The home's claim to fame was that Brad had remodeled the kitchen and took down a support wall without a permit. It had a fenced yard that contained his new dog and a small garden growing weeds mixed with cosmos and lettuce, which I found sad and charming.

When I asked if he needed help with the barbeque, he said that he did. In fact, he said he had no food to put on the barbeque, so we all went to the store, but I got stuck paying for all the food. I didn't mind. I was the captain of this crew and I wanted to take care of everyone.

At this point in my life, I was at the zenith of what I thought was success in the year 2000. I was a junior captain making about a hundred dollars per hour and I could fly about a thousand hours per year. I owned my car outright, I had no credit card debt, and I had seventy-five thousand dollars cash sitting in my savings account. I had no social life outside of work and I lived out of a suitcase. I was planning a three week trip to Kenya and was finagling my schedule to make it all work. You'd think I would be sick of traveling, but I still felt like something within me was lacking. That damn feminine mystique. I couldn't quite put my finger on it, but I needed to get outside of my comfort zone and try something new. I figured a safari to Africa would be something completely exotic and would fill the lacking in my heart.

What I really needed were a few close friends, but at the time I didn't realize something so simple was so important. I had no close friends anymore, but I didn't notice the sense of loss. I had a built-in social life at every layover. When I got home after being with people every waking and sleeping moment, I just wanted to be alone. I was too busy to fill my downtime with friends. Other women couldn't understand the passion I had for my career. My job fulfilled me. I wondered what women did a generation ago when they didn't have careers.

I was financially independent, which meant freedom, but I was exhausted to the point where I couldn't even relax. I felt if I slowed down, I'd lose the feeling. Pride, power, and money are a lethal, addictive combination. No matter what problem came along, I would whisper to my soul, "If you can captain a commercial airliner, you can do *this*! You can fix any problem and overcome any barrier. *You can do this...*"

My arrogant mindset allowed me to do two things. First, I went through my early adulthood never feeling like I *needed* a man in my life. Sure, I liked having a man in my life, but I never thought I'd have to depend on one, so I never viewed men through the filter of a potential wife and mother. The truth about aviation, which every pilot eventually figures out, is that you simply cannot have it all without a great spouse. My ego hadn't allowed this thought to enter into my filtering process. I just never thought I would have to ever rely on someone else for anything.

Second, I figured since I could pilot any make, model, and type of aircraft, I could manage any abnormalities that came along in a relationship. What's the worst thing that could happen? If I couldn't fix it, I figured there'd be a checklist so that I could still operate normally with something not working properly.

My self-induced power gave me the opportunity to pick someone so completely incompatible because I never had to consider him to be my equal. I had the power to love whoever I wanted and since Brad made me laugh, offered a completely different way of looking at life, and shared the core of who we were in aviation, I was ready to step off the deep end to feel the sensation of unconstrained freedom.

Every time I'd ever seen Brad at work, he was always trying to flirt with the flight attendants, so when I felt the first pass at me at the barbeque, I instantly assumed it was his mode of operation and I was just one among many. I'd heard through the grapevine that he had been dating a flight attendant for the last three months, and on a recent flight she had gloriously announced to the crew in the flight deck that she was sleeping with him because she had a ton of car issues that needed repair, and Brad would do it for free. I'd felt badly for him knowing she was only using him and willing to announce it to everyone at work.

Brad thought he was still dating his flight attendant, and I routinely reminded myself that he didn't know how she truly felt about the relationship. They had been dating three months and it was the longest relationship he'd ever been in, so *he* thought it was quite serious. I didn't think it was my place to tell him what she'd said to us in the cockpit so, instead, I accepted a few of his good natured passes and threw a few back at him. It did my heart good to see him blush, since he was usually the forward one. It also made my heart weak. Under the façade, there was vulnerability and softness that he didn't usually let show, and I felt empowered to bring that out of him. As the night moved on at the barbeque, and as the rest of the crew was playing Frisbee, our chairs got closer and the talk turned more serious.

He talked about his mom being divorced twice while he was growing up, along with his stages of loneliness as he transferred to three different colleges while trying to find his niche in the world. His parents had divorced when he was just five years old and, as is the trend, his dad was not a daily part of his life and only inserted himself to take Brad on road trips, which Brad remembered fondly. His dad was a longtime functioning alcoholic, so Brad has purposely stayed away from alcohol because he said he could feel his own tendencies of addiction pull him to the dark side. He had experimented heavily with drugs in college, and ultimately concluded that he should probably stay away from those, too. He also admitted to having emotional swings and attributed it to inheriting his dad's addiction issues. He said the swings were a constant pull side to side, but that he could deal with it by watching what and when he ate.

I'd always heard you should pay attention to how a son treats his mother because it is indicative of how he'll treat you. His mom was the primary topic of conversation and she was simultaneously a source of anger, frustration, pride, and humor. With hesitation, he admitted that their relationship was more of a love/hate pendulum. I'd never hated my parents, or anyone for that matter—keeping an unemotional attachment was my way of avoiding a bumpy ride along my flight.

Wanting to control every decision in his life, his mom offered unsolicited opinions on his life choices and denied all of his flaws. She was a strong woman with strong opinions, and her main blind side was that she believed Brad could do no wrong. It embarrassed him, but it also created an internal opinion of himself that was based on the view perceived by his mother.

Being the beneficiary of a parental college scholarship, Brad put himself on the seven-year Bachelor's degree plan. He finally found his stride at the University of North Dakota in their aviation business program, and decided he wanted to be an aircraft mechanic. However, the curriculum required that he get his private pilot's license, even though he wanted to be a mechanic. I remember being shocked as Brad laughingly recalled showing up to his lessons so hung over that he was probably still drunk. It was so different from the passionate focus I had given to my studying aviation.

The fact that he was in a band probably hindered the ability to blend musician's hours with the strict routine of aviation. Predictably, he failed his private pilot check ride and had to do a retest to get his license. At least he had a private pilot license to show for the effort.

I was shocked at his cavalier attitude towards aviation. I'd spent years giving it the upmost respect, while he laughed at those who did. He was the veritable yin to his classmates' yang. They wore military haircuts and went to bed early, so Brad wore his hair in a ponytail and stayed up late. As a conformist and having obeyed all the rules all my life, this bad-boy, mock-the-establishment attitude was intriguing to me. It was so unlike me — I was fascinated and enthralled with this new perspective.

The chord that struck deepest during our conversation was Brad's acceptance of his childhood pains. He said he was thankful that he had watched his parents go through their divorces so that he would be a better husband and father. He talked about spending years trying to understand why they got divorced so he wouldn't have to repeat their mistakes. I was touched by his sentiment. While he'd spent years trying to analyze his parents' divorce so he could be a better partner, I'd just readily accepted life's events at face value.

By the end of the evening, he felt more real to me than I did to myself. I was focused on being some*thing*, an airline pilot, whereas he simply wanted to be someone to somebody. All I knew for sure is that I wanted to get to know this someone better.

11 Find the Best Altitude

1. At high altitudes, super cooled water vapor leaves contrails (not chemtrails)
2. Polar jet stream winds are usually found at 25-30,000 feet
3. Winds in the jet stream average 100 mph, which is great or horrible
4. The winter gradients can produce 200+ mph winds, which is phenomenal or can make you run out of fuel

The winds aloft are important factors in flight planning high altitude jets. Commercial airliners generally operate between 30-40,000 feet. Corporate jets fly a little higher, 35-50,000 feet, since money always takes you a little higher than the rest of the world. Depending on the time of year and hemisphere, the jet stream can be calm or rage with winds in excess of 200 mph. With headwinds like that, it's sometimes necessary to include a fuel stop.

I once made it from Las Vegas to Denver in a Boeing 727-200 in an hour and five minutes, block to block. We knew the forecasted winds were high, but when we settled in at the perfect altitude, the jet stream was pushing with more might than predicted. I'd never seen the ground speed so high, and I had to actually call back to the flight attendants and tell them to hurry beverage service because we wouldn't have time to get it done.

While you're sitting in the passenger seat, those wind speeds are imperceptible. Since you don't have anything to reference your movement to, an extra hundred miles per hour can't be perceived from inside the aircraft. But to the observer on the outside, it's easy to see that the aircraft is zooming faster than normal. It's kind of like being in a new relationship. The speed feels normal on the inside, but to the others around you, they're wondering why the hell you're going so fast.

My first official date with Brad was a Neil Young concert at Red Rocks Amphitheater in Morrison, CO. Brad loved to remind me, and anyone who would listen, that I was the one who asked him out. It was a modern fairytale romance with a twist. This time it was the rich airline captain, who happened to be a woman, hitting on a mechanic.

When I was handed my September schedule, it included a string of six days in a row off. I had so much fun with Brad at his barbeque that I decided to see what he was like on his own. I knew Brad played guitar and had been in a band, so I figured music should be on the checklist. I had always heard about Red Rocks, and it was definitely on my bucket list. I couldn't believe my luck; Neil Young was playing the weekend I had off and there were still tickets available. I didn't even bother to ask Brad first, because I was going to go even if he couldn't go with me. I would just sell his ticket when I got to the concert.

Fearful of appearing too bold to just call him up for a date, I used the excuse that a friend and I were going to go to the concert, but she backed out, which left me with an extra ticket. The story took the pressure off of both of us and didn't necessarily make it appear to be a date, but more of a backup plan. He was officially broken up with his flight attendant girlfriend by then, so I tried to keep it light. I kept getting his answering machine so I finally just left a message, explaining about the extra ticket. He called me two days later and said he'd love to go. He even offered to let me stay at his house, and made sure I knew that I was sleeping on a futon. I was flattered by both the offer and the gentlemanly act of keeping my honor.

I always traveled as light as possible, and when I left Minneapolis, it was muggy and hot. Never doubting that it would be the same or even warmer in Denver, I packed light clothes and the only shoes I had were the white Keds on my feet.

It snowed at the concert, and it was only September. Not just a light dusting of snow, but an occasional white out and blowing horizontally. It started out as a hard, cold rain, and I had lost all feeling in my toes by the time I got the first whiff of ganja in the air. I shivered and froze my way through the entire concert and when it was over, there was a mad rush of the crowd to get out. Brad and I kept getting separated, so he reached back and grabbed my hand and held on. It was warm and strong and as subtle as a gut punch; I realized I wanted it there.

I slept on the futon as promised. His dog, Phlap, who was not much more than a year old, wasn't allowed to sleep on his bed, so she was in the family room with me. Correction, she was in the family room *staring* at me. I kept shivering because Brad didn't have the heat on in the house and I was still cold soaked and frozen from the concert. Brad was warm and comfy in his heated waterbed, so he never gave it another thought that the one thin blanket he'd given me wasn't going to keep me warm. Since I'd been around men as their workmate or roommate, I was used to not having a man worry about my comfort.

Since the dog and I were both shivering, I whispered for her to come onto the futon with me. We both knew she wasn't supposed to be on the furniture, but we both needed each other's warmth. The dog spooned with me and I was finally able to relax my muscles long enough to get a couple hours of sleep.

Our second date, the next morning, was going to the dump. There was a once-a-year recycling event that took used motor oil for free. Brad had saved up all the oil from his oil changes all year, and this was the only place that took it for free, so he asked if I wouldn't mind coming with him. We sat in the car and waited in line for two hours, but the minutes were filled with flying stories and gossip about flight attendants, pilots, and how great we were.

A young relationship and first dates hold so much promise. We're perfect in that moment, and we see ourselves as our new partner sees us; new, unblemished, and infallible. I'd had two serious relationships up to this point and a few in between, but there had always been some insurmountable impasse that allowed for gentle breakups with low drama. My relationships went out with a whimper instead of a bang. When I met Brad again in Denver, I was light and free, and ready to find my perfect fit, but I never thought I would be anything else to Brad other than a fun weekend or two. He was so different from me, that I was intrigued. I had spent so many years rigidly following my goals that I forgot that it was okay to just relax once in a while. I wanted to experience being with someone who disobeyed the rules. It was the perfect cliché for the bad boy to good girl ratio. Brad knew how to relax and have fun, and I wanted him to teach me how.

I had to catch my flight back home the afternoon after the concert, so before getting into my rental car, I decided to give Brad a hug and thank him for a great concert and for letting me stay on his futon. He gave me a big bear hug back and held it there just a questionable moment longer than a friend would. I know we both thought about it, but we couldn't make that transition to a kiss without embarrassing ourselves in case it wasn't what the other wanted.

In the ensuing weeks, the majority of my trips departed out of Denver International. With each layover came a new invitation to a restaurant, or to hear a local band, or hike an unexplored park. The official base in Denver had yet to open, so the company covered my expenses at the crew hotel. Brad would pick me up, we'd go have fun, and he'd drop me off. We spent hours exploring the

underground music cafes—the more mysterious the better. I
wanted to see it all.

My favorite outings were long hikes in the mountains with
his dog. We'd try exotic food restaurants on the way back from
hiking, and we always kept an eye on who was scheduled to
play at Red Rocks. I gladly paid for our dates. I paid for
everything and never thought twice about it. I earned it, so I
could spend it however I wanted. It was a powerful feeling, and
it made me feel good to spend it on someone. For the first time, I
had someone and something to look forward to that was
different and exciting, and nothing like me.

Several dates and make out sessions later, Brad invited me
out to dinner and to stay at his house again. "...and you're not
sleeping on the futon. You're sleeping with me..."

My sexual relationships had always been Midwestern: fun,
awkward, and brief—the relationships were long, but the sexual
encounters were forgettable. I didn't hold that much value on a
good sexual relationship because I really hadn't had one. I
appreciated having a buddy or a friend more than what went on
behind closed doors. I put my passion and intensity into flying,
so I wanted sex to be casual and without drama. Just like a man.
I didn't complain about it, and it wasn't something that I longed
for. Rather, I put friendship and love as priority, and whatever
else that came with the relationship was a bonus. If I had an
orgasm or two, then woo hoo.

In contrast, everything about Brad was sexual. He
constantly turned a benign conversation into a raunchy analogy.
He talked about sex openly and wanted to experience everything
about it. He was bold and would look me in the eye without
shame when he talked about what he wanted to do. It was sexy
and erotic, and we had long conversations where Brad explained
how the physical connection between two bodies is more
important that the superficial reflexes of feelings, which could
change in an instant. It put me on edge and made me question
everything I'd thought about love and sex. It was jolting to think

of what I had been missing. It was also freeing to think that a higher level of pleasure could be achieved solely and simply from physical contact. The irony (or probably the reason) is that at twenty-seven years old, he'd only had two other sexual relationships, but that didn't matter to me.

For all these reason, I turned myself over to Brad. I had spent my whole life being in charge of everything that happened to me, and I was tired of it. I was broken down from trying to be perfect and single-mindedly reaching for the brass ring. I wanted to let someone else be in charge of me. I gave in, and the relief was so enormous, I knew for certain that I had found the yin to my yang.

A new relationship can go months before ever questioning it. Every bump in the road is smoothed away with excuses because you want to keep enjoying the scenery. You don't want the edges of doubt to creep in and spoil the fun, so you close the shades and look straight ahead. If asked, every woman in a long term relationship can remember the first fight or flash of anger that entered the relationship. For the most part, I always blew them off, but looking back on my life and relationship, there were always huge red flags flying at full mast. I chose to ignore them, and it cost me everything. Individually, these little moments were nothing, but combined, it should have been so easy for me to see Brad's pattern of narcissism that turned to his justification of abuse. Not being able to have empathy or see a situation as the other person might see it happens innocently all the time, but I remember the first time I looked at Brad and thought *what the hell?*

We were in a car accident. He had a pimped out Honda Civic that he drove when he couldn't drive the old Ford Fairlane. His Honda was lowered to the ground with an upgraded engine and big tires. I didn't think it was much to look at, but he said it got great gas mileage.

We were at a stoplight on our way to a ski equipment sale in downtown Denver when a big blue airport transport van slammed into the back of the car at around forty miles per hour. It bent the frame and totaled the car. Brad saw it coming in his rearview mirror but couldn't get the words out to warn me—he just moaned "nnnnNNNNNOOOOOO!!!" as we got clobbered. The moment the car stopped moving from the impact, Brad unbuckled his seatbelt and sobbed, "Oh *NO*, my car!" He never even looked over to see if I was okay. I felt sick.

The impact had snapped my neck back hard into the headrest. Luckily, the headrest did its job and it was just a sore neck, but I was quietly crying because of the shock of the moment and that my boyfriend hadn't even looked over to make sure I was okay.

Brad traded insurance information with the driver and walked around his car several times before deciding he could probably drive it home. During this whole time, he never stuck his head in the car to see if I was okay. When he was finally done, he jumped back in the car and said, "Whoa, can you believe what just happened? I can't believe my car got smashed. I love this car. I've been working on it for years, and I finally got it how I want it, and just like that, it's ruined." I was heartbroken by his behavior, but I never said a word. It stewed in the back of my brain, along with my sore neck, but I wanted to appear strong and nonchalant. *I'm an airline captain, so this is no big deal.*

That very same weekend, we went skiing. How many relationships have fallen apart at the top of the chairlifts or by the time the skiers had ended their ski run?

I hadn't been skiing for years, but I used to go every weekend in Minnesota and enjoyed it. Colorado skiing is nothing like Minnesota skiing. I was excited to go, but the anticipation was blended with apprehension because it had been so long and I had only skied once before in the mountains. On the drive up to Loveland, I told Brad I was nervous and thought I would be fine as long as he'd just stick with me for a few runs and remind me how to do it. What I was lacking was confidence, but I knew with a seasoned pro by my side, I'd be fine.

The view from the chairlift was incredible and surreal. The mountains, which I usually only saw from the air, towered over me. Their majesty took my breath away. I got off the chairlift without falling, which was a great start, so we headed down an intermediate slope that was long, but didn't look too technical. About fifty yards down the very first slope, Brad saw a black diamond run off to the right. Without stopping, he yelled to me, "I'm going to head down here—meet you at the bottom!" And with that, he was gone. I stopped dead in my tracks because I couldn't believe he'd just ditched me. We hadn't been skiing for five minutes and he was gone already.

As it turned out, the slope he went down lead to a completely different chair lift and it rounded the backside of another mountain, not the one I was on. I looked all over for him at the bottom of the run, but he was nowhere to be found. Neither of us had a cell phone with us, so I skied by myself all day. I saw him once riding up on a chairlift, but it was impossible for an ant to get someone's attention. Not knowing how long he was planning on skiing, and figuring he'd at least meet me at the car at lunchtime, I lugged my equipment back to the car and waited two hours for lunch—from 11 to 1 pm. He had the keys to the car, and I had given him all my cash and credit cards to put in his zipper pocket, so I had no money to even buy a hot chocolate. I couldn't warm up in the car because he had the keys. The lunch I'd packed for us was locked in the car, and I could see it sitting on the front seat.

Hungry and mad, I went back to the slopes and skied a few more runs, but I couldn't enjoy myself because I was focused on trying to find Brad. The lifts stopped running at 3:30, so I headed to the car and finally, about 4:00 pm, Brad came moseying back to the car with a smile on his face. He said the skiing was great. He informed me that since he had money, he decided to buy lunch at the chalet instead of coming back to the car for the sack lunch. I just stood there. I asked if he realized I had no money or keys to the car, and he smacked his forehead and said, "Dude, I'm so sorry. I was just having so much fun, I totally forgot. You're so mellow and laid back; I figured you wouldn't mind..."

So here's the thing, I just acted like a dude and said, "Whatever. Glad you had fun."

I was off-the-charts pissed because he was so inconsiderate, but I just swallowed it. I was his dude girlfriend — something I'd strived to be with my men friends. Just one of the guys. I had paid for his lift ticket, he took my cash and put it in the pocket of his ski pants for safe keeping, and that was the last thought he had of me being there with him. He knew I was nervous about skiing again, but satisfying his own pleasure overrode all thoughts. His self-fulfillment was all that mattered.

I didn't stand up for myself and say what I thought. I just let it go because I thought by not saying anything, I'd be the better person and the dude girlfriend you'd want to hang out with. I'd strived to be treated like a dude my entire career, which muddled my mind to what is expected from a relationship. I told myself to let it go. But, as we all know, it doesn't just let go. It lingers — forever — no matter how righteous you are. We can all do our Buddha imitations and say we know how to forgive, but we all still vividly remember it, and just the thought pisses us off all over again. You'll be cruising along at your altitude in life and then suddenly, you hit the jet stream and you're pushing against 200 mph winds. You'll finally have to admit defeat, land, and take on more fuel

We're taught that forgiveness is a practice for removing unhealthy emotions. Fuck that. If the other person does something wrong, why do you have to forgive them? Why do we have to suck it? Isn't that more unhealthy? Swallowing all that acid and bile other people hand you will eat you up inside. I'm of the opinion that the idea of forgiveness is an excuse to justify the feeling of the anger because we're not supposed to feel anger, especially women. We should just be angry about the things that make us angry and leave it at that. Sure, anger is an unhealthy emotion, but only if you don't move it onto the next stage of doing something about it. Buddha says that "Holding onto anger is like grasping a hot coal with the intent of throwing it at someone else; you are the one who gets burned."

But I say that if you move that hot coal fast enough, you might only get singed. Anger can be good. It can rise up in that part of your character that inspires you to do something about it. Or, you can push it down into the pit of your heart and let it smolder forever. But I didn't know all that back then. All I knew was this was a new kind of guy I was dating—the proverbial "bad boy"—and dating a "bad boy" came with different kinds of baggage. I hadn't figured out the trick of knowing when to land in time to avoid running out of fuel in midair.

The car accident and being left on the ski slope are just minor examples among thousands of the cliché "red flags" which your momma warned you about, but we knowingly ignore. Picking the wrong guy was a reflection of my inability to understand myself. I thought all those red flags were a warning meant for others, not me, because I could fix and fly anything. I was going to captain this relationship to my destination even if I was fighting strong headwinds for the entire flight. In retrospect, I wish someone pulled that red flag out of the ground and smacked me over the head with it. Repeatedly. It's not necessarily the actions in and of themselves that I was concerned about; it's the reaction and sentiment *behind* the action. He simply didn't think about my welfare at all. Your partner's inability to have empathy for you should always worry you.

For me, I had spent a lifetime of having empathy trying to understand men. As a woman working and living in their world, I didn't want to stand out or cause a fuss. I wanted to see what they see and be what they didn't expect to see in a woman. I had spent so much of my energy wanting to be like them, I forgot how wonderful being a woman is. I forgot that we are amazing creatures with our unique abilities and that in a harmonized world, men and women create a balance for each other. I forgot to stand up and be proud that I am a woman. Instead, I unfastened my seatbelt and started walking around the cabin, even though I could see a thunderstorm brewing in the distance.

12 Cruise Checklist

1. Seat back – reclined
2. Fuel burn – monitor and balance
3. Call flight attendant for crew meals. If you've pissed them off, check for spit
4. Now that you're comfortable, don't be lulled into a stupor

We've reached our final cruising altitude. The air is smooth, so I'll go ahead and turn off the seatbelt sign. You are free to get up and move about the cabin. In the flight deck, the autopilot is on and the flight engineer is balancing the fuel burn. The flight attendants have stopped complaining to us that the passengers are too hot, then too cold. I can see for miles, and now we have nothing to do except talk to air traffic control. But because it's my leg to fly, my first officer has to do all the talking. This is when I drop my seat back a bit, lean my head back and breathe in a moment of Zen. It's when we let our guard down that we are the most vulnerable and unprepared for an emergency, but those moments are so important in life, it's usually worth the risk.

I loved risking a brush against a growing thunderstorm. There is nothing more sublime than being at cruise altitude on a late afternoon at flight level 350 on a hot summer day. Watching the towering cumulonimbus clouds reaching for the stratosphere always made me feel so inconsequential, and I was always amazed that sometimes the air around the storms would be absolutely serene.

The strength of those late afternoon storms are hard to imagine since a cloud has no touch, no feel, no strength. It is the gathering of all those molecules of water and atmosphere that gives it force and it can turn into a deadly super cell in just a matter of minutes. It is the collapsing of these storms that causes the damage. All that strength reaching upwards, only to find the air too thin to sustain any more growth, causes the storm to change direction downward with conviction, creating straight-line winds, flash flooding rains, and pounding hail. The storm cells that reach the highest have the most strength because they have the farthest to fall...which proved to be a prophetic metaphor for my life.

The red-eye flight from Las Vegas to St. Louis was living up to its name. As we turned the Boeing onto final approach, the ragged edge of the sun was boring over the horizon just enough to strain our weary eyes. Most of the passengers were still in a drunken haze long after the flight attendants had run out of liquor. Like a young child on a long road trip, the lead flight attendant kept ringing the cockpit to find out how much further we had to go. I kept telling him we'd get there when we got there.

Captains get to choose which legs we want to fly. Copilots know that captains delegate the pathetic legs to them, so my copilot knew in Las Vegas, without even having to ask, that he'd be flying this leg. We had been on the road for five days, my uniform was getting ripe, and we were tired from holding up the image of being pilots. Besides, it was his turn to fly.

My copilot was new, but he'd proven himself over the last few days. I'd chuckle to myself when I'd glance over at him during a particularly difficult altitude crossing restriction or crosswind landing and he'd have his tongue wrapped around his lip in concentration. He was doing this now as we turned onto final approach on this beautiful, calm day of fall. I wasn't sure what was causing him to overextend his concentration, but exhaustion has a way of blearing your thoughts.

His altitude and airspeed were perfect as he called out his requests.

"Gear down."

"Roger, here they come."

"Flaps, thirty degrees. Final items."

I was so proud of his perfect stabilized approach. I relaxed and sat back to watch his beautiful landing.

"200 feet."

"50 feet."

WHAM!

In the two seconds it took for me to realize he was going to forget to flare, I couldn't get my hands to move fast enough to the yoke to slow the rate of descent. As we slammed into the runway, I could feel the landing gear groan into their sockets and we landed hard enough to drop a few oxygen masks in the back. It wasn't anything more than a firm landing, but for the passengers, I'm sure they thought the end was near.

I'm the captain. It's my fault. Even if the copilot makes a mistake, it's on me. Every pilot has had this bad landing. It is part of the initiation into becoming a good pilot, but when I looked over at my copilot, he was crimson and drowning in his embarrassment. We were both so sure he was going to grease it onto the runway that the outcome was out of the realm of our possibilities. He was wallowing in his misery, so I tried to lighten the mood.

"Well, that'll wake up the drunks back there! You probably did the flight attendants a favor by getting the passengers out of their stupor so they can deplane. I'm sure you meant to do that, but you do realize that the flight attendants are going to demand that you stand in the doorway and offer every single passenger a back massage…"

The flight engineer started to join in on the razzing, and I could see my copilot's lips quiver in the attempt to keep a smile away, and he began to lighten up a little. We opened the cockpit door as the passengers were deplaning at the gate, so they could chime in on the teasing.

About midway through deplaning, we could hear the grumble of a deep and drunken voice creep louder as he pushed his enormous mass into the cockpit. He was slurring his complaints until his breath got caught in the back of his throat as he saw me sitting there in the captain's seat with my long blond hair in a ponytail.

"Oh my God. There is a chick in the cockpit! I knew it. I knew there had to be some reason for that gawd-awful crash landing. Well, hell, no wonder why. Women can't and shouldn't be flying. Wait until I tell my wife about this. Hey, honey…"

It wasn't worth explaining that the male copilot made the landing. It never was worth explaining anything about being a chick in the cockpit. I just smiled at him and said I'd be out by baggage claim giving massages. He offered to take his shirt off right then and there, but he had left his suitcase in the aisle and the passengers behind him were stuck, so the flight attendants pulled him out of the cockpit.

My copilot and flight engineer thought this was hysterical. My copilot was also relieved to realize that most everyone thought I'd made the landing, so he smirked and said he was going to get in line for the back message behind the drunk.

"Fuck you," I laughed.

My shy copilot from Nebraska found the nerve to respond with a good-hearted, "Okay."

To which I replied, "Not after a bad landing like that. My back hurts."

"That's okay, I'll let you be on top."

And with that, we all start laughing until our red eyes fill with tears. With our veins flooded with exhaustion and adrenaline, it's hard to stop laughing because it feels so good. It's in these moments of humor and smack talk that my heart soars. I'm not offended. I am dauntless and I know I can hold my own, so I can tease about not being a man. When I'm in the cockpit, I am not a woman. I am a pilot. I am on top. I have earned my right to be a member of my crew and everything that it means.

Everyone's lives depend on our trust in each other, and even after my copilot's bad landing, I knew I could trust him. He knew he could trust me.

As we walked down the jet bridge together, we knew we had to put on our serious pilot faces to walk through the terminal. We all lived in different states, so we waved good-bye and knew we'd see each other again after our four short days off were over.

Thankfully, the flight I needed to catch home was only a few gates away. United to Denver. The flight was full, so there weren't any cabin seats in which to sit my weary ass. I had to sit in the jump seat in the cockpit that was designed by an inventor who learned how to duplicate the comfort of concrete.

I arrived in Denver at 6:40 a.m. MDT on the morning of September 11, 2001.

I had been awake for too long to know my name as I rested my head on my pillow. I was so tired, and it was cruel irony that I couldn't fall to sleep. I finally stumbled into unconsciousness and just as I was about to go over the ledge and find sleep, the ringing of my phone bolted me awake with confusion.

"Hello?"

"Oh good. You're home. Turn on the TV." It was my sister in Iowa. I told her I was so tired that I didn't know if I could even make it back to bed. Instead, I was going to curl up and sleep on the floor where I stood.

"Erika. No. Really. Something is going on. An airplane just hit the World Trade Center."

"What? Here in Denver? How can that be, the weather is good."

"No. In New York."

"Was it a single engine airplane that got lost? Is the weather bad? Is anyone else hurt?"

"Erika. I'm hanging up now. Just turn on the damn TV."

Well, that was rude. My sister just hung up on me. I turned on my old TV and just stood there watching and trying to comprehend what they were saying. Wait, what? What were they saying? How could it be? It was a beautiful New York day. How could an airliner have gotten so off course that it actually hit a building? Wait. Oh no. What the hell is that? Oh my God, it's another plane. Please. No. No. No.

Everyone remembers where they were at that crushing, tragic moment.

In my mind, I was sitting in that cockpit with the crew. I closed my eyes and my brain projected the image of what they might have seen. The image loop repeated, and I couldn't find the "erase" button. I am a pilot. My heart ached for the crew and their families.

For all of us, 9/11 was a profound moment. Something as simple as a few box cutters killed thousands of innocent people and changed aviation forever. I had the feeling that it could have just as easily been me who died that day. Life was precarious, and all I'd done with mine was fly it away. If it had been me in the cockpit of one of the doomed flights, what would I have left behind except a tragedy? I hadn't completed the full human experienced of life, love, or birth. I had spent my life thinking about what was next rather than fully experiencing the moment I lived in. My moments were dreams about what was the next airplane I would fly. How much money would I make? What's the next company I'd work for, where is the next base? What's the next superficial achievement on my checklist?

In the weeks following 9/11, Brad and I quietly held hands and talked about life, our fears, and our dreams. We compared bucket lists and combined our desires into one bucket. The conversation began a deeper level of thinking about our relationship and what our lives held for the future, together. We realized we had common hopes and dreams, and at the root of it was our shared passion for the aviation industry. I was deeply grateful to have found someone who understood my crazy work schedule, someone with whom I could share my fears and accomplishments. And because he was in the industry, we could truly sympathize with what we were experiencing. Since he wanted to become a commercial pilot, too, I was thrilled to be on this journey with him. He was someone I believed could understand me on a deeper level, since he wholeheartedly acknowledged that, at my core, I was a pilot first and a person second. He said that was what he admired about me—and I admired him for being able to accept me as I was.

Since we had similar broken families, we discussed how we would be different. We saw the stupidity of letting emotions and hate get in the way of making good decisions. More than most couples, we also shared an industry like no one else we knew. Aviation was our lives, so we had respect for each other's professions, despite the teasing. I admired Brad that he could troubleshoot a problem on the airplane, find the flaw and fix the problem. I was thrilled to see Brad guide my aircraft into the gate at the end of a long day. He would come up and talk about the mechanical troubles that the airplane had, and when no one was looking, we'd steal a passionate kiss in the cockpit.

Although our company acknowledged workplace romances happened continuously, it was still discouraged, so we kept it as quiet as long as possible. We forgot to follow our clandestine checklist, so our cover was blown when Brad rode along on one of my charter flights.

My crew and I were contracted to fly a college football team, and charters away from our normal routes required a mechanic to fly along. Luckily, Brad was assigned to my flight and was sitting in the jump seat behind my captain's seat while we were waiting for passengers to load. He was leaning forward reading a manual while he quietly reached around and touched my left breast. We tried to contain our laughter as I jumped and blushed. From the angle Brad was sitting in, no one should have been able to see what he did, except that this flight was at night and the reflection of his action bounced into the eyes of my flight engineer. He sat up, looked at us both and said, "Hey, what's going on with you two?" We just looked guilty, and it dawned on the engineer what was going on. We realized the news of our relationship would spread like wildfire, and accepted our fate. Within days, everyone knew we were dating. It was out there and we were proud of it. Our romantic lives as pilot and mechanic together had officially begun.

After 9/11, I decided to give up the townhouse I'd been renting in Greenwood Village and move in with Brad. I spent all my time at his house anyway, so the townhouse was just an expensive storage locker for furniture. He'd been asking me to move in for several months, and I finally thought what the hell? This is the moment, live it to the fullest. I was settled into my cruise altitude, so I felt comfortable unbuckling my seatbelt.

My cocker spaniel was getting up in years and I loved the idea of having a place with a doggy door, so I told Brad I'd pay his mortgage, which was the same as my rent, if he paid the utilities. We started playing house, and this time I didn't revert to my childhood and rip the head off the Ken doll.

In preparation for our togetherness, I had also cancelled my lifelong dream trip to Kenya. I had booked and paid for the safari months earlier, but it didn't feel right to be so self-indulgent during the thrill of new beginnings together. Brad didn't ask me to cancel it, but he acknowledged that the sacrifice showed just how much I loved him. It was an expensive trip, but I had almost six figures cash in my savings account. Leaving it at that level felt powerful, and Brad was humble when I said I'd send us on a different trip together.

Since aviation was shut down during the weeks after the terrorist attacks, I thought it would be months before I was back in the air. As it turned out, I ended up being one of the first flight crews that were in the air after 9/11. Unknown at the time as to who our passengers were, we did several contract charter trips for the Department of Defense, one of which was down to Guantanamo Bay, Cuba. We were mainly flying troops around, even though we didn't know yet who the enemy was. I was a captain, but since I kept my currency in all three flight deck seats, I was asked to cover some emergency trips as flight engineer. Realizing that the security of every pilot's job was in jeopardy due to the entire shutdown of aviation, I jumped at the chance. Only later did we all realize who our passengers were and why they were going down to Guantanamo Bay.

Even though I was able to work a few flights, our company was still sliding towards bankruptcy, and all scheduled flights were cancelled. Brad and I decided to take this time to be together, use our free pass travel and spend some of the money I'd set aside for Kenya. We wanted to show the terrorists that they couldn't stop us from living, and since we couldn't go to Europe, we chose to go to New Orleans instead. We wondered if traveling on a pass and sitting standby during this crisis was going to work, but we didn't have to worry. There were only fourteen people on the entire flight. As our plane headed south, I wondered how this aircraft could afford to operate with the income of just a dozen people (we were riding on a free pass). The devastating impact this would have on the aviation industry sunk in, along with knowing the domino effect that would take down many airlines in slow motion.

New Orleans was subdued. The nation was still in shock, and even rebellious New Orleans had a reverent quiet about her. We spent our days wandering the old neighborhoods, cemeteries, and museums. We finished our nights with Zydeco music and pizza at midnight. We felt guilty to be happy, but we were, and we thought the best revenge on Al-Qaeda was for everyone in the world to give them the finger and smile while doing it.

On our fourth day, I noticed that Brad was quiet and withdrawn, but figured he was tired. After an aborted trip to the Audubon Zoo, we decided a walk through a park would be better, given the oppressive heat and humidity. The oak trees were monstrous and spooky with the Spanish moss groping at their limbs. If you looked closely at the tree branches, there were hundreds of Huntsman spiders in their webs waiting for their prey.

Brad stopped under one of these trees draped in spiders and said he had a question to ask me. I watched as he bit his lower lip. I'd never intuitively known what was going to happen next more clearly than I did at that moment. I knew he was going to propose, and I didn't want him to. *It's too soon. Not here, not now. Our life is perfect; don't change it* I pleaded inside my brain.

The realization put panic and adrenaline into my heart, so I instantly said out loud, "Oh please, no!" His eyes got wide and he tilted his head because he hadn't said anything yet, but he plowed ahead because he thought I didn't know what was coming next. His eyes filled up with tears of emotion as he dug into his pocket. Before he found what he was looking for (the ring), his trembling hands reached for mine and held them while he collected his thoughts. When he began to speak, his face was filled with an intensity I'd never felt before. "Erika, I love you so much," he said, looking me straight in the eyes," and I think that we could have a great life together. I have never, and will never, meet anyone like you again…I was wondering if you would marry me."

A flood of heat coursed through my veins. Spoiled by fairy tale books and Hollywood romance movies, I figured I just didn't want him to ask me when I was close to passing out from heat exhaustion with spiders looming inches from our heads. But there it was; the beautiful, life changing offer. The question. My moment. The future. He was the symmetry to my narrow balance-beam life. He would be there to catch me if I fell. This could really be a good life together. 9/11 enforced the idea that I should live in the moment, and in that moment together we were invincible. I was tired of being the captain of my life, and I wanted to fly with just the responsibilities of being a copilot. I wanted a captain. Of course, I said yes.

He finally found the ring and placed it on my finger. We hugged each other like our lives depended on it and kissed with the passion of Adam and Eve to seal our fate.

We planned a July wedding and hoped we'd be able to get time off from work. In the meantime, I picked up as many extra flights as possible and bid the heaviest flying lines to cover the upcoming costs. As usual, I was away from home most weeks of the month and rarely saw Brad. My focus was getting flight hours to earn enough money to pay for our wedding. Never once, from my first solo to my Boeing 727 captain's check ride, had I ever considered what would happen if I couldn't fly. Flying defined me. I was nothing but a pilot, but something happened two months before our wedding that planted a seed in the back of my mind and shook the foundation of who I thought I was. It was something that made me wake up and realize how precarious life is. In an instant, life can change forever with the simplest of twists. I had bought a horse.

His name was Tuff (aptly named, I might add) and I boarded him at a stable about a mile down the road. His history was unknown, but I purchased him from a desperate man who was moving to Australia. I swear he must have drugged the horse the first time I rode him because he was the most docile creature I'd ever met. Within two days, however, he was as calm as a wild mustang on BLM roundup day. I realized he was going to need time and patience, but I was in no hurry. Brad and I would drive over and visit him almost every day.

I had a trainer start working with him, which dismayed Brad. He couldn't imagine why anyone would own a creature just to play and look at it. He wanted the horse to be ridden, not a pretty lawn ornament, and after just three weeks as we're driving to the stable, Brad grumbled that, "If you don't ride that fucking horse today, I think we need to talk about why you have a horse."

Three weeks. My goal was to be able to ride him within a year, so I was shocked to think Brad thought now was an appropriate time to give it a go. I wanted to show Brad that having a horse is a good thing and, at some point, I wanted him to have a horse, too, so we could ride together. I didn't want him to be soured on the whole idea so quickly. I wanted this to be a good experience, I wanted it to work. I threw away my common sense checklist.

The stable owners had wanted me to sign a release of liability to use the arena next door. I realized I forgot the slip as I was walking Tuff and getting him used to the reins and saddle I'd bought for him. Not even in my wildest dreams was I planning on riding, but Brad looked at the saddled up horse and said, "Well, this is a perfect time to ride this fucking horse. Jump on him and ride back to the car and get the slip." My heart stopped at the challenge.

"Nah, I'll just walk him up there. I'm getting him used to the equipment."

Brad rolled his eyes and laughed at me. "You've got to be kidding! You have a horse and he's tacked up and you're going to *walk* with him back to the car? Are you insane? I don't get it. Do you want a horse or not? What's your problem?"

I knew I shouldn't have done it, but I was pissed and wanted to show him that I knew what I was doing. I did know what I was doing by *not* riding him, but I jumped on instead.

Tuff didn't seem too concerned that I was now riding instead of walking him. I sat up there on his back trembling with fear and pride at being laughed at. As we were riding up the side road back to the car, an unfamiliar Boxer dog came running out of an out-building and spotted us. It was a visiting dog that hadn't been around horses, so he started running right towards Tuff and me. It took my horse half a second to decide he was going to get eaten by this dog, and bolted into the dense woods. In an instant, I saw Tuff lower his head, and my reflex told me he was going to try and buck me off, but as it turned out he was ducking out of the way of a guide wire off a telephone pole. I just misread the cue.

He ducked and I had pulled straight up on the reins thinking he was going to throw me, so the guide wire hit my raised hand first and it boomeranged me off the back of the horse. I landed flat on my back and it knocked the wind out of me. I lay there hoping I could move, and a wave of relief washed over me when I realized I could sit up. I put my left hand down to leverage myself up so I could stand up but before I could rise, I felt a sharp pain shooting from my fingers to my shoulder. I looked at my left hand and paled when I could bone sticking out of my ring and pinky finger.

"Oh, that can't be good. Oh, no...Brad! Help!" He'd already seen the whole thing happen and was running up the hill to retrieve what was left of me. We drove to the local doctor (this is on a Sunday, as Murphy's Law would have it) and after one look, the doctor said there was nothing he could do. He had given me a shot of morphine as soon as I walked into the clinic, which now required a thousand dollar ambulance ride to Denver because he couldn't release me after a shot of morphine.

Before they wheeled me into the operating room, I looked the surgeon in the eye and said, "I'm a pilot and I'll die if I can't fly anymore. Please do a good job." The doctor said he'd do such a good job that he'd let me be his captain. They operated and stuck three pins in my fingers, which extended out of my hand. During the months of recovery, I could make myself almost faint just by looking.

When I first woke up after surgery, my hand was bandaged so heavily I couldn't tell if it was a stump or if all went well. I was in the hospital for three days. Brad stayed until I woke up from surgery on the first day, then left. I didn't see or hear from him the whole next day until dinner time. I had no idea where he was. I lay in my hospital bed thinking my career, which meant the core of who I was, was done and over forever. Meanwhile, Brad had decided to go to Bandimere Speedway without so much as a phone call to inquire if I was okay, or to tell me where he'd be for the day. As my dinner was being brought in, Brad showed up in his stinky racing clothes. He told me he'd been at the racetrack all day and forgot to call to let me know where he was and, oh by the way, he was also starving, so would I mind if he had some of my dinner? He ate my entire dinner, kissed me on the cheek and said he had to get home and change his clothes and feed the dogs. I was crushed.

The next day, the operating doctor came in to check on me. He said the surgery went well and that with extensive physical therapy I would be flying in as little as three months. "Three months? No way! I can't be gone that long." I had never been away from flying that long. Flying *was* me, and I didn't exist unless I knew I could fly.

I was back to work in two months. I went to physical therapy religiously and basically just spent that time building up the strength in the rest of my hand since my two fingers were worthless. They still are. Crooked and mangled and permanently at an angle, they are a constant reminder of the stupidity of my pride.

The Boeing 727 has a tiller that steers the aircraft when taxiing on the ground and you have to use your left hand to operate it. It's not especially heavy, but I'd lost my hand strength, and two fingers didn't work, so I worried that I couldn't maneuver it. I needed to find out before I went back to flying, so I decided to tag along with Brad for one of his night shifts as a mechanic just to make sure I had enough strength to turn the tiller full motion. The mechanics reposition the aircraft at night, so taxiing the aircraft would give me an opportunity to test myself. After all those weeks of therapy, my heart was chomping at the bit, and I was more than eager to put aside my anxiety dreams about forgetting how to fly.

Tears of fear and frustration rolled down my face the first few minutes because I just couldn't hold the turn. The tiller would pop back into the neutral position while I was trying to turn. Brad quietly put his arm around my shoulder. "Come on. I know you can do this. Try gripping the tiller in a different position so you can use your body as leverage." I braced my left leg against the side of the cockpit wall and used my whole arm strength rather than my hand—and it worked. I moved the aircraft from the maintenance hangar to the gate. I called crew scheduling the next day and informed them I'd be ready to bid a flight line next month. I knew I had to go to recurrent training before I was back on the line, so I got in a few more days of physical therapy. I also had my medical certificate renewed, and I downplayed the accident to my flight physician. "Oh, it was no big deal, I just crunched a couple fingers, but they're fine now."

The story didn't end here because, once again, Karma reared its head to equalize the experience. Just two weeks after I'd been released from the hospital, Brad informed me that he was going to ride Tuff. He was convinced it was my bad horsemanship that got me hurt, and he wanted to show both the horse and me who was in charge.

Brad went for an ambulance ride, too. Tuff threw him and the saddle off in less than eight seconds. It just knocked the wind out of him but, not to be outdone, he demanded a ride in an ambulance. Not even a bruise! It made me think of how he'd pulled me to my feet before I even had my wits about me, with a bone sticking out of my hand, no less. Brad told the ambulance driver that he "for sure broke something." They put him on the backboard with a neck collar and he got carried to the ambulance.

I sold the horse two weeks later. I was honest with the new buyer, and he was confident he could train him. I heard through the grapevine that the new owner "decided" to just walk this horse around instead of ride him, too. Tuff colicked a year later, and his bucking days were over.

A year later, I bought a kind, small horse named Riley. Such a gentle spirit, he helped me reconnect with my passion for horses. Those few moments at the beginning always triggered a splash of fear when my butt was in the saddle, but he taught me how to trust him. Brad forced me to sell Riley when I started my business the following year, but I am thankful this sweet horse gave me an opportunity to heal.

During those days of recovery and realizing how quickly my career could end, I forced myself to envision what life would or could be like outside of aviation. It was all I knew or thought about, but for once in my life I forced myself to open a tiny door that had a tiny sign whispering, "Back Up Plan." I had never even considered it, but once I confronted my initial fear, a quiet calm settled over me. Somewhere inside, my soul gave me a taste of foreshadowing that I would still be okay if I couldn't fly.

I still had ugly, distracting bandages on my ring finger for our wedding, so we used my right hand for the ring exchange. How ironic that of all the bones in my body, it was my wedding ring finger that received the most damage in the accident. The photographer printed our photos in reverse so it looked like the rings were on my left hand, but you could still see the ugly bandages. We had been married the following July after the proposal in September. I did most of the planning and paid for almost everything since I had the bigger bank account. My flight schedule was getting busy again and Brad didn't have many vacation days, so after a fun and casual wedding at the Evergreen, Colorado Lake House, we took a three day honeymoon to the mountains and went right back to work.

During the honeymoon, we dreamed of traveling the world, and Brad mentioned once again that he wanted to become an airline pilot. He said he'd always been jealous of me being a pilot and that he was going to go back and get his ratings. I thought it would be exciting to have a spouse who knew all the nuances of what it took to be a pilot, so I offered to help him get there. We both agreed that once we got settled into a new house together, he'd get started on getting his licenses.

I combined the rest of the money I hadn't used for my canceled trip to Africa with my savings and put together a sixty-thousand dollar down payment into the purchase of a house in Evergreen, Colorado. Even though we were now living in the mountains outside Denver, it was worth the extra commute time to wake up and find elk lounging in the front yard. This was what we had dreamed about. Work hard, play hard, and living in the mountains. Never before had my maternal instinct spoken before, but in the back of my mind, I thought we had the perfect foundation for starting a family.

13 Warning Indications

1. The cockpit has warning, caution, and advisory lights and audio warnings
2. Red warning - most urgent, requires immediate response
3. Amber - may become urgent if not addressed
4. Green - good
5. Blue or white - indicates routine operating functions
6. Illumination of a red warning light - followed by pilot audio response, "Oh, Shit"

The most famous warning light changed the aviation industry for the better, but it was a hard lesson to learn. In 1972, Eastern Air Lines Flight 401 crashed into the Everglades killing 101 people because a light bulb had burned out.

On approach to landing into Miami International Airport, the first officer of the brand new Lockheed L-1011 extended the landing gear and noticed that one of the green landing gear indicator lights did not illuminate. The pilots cycled the gear, but could not get a green down and locked indication. They told air traffic control they wanted to depart the traffic pattern and enter a holding pattern to work on the problem. They headed out over the Everglades, in the dark of night, to fix a tiny problem. Even if the gear was not down, they could manually extend it.

Once they got into the holding pattern, the captain told the first officer to put on the autopilot and he then sent the second officer down to the avionics bay to confirm, via a small viewing port, if the gear was, indeed, down. For eighty seconds, the plane maintained altitude. Unknown to them all, the autopilot had not captured or somehow departed from the altitude setting so the aircraft began a gradual and unnoticeable steady descent while the crew tried to figure out why they didn't get a green light. They also didn't hear the audio chime warning them that they were off their altitude setting and since it was at night, they had no instant point of reference that they were descending.

The perfectly good airplane hit the ground at 227 mph. Since it was in mid-turn in the hold, the left wingtip hit first, then the left engine, then the left landing gear. It was discovered later than the light bulb they were worried about was just burned out and that their gear was down and locked.

This accident created the "situational awareness training" that we still have today. The error was just so simple, yet so deadly. One single indicator distracted everyone to death.

Having children is one of those topics that you can sit and describe for a million hours, but until you have children of your own, you'll just never know what I'm talking about. It's a waste of words.

The baby discussion was broached after we got engaged. We spent many long nights talking about how that would look. I strongly believed that if someone chose to bring a child into this world that it was up to the parents to make the sacrifice needed to raise the child themselves. I had several friends who did the child care route, and I firmly respected their choice, but I couldn't see why you would have a child, only to have someone else spend the majority of their waking hours with them. I'm sure my being adopted propelled that feeling of responsibility, and I was passionate about making sure that any child of ours would be raised by us. This was the promise I made to my unborn children, and Brad assured me he agreed completely.

We discussed how it would work to have Brad continue working his mechanic position at the airlines, but he despised his job and because of his schedule, he had to sleep during the day. Delegated to always working the night shift (the planes flew all day so most mechanics work at night) and in extreme weather conditions, it was easily decided that I would continue working and Brad would be the stay at home parent if we decided to have children. I made twice as much as he did, so it was the logical decision. He daydreamed about the new scenario and excitedly explained that he had several ideas that he wanted patented. He also loved working on his race car, so he thought this was going to work out well for all involved. He could stay home and be a famous inventor, while I brought home the proverbial bacon, thank you, Gloria Steinem. He was giddy with the possibilities. So was I. Our lives were perfect, except that I didn't have a green down and locked indicator.

I had spent eighteen years trying not to get pregnant and it blew my mind the first time I thought about actually trying to get pregnant on purpose. Brad had wanted to start right away and I thought that since I'd been on birth control for so long that it would take some time for the chemicals to get out of my system. I figured at least a year before I'd actually get pregnant. Wrong. The first month off the pill I got pregnant, but it took me awhile to figure it out.

My sister had jokingly wrapped a wedding present to us with a few pregnancy test sticks attached to the ribbon, still in the plastic wrapper but not inside the original box. I had kept them as a memento of our wedding. Never thinking that the reason for my late period was anything more than exhaustion, my body and brain told me otherwise. I had a dream that I was pregnant and when I woke up, the rush of realization gave me tunnel vision.

I remembered the joke pregnancy sticks tied to our wedding present and I wondered if they might work. There were no directions attached so when I used one of them, it came up as two negative signs so I thought that meant I wasn't pregnant. It told me twice that I was not pregnant, right? I was slightly relieved. I was in the grocery store a week later with

Brad and the last aisle had all the family planning products, one of which was the same pregnancy test that I'd taken. I picked up the box and turned it over. The directions explained that the results were simple: if the symbol in each window matched, you were pregnant! I had two negative signs so I thought two wrongs would never equal a right.

I was in aisle twelve at King Soopers when I figured out I was pregnant. I explained the story right then and there to Brad, and we burst out crying with tears of laughter and joy. We hugged each other, and I'm sure it was quite disturbing to the other shoppers trying to grab a box of condoms.

As recommended by the old wives tales, we didn't say anything for the first obligatory three months. I continued on my same flight schedule and was actually trying to pick up as many extra flights as possible because Brad constantly reminded me about the pay hit we'd have to take while I was on maternity leave. I planned on being one of those moms who would have a baby and joyfully go back to work. They exist, right? Who knew how a baby could change your life. Babies come with red annunciator lights. They are the most urgent warnings and require immediate and full focused attention.

Morning sickness also comes with a red warning light. Everything I smelled, looked at, or thought about made me sick. I craved Pop Tarts, but would gag at the thought of chicken. You can just imagine how well I did in the airplane lavatory. Each morning, I'd walk with the crew into the airplane and excuse myself to the restroom. I was going to throw up no matter what, so just simply walking into the ghastly smell of the restroom would just start the sequence. I avoided eating during a flight and stuck to pretzels and ginger ale. I was able to manage it so that I never threw up when I had passengers onboard, but it took all my strength and concentration to take my focus off my body and put it on the task at hand.

For the passengers on my flights during my pregnancy, they were the safest flights I've ever flown. Every move I made was for the safety of me and my baby, so my passengers got the peripheral result of my overly anal retentiveness. I drove the other pilots crazy because I turned off the radar unless I absolutely needed it. I just kept thinking about all the passive radiation bouncing around in the flight deck, and adding the radar beam to the mix conjured up thoughts of extra limbs and eyes.

I flew until I was eight months pregnant. Yes, I know. I shouldn't have. I was sleeping on a hide-a-bed at the crash pad, at eight months pregnant. I was commuting and working a full schedule up until the last moment. I was a walking mass of change being held together by a lifetime of focus.

The topic of my pregnancy was never mentioned, and I know it made everyone uncomfortable. There was no policy, no uniform adjustments, and no standard procedure for this. My pregnancy was handled like I had a disease that would be cured in nine months. They forgot this disease also had a lifetime of side effects.

I am five foot eleven inches (well, I was before I got pregnant), so I was able to hide the extent of my pregnancy with a suit coat and aviation sweaters, and they never asked when my due date was. I wasn't sure when I should stop flying, but I figured when I couldn't pull back on the yoke or get out of the emergency exit, I'd call crew scheduling and tell them I was too fat to fly.

My maternity leave had to start before most women. I really couldn't safely operate the airplane during an emergency with my stomach in the way of the yoke and indicator lights. I called (s)crew scheduling to tell them, and they asked that I fly three more trips. What part of "I'm not safe to fly" didn't they understand? I had already waited too long, but it meant that my baby would be just two months old when my maternity leave would be used up. Crew scheduling happily reminded me of that when I went on maternity leave.

It was during these final months of happy anticipation and introspection at home that I first felt a shift in the relationship with Brad. Never having spent this much time alone together, simple disagreements escalated into arguments, and Brad learned quickly that calling me a "fucking cunt," or his favorite, "stupid fucking bitch" would take my breath away, and he would win the argument by default. I was shocked into silence and stopped the argument immediately by walking away.

I'd never been called that, and it was particularly shocking because it was in response to such benign things. He'd taunt and say, "Oh yeah, just walk away. You're just proving you're a weak, dumb bitch." Afterward, he'd laugh and give me a hug while saying, "God, you're acting like you're having your period, but obviously not..."

Here I was, eight months pregnant and being called names no one deserves to be called. I spent the last of my pregnancy an emotional wreck, constantly in tears. Is this truly part of a relationship? Do people do this to each other? If someone does this, will it ever stop? Since I was always traveling while we were dating and in the first few months of marriage, we always had the rush of excitement of seeing each other. Now, we were with each other from sunrise to sunrise, and the sun was only shining meekly through the overcast.

After twenty-six hours of labor, six hours of pushing, and no drugs, I ended up with a cesarean section because my daughter had an enormous head (I tell her it's all those brains in there) and refused to turn around, so she got stuck in the birth canal sunny side up. Every time I had a contraction, her neck and head would bend to create a ball that simply got wedged. The warning lights on the baby monitor started screaming louder than I was, so into the operating room we went.

When I hear birthing stories, my fascination always turns to how the husbands handled the situation. I believe that how they handle this situation is indicative of how they handle everything else in their life.

My water broke about 10:00 p.m. and the contractions were faint and about eight minutes apart, so there was no rush. But because we lived an hour away in the mountains, we got ourselves down to the hospital right away. By 6:00 a.m., the contractions were about four minutes apart and stayed that way most of the day. By 3:00 p.m., they were about two minutes apart and their strength was breathtaking, but I was progressing slowly. Shortly before 6:00 p.m., my husband walked up to my bed in the delivery room and announced that he was exhausted and hungry. His mom, standing beside him, put her hands on his shoulder and said, "Oh, Brad, I'm sorry. I should have brought you dinner. You must be beat. Let's take a break and pop out for some dinner."

I had already been awake for thirty six hours (Brad slept most of the night on the cot in the room and had a nice breakfast and lunch), and Brad tells me he needs a break for a while? He actually left the birthing room as the nurses were coming in to instruct me to start pushing. He shrugged his shoulders and said he had to get away from the commotion for a while. He came back an hour later and since I was still pushing, he said, "See, I didn't miss a thing."

While they were giving me an epidural, I wondered why the fuck they couldn't have given it to me about twenty hours earlier. Within ten minutes, my body was released from my mind, and I lay on the surgical table with the doctor telling me I'll feel pressure and pulling. I did, and compared to the previous pain, I didn't care. My daughter was "born" at 12:13 a.m., and she was the color of a Smurf. Big and blue, but as life can be, she changed from blue to pink in a matter of moments as she gathered her strength to give us her first wail.

My eyes well up with tears just remembering the moment they put her in my arms. Why the hell is everyone looking for the meaning of life? It's right there, in that moment, when you realize why we exist. There was an actual pathway created in my brain at that moment that connects mother and child. Even now, if I see that either of my children are in danger (or if my brain even thinks they *might* be in danger) or about to get hurt, I have an actual physical contraction. My kids think it's hilarious and after an injury, they wipe their tears and ask, "Mom, did that give you a contraction?" They smile because it always does. It's an intense, painful contraction. What better example of Mother Nature's power than having an uncontrollable physical reaction to something your eyes and brain see? It didn't exist until I'd given birth, but it created an automatic warning indicator system within my own body. That instinct was created at that moment of birth and it may not always happen for everyone, but it did for me. It's strong and deep and no matter how much a father loves their children, it doesn't compare with the power of connection between mother and child. You can't always have equal rights.

Brad was bursting with excitement and emotion. Usually joking and teasing the nurses, holding his baby girl moved him to tears and silence. He could hardly speak as a new range of emotions he'd never experienced before flooded his mind and body. His face was framed with joy and pride. Since I was recovering from a birth and a surgery, Brad proudly carried her for as long as the nurses would allow. He held her, sang to her, and told her that he would always be there to protect her. He was kind, gentle, and healing to me. He helped me take a shower and brushed my hair as we conspired to get out of the hospital as soon as possible so we could block out the world and be at home with our baby.

We left the next morning, and it was the safest car ride we've ever taken. Brad came to full stops at the stop signs and went ten under the speed limit. We were giddy with joy. Neither of us could believe what a little six pound baby could do to our souls. You just want to be a better person once you've held your own child.

We named her Lindsey, and she had already traveled thousands of air miles before ever taking her first breath. She was blue eyed, strong, and colicky. My mom reminded me that I was colicky, too, and that it was poetic payback. I felt horrible that I couldn't soothe her. Each time she reached that level of hysterical crying where I thought I would start crying hysterically, too, I would run through my checklist. Has she been fed, does she have clean diapers, soft clothes, burped, still breathing? Yes to all. I finally learned that sometimes she was just going to have to cry. And she cried and cried and cried! There is nothing worse than being sleep deprived for days on end and have a baby that can't tell you what's wrong except by crying. It's their only warning system, and they don't come with clear indicator lights.

It was the eighth night of Lindsey's life that my husband first hit me. It was sudden and shocking, and it didn't come with a warning light.

On this eighth night, Brad had gone to bed about 9:00 p.m. and Lindsey usually started her colic fits about then. It was now 2:00 a.m., and I had not been to sleep yet. Lindsey had gone from crying to cooing to nursing to crying again. I had not had more than two hours of sleep in a row over a week and my brain hummed from the torture.

I was trying to let Brad sleep because he had to go to work in the morning, but our small three-level mountain home was open and airy, and sound carried well—and Lindsey had hit a rather high pitch. I had just given her a warm sponge bath, put her in clean diapers and clothes, and she nursed about twenty minutes. There was nothing else to do except to let her cry it out before she fell asleep, but unbeknownst to me, Brad was tossing and turning unable to sleep with the crying.

I was walking her around her room with her head on my shoulder when Brad came in, bleary eyed and angry. He didn't say a word as he just walked over and took her from me. For a moment, I thought he was going to walk her around for me. He'd helped walk her around on the previous nights, so I just handed her over. What actually happened is that he put her down on the changing table to change her dry diapers. The moment he laid her down, her crying intensified to hysteria. I immediately walked over and tried to explain. "I just changed her. She has dry diapers. She just needs to finish crying this one out, so please don't get her more worked up. She just needs to be comforted so she can relax and fall asleep. Stop! Don't take off her pajamas! What are you doing?"

While I was explaining this to him with a draining amount of patience, I had walked up behind his left side and was looking over his shoulder to see what he was doing and to try and convince him to stop undoing the clothes and diapers that I had just put on her. I'm sure my tone was not kind; I was at my wit's end, but at that moment, I felt his elbow wallop into my cesarean section incision with such force I dropped to the ground. He looked over me and said, "Don't ever fucking tell me what to do. You can't get her to stop crying so you must be doing something wrong, and I can't wait any longer to find out what the hell is wrong with her! What's wrong with you that you can't get her to stop crying? You're her mother for Christ's sake!"

With this, he plopped Lindsey back onto the changing table, stepped over me to get out of the room, and went back to bed. He left Lindsey screaming on the changing table and he left me on the ground with half my incision peeled open and bleeding. I lay curled in a ball for what seemed eternity before I felt I could move again. I looked down and my nightgown was covered in blood, but all I could think was that Lindsey was crying so hard, she might fall off the changing table.

When I attempted to stand up, I thought it quite possible that my guts would drop out—the pain was mind-numbing. C-sections feel like that anyway, and as I lifted my nightgown I was relieved to find my guts intact, but saw that the wound was bleeding badly. Thankfully, it didn't appear to be anything worse than some stretched stitches. I put a diaper on it and applied pressure. It stopped bleeding after about twenty minutes. I self-diagnosed that since it stopped bleeding, I must be okay.

I wasn't okay. Not in any sense of the word. I had never been hit before. Sure, my sister and I took swings at each other when we were kids, but it wasn't in the scope of my imagination that this man whom I loved and adored would do this to me, especially when we had just had the most incredible experience of bringing a baby into the world. We were supposed to be a team for better or worse. These things only happen to other women who do bad things. Or those who live in trailer parks or low-income housing units. I was so naïve. My mind started taking inventory of what bad thing I had done. I talked it over with my internal committee (we all have one, have you talked to yours lately? It's usually the justification committee that I ended up talking to) and they were confused, too. *He must've been so tired he just had no idea what he was doing. We're both so tired we can't think straight. He'll apologize in the morning. He'll tell me something to make it okay. It has to be okay. You just had a perfect, beautiful baby with your husband, and you are a team. There were no warning lights and your cruise checklist is supposed to be nothing but smooth flying. He's never hit you before, and there is no way he's going to hit you again. Our life is just too perfect. Why in the world would he get so angry to actually hit me?*

When the sun rose the next morning, Lindsey was still sleeping, so I was, too. I didn't hear Brad leave the house so I awoke to find the bed empty. I thought he must be feeling badly for what he'd done. I was sure he'd left a note downstairs or something to let me know he was sorry. There was nothing. He said nothing. He came home that day and I had dinner ready, and we ate, and he said nothing. I said nothing. It was the beginning of nothing, nothing, nothing....

14 Engine Fire, Failure, or Separation Checklist

1. Fly the airplane
2. Fly the airplane
3. Fly the airplane
4. Land

If you're reading this checklist, the proverbial shit has hit the fan. Try taking a deep breath and remember one thing; just fly the airplane. Your main goal at this point is to control the airplane in a forward path and then, if there is a fire, to put it out.

When an engine fails on any aircraft with more than one engine, the sudden loss of power is amplified by the fact that the other engine is operating at full power. The aircraft wants to yaw (pivot) immediately towards the side of the failed engine. The overcompensation is a deadly tendency, especially right after takeoff when your aircraft is at its heaviest and the other operating engine is at full power. It is counterintuitive, but in some aircraft it's necessary to pull back the power on the operating engine to overcome yaw, if it's severe, while you are trimming the airplane to compensate for the new line of thrust.

You'd think it would be obvious to determine immediately which engine failed, but it's hard to maintain directional control right after engine failure, and it might take a moment to figure out which engine quit working. Pilots are trained to remember that the dead foot (not holding down the rudder) determines the dead engine, and depending on what type of aircraft, the effect can be mild to extreme. Everyone thinks a twin engine aircraft is safer than a single engine, but with an engine failure at takeoff in a light twin engine, having a second engine often means you plow into the farmer's field a little farther away and at a much faster speed.

The well-publicized video of the TransAsia crash in Taiwan sums it up. They had an engine fail right after takeoff, which shouldn't have been that big of a deal, but in the ensuing chaos, they accidentally shut down the operating engine. The question in the media was how a pilot could shut down the wrong engine. The answer is: easily, and every multiengine pilot knows it could happen, so we all train for it.

When the engine failed, it wasn't the dead engine that was their primary concern, it was the good engine operating at full takeoff power that was trying to yaw and turn them into the dead engine. Subliminally, in the moment of mechanical pandemonium, they pulled back the power on the good engine so, for a few moments, they were moving straight ahead and had control. That moment of Zen led them to believe they were shutting down the correct engine. In this case, they shouldn't have done anything except fly the airplane, come back around, and land where they just took off.

All the engines of my life were running at full throttle and I forgot how hard the yaw would be when one failed. I'd repeatedly trained for engine failure, but when it happened, I forgot to put my foot down hard on the other rudder to regain my directional control. I just let the operating engine yaw into the dead engine and plow me deep into the earth.

Brad never did say a word about hitting me. Life went on, but I felt betrayed. Considering everyone I'd ever known in my life, I had never had a violation of trust like what happened that night. In the big scheme of events in the world, this was nothing, but I never for one moment thought he would ever hit me and treat me with such disregard. I assumed there was an unspoken contract between partners that no matter how mad you are, you still don't hit someone, especially eight days after that someone gave birth to your daughter. He was my best friend and ally, and having him strike me was completely out of the realm of possibilities. When it happened, I could do nothing but try and justify it.

In that moment of impact, Brad became something else in a blink of an eye. It not only changed me and how I viewed him, but it changed him and opened up a strength and avenue of dominance he didn't realize he had. After that day, all he had to do was make a quick motion like he was going to hit me, and I'd flinch and shutdown. I couldn't stand the thought of him even having the idea that he was allowed to hit me. I didn't care about the physical pain, which was temporary and minor; I was worried about being able to love someone who might hit me in the future.

What I learned to do in situations where I couldn't accept what was happening to me was to tell myself how much worse other people had it. I justified it. It's a very woman thing to do. I didn't actually know anybody who'd been hit by her husband, so I told myself that millions of women must be in situations much worse than this. I figured the scenario of *Sleeping with the Enemy* must happen all the time and none of us know it. I had a nice house, healthy child, and food in the fridge. Just live with it. If I couldn't find resolution with that, I'd take it to a multi-national and cultural scale (must be all those years of my mom telling me I was ungrateful for not eating my dinner. "Just think about all those poor, starving children in Africa who would love to be sitting where you are." Oh, the guilt!). That way, I could remind myself of those poor women in Iraq, Iran, and India who would trade places with me in a heartbeat. And it's true. The problem with that was I lived in *this* here and now and when I look back, I realize how I began to change after that first strike. I was ashamed of myself for making the wrong choices, and it began a cycle of destructive self-talk that eroded who I thought I was.

I don't know who changed more — him or me.

He never apologized for hitting me, but what he did do was suddenly start helping out with chores. Even when I was working full time I still did most of the household chores, but all of a sudden he was pitching in without me even asking. He did some laundry, and he even brought home takeout one night, which he had never done before. I never knew the simple relief of not having to cook a meal could be so uplifting. He remembered to call when he was running late, and thanked me for making dinner. All those little things you should do anyway, he started doing with an obsession. We'd sit down every night and without looking at me, he'd say, "Thank you for making dinner."

He became a trained robot and, out of duty, said all the things he was supposed to say, and we both pretended nothing happened. He was kind and sweet that following week, and it was possible to convince myself that it was a momentary lapse of reason and that he was showing how sorry he was by overcompensating in daily kindness.

It lulled me into a sense of security because I truly felt he was sorry for what he'd done, even though he didn't say it. I tucked the incident into the back of my brain as an unfortunate moment and shame on me for even thinking that one incident should change or redefine our relationship. Even though he hit me, he was acting like such a good husband. Maybe it was worth taking a hit if we could have such a nice relationship.

Lindsey was eight weeks old and crew scheduling reminded me it was time to go back to work. There were still several company pilots on layoff, so I was able to convince the chief pilot and crew scheduling to call a furloughed pilot back to work and extend my maternity leave for another month. They made sure I understood it was just one more month. It was unpaid leave, but I was so deeply in love with my new baby that the thought of leaving her for even a few minutes sent chills down my spine and acid into my stomach. How was I ever going to go back to work? My entire body ached at the thought of being away from her for more than a few hours.

I had to push the doubts aside because I had made a deal with Brad and our baby. I chanted the mantra over and over that a lot of women work full-time and their children are fine...right? Lindsey would have the luxury bonus of a stay at home parent— it just wouldn't be me. She would get to stay in this glorious mountain home and not have to spend a moment in daycare.

Problem was, ever since Lindsey had been born, Brad was tentative around her. At the first whimper or squirm, he would hand her over, but it was because I was there. I figured if I wasn't there, he'd have to step up and learn how to fix a baby. He was a mechanic. He knew how to troubleshoot a problem. It's easy, just follow the checklist. Even though Brad had not spent any significant time alone with Lindsey, I knew if I could do it, so could he. He was excited about being a stay-at-home dad, and how hard could it be to fix a fifteen pound human?

Brad turned in his notice at work and joyfully burned his mechanic's uniform. He had already used his paternity leave (unpaid time off, but you are allowed to use your sick and vacation time up) to build a greenhouse, and he was looking forward to staying home and tackling more projects.

I was jealous that he was going to get to be the stay-at-home parent, but I knew in my heart that we needed to be financially durable, so I was going to willingly make the sacrifice to keep our family structure strong. I put myself in this new mindset, focused on the plan, and made my checklist—never once thinking I would need to deviate from it.

Since I had not flown for four months, I had to go back to Minneapolis for recurrent training before I could go back to work. I was already having anxiety dreams that I showed up at the airplane and had no idea what I was doing. The nightmare would begin as I got off the crew bus and realized that I had forgotten my uniform and clothes for my week-long trip. As I crawled into the cockpit in my shorts and t-shirt, I'd get the airplane started, and during the takeoff roll I'd realize I didn't know what to do next. It was at that moment in my dream that the terror of completely forgetting how to fly would set in, but I was too embarrassed to tell the other crew members that I didn't know what to do, and I'd wake up drenched in sweat and my heart in my throat. I always knew what to do in real life, so my brain knew how to create the perfect nightmare.

The first step of going back to work was in motion and I was leaving my baby for the first time. I cried all the way to the airport. I cried the entire night before, during the flight, and the entire first night in the hotel. I was determined to breast feed for a full year, so I pumped every two hours to keep the milk supply going. I was narcoleptic tired trying to prepare for my upcoming simulator training, but I'd been informed by the chief pilot that I would not be returning as captain, that I'd been demoted to first officer. That was my punishment for having a baby. They really didn't give me a reason; I was simply instructed to prepare for recurrent training as a first officer. I was completely pissed off, but figured it was only temporary and was politics as usual. They were going to use me as a way of deterring the other women who had entered our pilot herd to stay away from the mommy track. It took the burden off of me to study for the captain's check ride, so the feeling of "fuck you" was mutual. I was still a junior captain and low on the seniority list, so I figured I might have to bounce between first officer and captain for a few months.

Four days. That's how long it took for an entire life's worth of planning to come unglued. On my fourth day of training, I was slammed. I was informed that I was suddenly expected to pass the captain's check ride or be passed over permanently for a captain's slot in Denver. They made sure I knew that I would not have a captain's bidding schedule, but I was expected to pass the captain check ride. I couldn't say no. I was already flying as captain, but shit, I really hadn't studied to that level, and I hadn't flown for four months. I was rusty, disconnected, and I was missing my child to the point of dysfunction.

I spent the entire day locked in my hotel room trying to review everything there was to know about aviation—which seemed like a lifetime of knowledge. I usually liked to unwind before my simulator sessions, but I had a 10:00 p.m. captain's oral and simulator check ride I had to pass, so I studied straight through dinner.

At 9:10 p.m., the phone rang. It was Brad.

He didn't get past "Hi" before I interrupted him. "Hey, Brad, I'm in a huge hurry. I found out I am being given a captain's check ride and the van is picking me up in twenty minutes to go to the simulator," but before I finished my thoughts, I took a sharp intake of breath thinking maybe something was wrong with Lindsey and that's why he was calling.

"Wait. What's wrong? What's up? Is everything okay?" I instantly dove into panic overload.

"Yes, there *is* something wrong," Brad stammered. "I can't do this. I just can't. It's not what I expected, and I think I'm going to hurt her…"

"Wait, what? What are you talking about? Can't do what? Is Lindsey okay?" I just couldn't piece together what he was saying. My mind was focused off in the distance, and I couldn't draw it in.

He took a deep breath and his tone changed. In a firm voice he said, "I can't be the stay-at-home dad. I just can't. It's not right. You have to come home, and we need to figure something else out. This isn't going to work for me…"

I knew the feeling of fear and self-doubt of being home alone with a newborn. It was absolutely terrifying sometimes, so

I just figured he needed a boost of confidence. He was in a weak moment, and it was going to be okay. During my first full day of recurrent training in Minneapolis, I had called him on what was to be his first day alone with Lindsey, only to find out that he'd gone to his mom's house. I called Bernice's house, and found that Brad was sleeping. He spent the first two days at his mom's house with Lindsey, so he hadn't even been alone with her until this particular day.

"Oh, Brad, you're just having a bad day. I know how that goes. It'll be okay, just give it some time. You'll get used to it, and you'll learn what to do to soothe her. It just takes practice. Sometimes she just needs to cry."

While I was saying the last few words, he was overriding me by saying, "No, no, no. NO! I have thought about this. I can't stand staying here all day listening to her cry off and on. I'm all jittery and I'm afraid I'm going to hurt her." All I could think was that he meant he'd hurt her by mistake. That's not what he meant, and I was too dense to catch what he was truly admitting.

I was peeved at this intrusion when all I should be thinking about is the next four hours. "God, Brad. I'm about to step into the simulator for my check ride. I'm a wreck and can barely concentrate as it is. Can this wait until tomorrow? Please?"

"I'm sorry if this is fucking inconvenient for you, but I want you to know that when you get home, things are going to change. I'll see you tomorrow night when you get home. Good luck on your check ride…" and he hung up.

I was trembling as I gathered up my flight bag. All of a sudden, his words screamed in my brain…"I'm afraid I'm going to hurt her." I thought I was going to throw up, and with one of the most important check rides was just minutes away, I was coming unhinged.

Never before had I not fully prepared for a check ride. I thought I'd teach them a lesson by just prepping for a copilot's check. Duh, who was I hurting? Now my job was on the line and the phone call I just got threw me so off balance, I felt like I needed to be caught.

To this day, I'm still embarrassed by my weak performance that night. We all have bad days in the simulator, but I was ashamed of myself. I felt I was letting down every woman who was going to come behind me who wanted to be a mom. Was it true that we just can't have it all? Maybe our definition of "all" changes over time, because I just didn't want this.

I fumbled through the oral exam and barely survived the simulator session. Thankfully, I had taken check rides with this training captain before so he knew what I was capable of—and this wasn't it. I think he passed me out of pity. I was still safe, was within the margins of error, and didn't crash the simulator even under dire circumstance, but it was complete slop. The captain never asked what was going on, but since he was a father, I assume he just thought I was having a tough time being a new mom. I was. I was having a fucking tough time with everything. I promised him that I would go home and study my ass off. I knew enough to be safe and pass the check ride, but that wasn't my style. I always wanted to know more than the next guy, and being average wasn't okay with me. I didn't want to just fly, I wanted to soar.

I came home completely defeated. I had to explain to Brad that I wouldn't be able to hold a captain's line right now and that I'd be bidding first officer. I knew the situation was political and temporary and after a few months I'd be back to holding a captain's slot. I babbled and made small talk in anticipation of the heavy discussion that Brad said was due. I dreaded the answer, but finally asked the loaded question while smiling, "So, how'd it go with Lindsey?"

Brad didn't say anything. Instead, he walked backwards towards the couch and sat down. His eyes told me to have a seat so I took a deep breath and sat down.

"I'm sorry. I can't do it."

"What? What are you saying? I don't understand. What can't you do?" I asked it, but I already knew. The hopes and dreams that the giddiness of fresh relationships spawn, was about to go over the bridge. Our plans that were sublime in the making were now being held up with false hope, and the pressure was building to a level where something had to give.

"Look. I'll just say it. You're not going to change my mind. I'm not going to be the stay at home parent. I'll be honest. It's just too hard. I know that sounds lame, but I really think I could hurt her. I don't want that to happen. I love her and I love you. I love you both with all my heart, so we've got to figure something else out. I'm sorry." The tears that were threatening exposure finally spilled and the sight of them running down his cheeks broke my heart. All I wanted was the best for my family and in the end, my job was just a job. If I could find another way to earn an income, I would do it.

At that moment, I didn't give a flying fuck about flying. My momma bear instinct went into overdrive and I responded with how I truly felt. "Brad. Don't worry. We'll figure something out." As my words melted in the air, that tiny door that I'd once opened that whispered, "Back-up Plan," expanded wide enough that I could see myself stepping through. The idea of being there to raise my child inspired me to push the door open wider to see what was on the other side.

After being away from Lindsey for five days for the first time, I gladly volunteered for nighttime baby duties. It was during those lonely hours that I projected how a new plan could make it all work. I looked into my child's eyes and it truly didn't matter what *I* wanted anymore. I would gladly give up everything to make sure she was safe and loved. I was done leaning in.

During one of my furloughs after 9/11, I had casually thought about starting a side business that might help me during the ups and downs of the airline economy. Never thinking I'd make a living from any other source, I just thought a side business might generate a little fun money or gap money should I get furloughed again.

During my perusal, I'd found one particular business that wasn't retail and had low overhead. The owner was selling his business plan structure like a franchise, so I pulled out the information again and reviewed it with the idea that it was going to be my one and only source of income. I called the owner and after a lengthy conversation, I knew we could make this work.

I presented the whole idea and plan to Brad, and we were both ecstatic at the idea of controlling our own schedule and our own lives. In the back of my mind, I was still clinging to the hope that Brad would come around and say that he thought we could still start this business while he took care of Lindsey, just while I was on my trips. The last of that hope was severed when Brad firmly explained that there was no way he was going to work on starting up a business while watching a newborn. It couldn't be done. If we were going to do this, we were going to do it right and put everything into it—which meant he needed me to stay at home and be a mom and support him.

In exchange for me being the stay-at-home parent and taking every penny I had in my savings and retirement accounts to buy a construction warranty management business, Brad said he would run the day to day operations of our new company. I would work behind the scenes doing business development, getting the office together and finding leads on new home builders. I could work from the home office and Brad would run the office in Evergreen. He promised if I left my career, he would take care of us, forever. He would build the business, and I would build our family.

Still nervous about just quitting, I secretly called the chief pilot's office and repeatedly left messages, asking for a meeting or a phone conversation. Days passed with no response, so I wrote my company a letter asking for an unpaid leave of absence for just a few more months. I didn't want anything from them except to hold my seniority number. They wouldn't have to pay insurance and I even said if there was an expense associated with holding my slot, I'd pay them for it. I was even willing to slide down to a lower seniority number for each month that passed, but they didn't even give it a moment's consideration. Absolutely not. When I reminded them we still had pilots on furlough, they still said no.

Since Brad received his pilot's license in college, he knew everything there was to know about being a pilot. He knew that once I turned in my notice, I could not easily go back. Aviation is all about seniority, and I would have to start all over again—at the very black bottom. I planned on returning to aviation, but we both acknowledged it would be an uphill climb again. I figured I did it once, so I would just do it again. I would have to switch companies, because airlines rarely take anyone back. They correctly figure that if they dump hundreds of thousands of dollars of training into someone, they better not ever quit and walk away. It was unheard of. It's like the mafia; once you're in, you stay in and the only way out is to wait until your age allows you leave, and even then, you'll bore everyone by talking about it. No one quits the airlines.

I quit the airlines.

I wrote them a nice letter and gave them my two weeks notice. To thank me for my years of service, they allowed me to show up for my last trip on Halloween, but they had a secret replacement pilot there waiting to take the trip away from me. I walked up to the gate to savor my last trip, and there was a junior copilot standing there who guiltily informed me crew scheduling decided to put him on the trip instead. Oh, I suppose they thought I might pull something, since I was so insane to quit. They covered their ass by having another pilot there. They said I could still fly the leg if I really wanted to, but you know what? Fuck that. Fuck them. I got paid *not* to fly the trip, so I gave my crew a hug and said I was going home to Evergreen, to sit on my deck, with my baby in my arms, and I'd wave as they flew overheard on their way to Las Vegas. And that's exactly what I did. Well, not exactly. I did sit on my deck and watch the airplane go overhead, but I didn't wave. I gave the blue tail the finger as I watched it lumber to its cruising altitude over Evergreen, Colorado.

While Brad was out in the world starting our new business, I was now at home, forever in awe of our baby girl. My attention and energy I had shared with the world was now turned to one little creature. I would stare at her for hours because I was astonished that my body could actually make this gorgeous, squirming handful of flesh and blood. I couldn't wait for her to talk to me. I wanted to meet her, to know her. I wanted everything for her, and I made little vows every day that I would always do the right thing for her and provide her a good home. That last part is hard to do when you're out of money, but I was beginning to learn the meaning of home wasn't just about money.

The first year, we made $2,800 in taxable income. We went from $150,000/year combined income to poverty income in a matter of months. Of course, this change in income triggered an IRS audit which was painful but as it turned out, the IRS owed us another $4,000 — guess the IRS agent didn't have *that* on his checklist.

During this time, Brad thought maybe learning the stock market and doing a few day trades could help supplement our income while we were getting the business established. He came home one night and informed me that he had signed up for a stock market course with his dad. I figured the class would cost a couple hundred bucks and would just give a few pointers to get him started.

The truth was that it was actually $11,000 for a two week course that smelled of scam in the fine print. After the first class,

Brad came home psyched up and said there was a way to set it up, which guaranteed there would be a limit on how much you lost, if any. The system had built-in checkpoints that would kick you out of a trade if it looked like it was failing. He never bothered to tell me the cost of tuition or confirm that he would set up the stop limits. He told me that trust was a huge issue with him and that I really hadn't done anything to show him that I trusted him, so it was vitally important to trust him on this and just enjoy the profits. Since my entire savings and retirement accounts were nearing zero, and our income wasn't doing much better, I was getting nervous. This Hail Mary income gamble sounded so good, even if only half of it came true. Brad kept assuring me that I'd done my part by buying the business and living off my savings: now it was his turn to show me he could bring home the bacon.

Within six weeks, he'd lost tens of thousands of dollars and *my* stocks. I had agreed to let him do some trading on my Options Xpress accounts and he guaranteed me that he couldn't lose money — or if he lost, it would be minor. He kept gambling, trying to earn it back, but he just sunk deeper into the losses. At the time I discovered the stock loss, I had no idea of the cost of tuition or the actual cost of the lost stock.

It was our first huge fight. It was the first time I raised my voice to him. More than the money, I couldn't believe he was so deceitful. He hid the actual cost of tuition and tried to turn it on me by saying it was my fault for letting him have access to the stocks and money.

"God, Erika, you shouldn't have let me use it if you were going to be this mad if I lost it! This is the stock market! You know it's not a sure thing!" It's not a sure thing if you don't actually set the parameters to get out, like I assumed he would. He was so sure he was right that he pulled the stops and kept riding it down. I was so caught up in his dream that I forgot to remember that, of course, he could lose it. I just didn't think he'd lose it all. I just didn't think, so in the end, I figured it was completely my fault since I'd made the false assumption.

I was scared. We were out of money. I'd spent all my savings to start the business and to live on for the first year. Lindsey and I spent our days just going to parks and playgrounds, and I never spent a penny on anything I didn't need. I helped Brad when he asked for help, and I shopped at Goodwill and the discount racks at the grocery store. He kept reassuring me that his salesman skills would land a big client. In this business, just one big client could be the difference between poverty and prosperity, and we'd been so close several times. One even signed on the dotted line, but filed bankruptcy three months later. If it had gone as planned, we would've netted close to six figures on just one client. Success was so close, we could taste it. Brad was working really hard, and I respected his endurance and perseverance when every potential client was saying no.

During this despair, I had mentioned the possibility of going back to fly corporate aviation. I always intended to return to aviation anyway, and since I had a few friends in the business who had recently tossed out offers, I figured it was worth a follow-up. I was still on the edge of currency (you have to keep your ratings current with hours in the air, takeoff/ landing practice, and instrument flying) and it wouldn't be too hard to get back in the air.

Brad looked me hard in the eye to make me understand that he couldn't work from home or be responsible for taking care of Lindsey while he was working our business, so I brought up the idea of a nanny. There is no such thing as daycare to accommodate a corporate pilot's schedule, so it would have to be a nanny. I told him I'd probably earn enough to have a live-in nanny, but he said no way would he let anyone stay in the house, or be there when he was there.

Another difficulty with aviation is that you never know when you'll have a huge weather or mechanical delay. In the past, I would sometimes get home days late. How was I going to get care for Lindsey? Brad wouldn't do it or let a nanny live with us. I said I could go back to work just until we got some steady clients and our finances stabilized. If I didn't go back now, my currency would expire and it would be harder and harder as each week passed. It was now or never. Brad was a licensed pilot and knew the rules and terms. He knew the intricacy of the aviation world, but he was astonished that I even mentioned going back to flying.

This conversation lead into the discussion about trust again and he let it be known that he was deeply offended that I thought he couldn't make our business prosper. He said it was because of my negative attitude towards his ability that our business wasn't thriving, and that if I just put my full trust behind him, then things would get better.

I wanted to believe. I knew Brad could sell snow to an Eskimo. He was a natural bull-shitter and salesman. He could get you to smile even when you didn't want to, and he could be standing on hot coals and look you in the eye with a smile and say he was cold. I wanted it to work, so I said I'd set aside the idea about returning to work, but I don't think he was convinced. His ego was wounded to think his wife would go back to work to pay for his mistakes.

15 Unidentified Indications of Impending Failure

1. Aircraft components fail in unique individual ways
2. No one knows how or when they will fail
3. The only guarantee is that even the strongest components must eventually fail
4. It ain't gonna fix itself

A Boeing 747 has approximately six million parts, give or take a few bolts, not including the 250 miles of wiring. Engineers understand that items will eventually fail, so all aircraft are designed to have their major or moving components fail to the "safe" mode/function so as to not damage other devices or put personnel in danger. This fail-safe concept is used in all fields of engineering, like having a dead man's switch on a lawnmower or Jet Ski. Since many types of failure are possible, it must be specific to what failure a component should fail into—either the "safe" or "secure" mode.

If, for example, a building catches fire, a fail-*safe* system would unlock the doors to let firefighters in. A fail-*secure* mode would lock the doors to prevent unauthorized access. One would think that safe and secure are both positive traits, but it always depends on the situation.

Two days before the New Year, the sun had finally powered through the clouds. One of Lindsey's first Christmas presents was a crystal ornament that refracted rainbows around the room when placed in the sun. I hung it up in her window that morning and laid her on a blanket in the middle of the room. She had been kicking and squirming, but when she saw the rainbows, she stopped in mid-movement and held her breath. Her eyes opened wide and she squealed in delight at the sight of a thousand rainbows dancing on her walls and ceiling. I took off her pajamas and let her move around with just a diaper on. She loved the sensation and freedom of being half naked after months of winter clothes, and the sun was warm on her skin. Since she was content and safe, I left the door open and walked down to the computer room where Brad was working on setting up our new QuickBooks program.

Brad was holding his head like it would explode. I understood because that's how I felt in class trying to learn QuickBooks. I sat on the bed behind him and he started asking questions about getting the program set up. Unfortunately, the class I took was just one day and they only discussed how to use an existing program. For every question he asked, I had to answer that I didn't know or wasn't sure. He had been sitting for hours and his frustration was at its maximum level, but I didn't realize this until he started talking.

"I just want to know how to get the new checking account going and to have it track expenses!"

"Well, try clicking on this and see what happens…"

"I've already tried that three times and it's not working, damn it!"

"Okay, take it easy. Why don't we look it up in this QuickBooks reference guide? Have you already tried looking it up?"

As soon as I said it, I knew he'd be mad. I knew that he didn't really want my help and he was just venting his frustration. As soon as the words left my mouth, my insides recoiled and I felt the intense urge to bolt out of the room.

"No, I haven't fucking looked it up! That's why I paid money for you to take a QuickBooks class—so I didn't have to look it up. You're supposed to fucking know how to do this! I knew I shouldn't have let you go to that class. I should've taken the class myself so I wouldn't be sitting here for hours just trying to do the basic shit that you should know!"

With this, I just got up and walked out of the room. While I was walking away, he yelled, "Where the hell do you think you're going?!"

"I'm not going to sit and listen to you insult me. You're acting like such a dick!"

I called him a "dick." Not off the charts nasty, but yes, not nice. The catch is that I'd never called him a name before. In the past and on numerous occasions, he had called me a cunt, a stupid fucking bitch, and a dumb shit...yet "dick" offended him. I could hear the chair crash into the desk as he bolted to his feet in an instant.

"What did you say?"

"I said you were acting like a dick — and you are!" I wasn't going to back down this time. He was being ridiculous about a damn computer program.

"I wouldn't be acting like a dick if you weren't so stupid! If you just knew how to do this like you said you did, then we wouldn't be yelling at each other!" I didn't know how to respond so I turned around and fled up to Lindsey's room.

Lindsey was still cooing and smiling at the infinite number of dancing rainbows racing around the room. I walked over and kneeled down on the blanket with her and started talking to her, but I could hear Brad coming up the stairs. She needed a diaper change so I planned on just ignoring him and work at the task at hand as a way of not engaging in this crazy conversation.

I think the mere fact that I was ignoring him made his mind leap from rational to utterly illogical, and I could feel sweat breaking out on the middle of my back where I hold all my stress.

He walked to the opposite side of the blanket and kept berating me for not paying attention in class. His voice was rising and I kept giving him the crusty eye more or less to keep his voice down. Lindsey had definitely stopped smiling and was looking intently at Brad as he brought his face closer and closer to my face over the top of her.

When he was about three inches from my face, I could smell the stress on his breath as he contorted his face up and raised his upper lip as he spat out, "You are just such a stupid, fucking bitch. I can't believe I married you..." He held his face in front of mine waiting for a response.

That moment, that exact moment, I felt it. "It" is an instinct that comes from the gut of your soul that says enough. My fail-*secure* system kicked in, and I wasn't going to allow further access. The variable was our daughter. He'd said this in front of our baby girl, lying on her blanket with rainbows dancing above our heads. It was too much. I took the heel of my right palm and pushed his forehead back and yelled, "Back off! Right now!" With that touch of his flesh, my life as I knew it ended.

Before I could process what I was seeing, Brad jumped over Lindsey and football tackled me into the corner between the wall and the crib. The force of the impact sent the back of my head into the wall hard enough to give me tunnel vision. As I slid down the wall, he accelerated the momentum by pulling both of my ankles out from underneath me. He changed his grip and dragged me out of the nursery by my ankles, right in front of Lindsey.

Something inside, some loose piece of rational thought floating around inside, made him turn around and close the door so that Lindsey couldn't see what he was about to do next. In the time it took him to let go of me, turn around and close the door, I tried to get up and run away, but the only way out was down the stairs.

I got to the second step before I felt the kick to the middle of my back and my forward momentum propelled me down the rest of the stairs at incredible speed. I flew down the stairs. I lay dazed for what seemed a split second before the sight of Brad filled my field of vision. With white lips and dilated pupils, it was a stranger who reached down and grabbed my wrists and stood me up faster than I thought possible. The head rush was enormous and my vision blacked out for just a moment but, as in a dream, I could still hear what he was saying.

He was shaking my body like a rag doll and telling me that he couldn't believe anyone loved me and that he certainly didn't because I was "too stupid to be loved. Look at you. You don't even have any friends here. You're all by yourself and you better fucking treat me right because I'm all you have! You have no job, no friends, no life…" During this tirade, he was shaking me and twisting my wrists with increasing force as I tried to pull away.

Lindsey's wail brought me back to my existence. I opened my eyes wide to try and focus, and what I saw was frightening. Brad's face was blood red, but his lips were completely white and his eyes were dilated like a shark. It was as if a demon had entered his body and pushed out everything that could be good in Brad. He was gone in that moment, and I was faced with an intruder into the lofty life I'd worked so hard for.

My fight or flight instinct told me I couldn't get away and I was going to be severely, physically damaged unless I did something right now. Right now! Fly the fucking airplane. The way he was holding my wrists, I could've kicked him in the groin, but I chose to do something I'd never tried before on a person. I spit in his face. My sweet grandpa laughingly taught me how to spit, and his lessons paid off in a way he never imagined. I hit Brad right in the eye with a wad of spit and he was so completely shocked, he let go. Now I know where the term "spitting mad" comes from.

The moment he released me, I ran upstairs to Lindsey's room and locked the door. I sat down with my back against the door trying to collect what was left of me. Lindsey didn't make a sound. She stared in amazement at my behavior, not quite sure what to make of the fear that emanated from my being. Her little mouth made an "O" as I tried to smile at her with fear in my eyes. I confused her instincts. I smiled at her, but she knew something was extremely wrong. In an instant, her face contorted and she began to cry.

On shaking legs, I walked over and scooped her up into my arms. I buried my face into her smell, her comfort, her warmth. Her existence soothed me as I tried to soothe her. As her cries turned into little hiccups, I heard the stomping of feet coming up the stairs to her room.

I felt his presence before he let it be known. He stood outside the door and with all the power and passion of his thirty years, he started pounding on the door. Lindsey was instantly startled and jumped in my arms. We both jumped.

"Open this door. Right now! If you don't open this fucking door, I'm going to call the cops! Open the fucking door, open it, open it, open it..."

I prayed. Please call the cops. There was no way in hell I was ever going to open that door. That door was shut, never to be opened to him again. He just kept pounding on the door. I looked over at the phone lying on the shelf. I would never dream of calling the police, but I thought the one woman who might know what to do could be on the other end of that phone line. I dialed Brad's mom for help.

Bernice was at work, and I knew this drama would be upsetting, but I was terrified and didn't know what to do. I thought if Brad knew his mom was on the phone, he might calm down or at least stop what he was doing. If a mom couldn't do something about this, no one could.

The front receptionist started speaking but I interrupted and said, "Bernice's office, please." The hum of being transferred zinged in my ear.

"This is Bernice."

"Bernice, this is Erika. I need your help, right now. Please. I don't know what to do. Brad and I got into a terrible fight and he's out of control and I'm scared. Can you please come up? At least take Lindsey for me? I need to get her out of the house."

Brad heard my voice and stopped pounding on the door. "Who the fuck are you talking to?" I put my hand over the mouthpiece and I said, "I'm talking to your mom."

"My mom?!! You're talking to my mom? What the hell is wrong with you that you'd call my mom?"

"I don't know what else to do! You won't stop scaring me. I'm scared! I just want you to leave me alone!"

He did stop. He immediately bolted down the stairs and I could hear the office door slam. In the meantime, Bernice had heard this conversation and her voice jolted me back to the fact that the phone was at my ear. She didn't ask if I was okay or anything, she just started in with a lecture.

"Erika, you have to remember that Brad doesn't think the same way we do. You have to remember he is a sensitive person who uses a different side of his brain. He is a left-handed creative person, and he just can't process his anger like everyone else. He has to let it out. You just have to let him be. I've learned this because he used to put holes in the wall as a child. It's mostly just a threat, but he won't hurt you. Once you learn to just accept Brad the way he is, he won't fight you like this. Just go along with him and you'll be okay. I learned way back when Brad was in high school that if I just accepted Brad the way he is, then we didn't have anything to fight about and we got along great. I was like a friend to him and that's what you need to learn to do too. Just accept him the way he is…"

Her response was almost as shocking as his behavior. He had just tossed me down the stairs, and she was suggesting I "accept him the way he is"? I thought she would condemn the behavior, tell me to put him on the phone so she could talk to him but, instead, she justified his behavior and made me feel like I'm the one who is wrong.

"Can you please still come up? I think if he knows you're coming over, he won't hurt us." I was truly afraid and didn't know how to get out of this situation.

"Oh, Brad won't hurt you. He just puts on a big show. All growl and no bite."

"But, Bernice, he tackled me into the wall and knocked me out and then pushed me down the stairs..." She interrupted my attempt at recalling the story. She didn't want to hear it.

"Erika. I'm sure you're fine. I'm not coming up. Just tell him you're making tacos. Give him something to look forward to. I'll see you next week. We're doing the family photo shoot at my house. Make sure you wear a blue shirt. I'll talk to you later." She hung up. I still cringe when I see that family photo.

A half hour had passed since he'd tackled me in the nursery. He shouted if I was off the phone and I simply responded, "Yes".

He shouted back, "GOOD!"

I sat down on the futon in Lindsey's room and nursed her for a few minutes. It took a few moments for the milk to let down, but when it did, I felt the euphoria of a nursing mother. There is a chemical that can be as calming as valium, which is released into your system as the milk swooshes into your breasts and you connect with your child. It was intense after the emotional trauma that my mind and body just experienced, and I breathed deeply into the sensation.

The milk I was sending was probably full of endorphins and adrenaline, and Lindsey didn't nurse for long. She started squirming and stopped nursing even though I knew she was probably hungry. It was lunch time and she had just started eating a few spoonfuls of oatmeal a few days before. Before heading to the kitchen, I took a baby wipe and dabbed at the wet spot on the back of my head where the blood had leaked down my neck. The wipe came away full of bright blood, but it wasn't flowing and it felt like it was already stopped bleeding. I cleaned myself up and, like a good pilot, assessed my situation.

I didn't keep a clock in Lindsey's room (it would taunt me in the wee hours of the night, laughing at me that I was the only person in the world awake at 2:30 in the morning). I wasn't sure of the time, but about fifteen minutes had passed since I'd heard Brad's voice. He was still in the downstairs office, so I quietly opened the door to the nursery and peeked down the stairs.

The door to his office was closed, so I quietly took Lindsey to the kitchen to make her some oatmeal. She watched in anticipation as I pulled down the box with the Gerber baby on it. She was bouncing in my arms and smiling as I got out the little bowl and spoon. While walking across the kitchen to set up her high chair, the beep of the microwave went off at the same time I heard the office door open.

In an instant, the footsteps went from walking to running. Brad bounded up the stairs in two leaps and ran straight towards me. My feet stood planted like an oak. I couldn't move. With shark eyes still blazing, Brad instantly started grabbing Lindsey out of my arms. He didn't say anything at first. He just started pulling my fingers back to get me to release her. The terror that flooded my body when I realized what he was doing was like nothing I'd ever experienced before. It was sheer panic thinking he was about to hurt my baby. I pleaded over and over, "Please stop, please stop, please."

Brad grabbed me around my underarm and squeezed into my armpit. "I'm going to hurt her if you don't let go of her. Give her to me right fucking now or you're both going to get hurt! You're totally out of control."

He was blocking the exit from the kitchen and there was no way out from the kitchen. The intense fear had caused my bladder to release. I had been in life or death situations in an airplane, but nothing ever scared me like this. This was pure terror, and I was humiliated.

As I turned my body to put flesh between myself and Lindsey, I saw a movement out of the corner of my eye. I could see something coming down my driveway. It was a car and as I forced my eyes to focus for more than a moment, I saw it was a police car.

Thank you, Sweet Jesus. One of my neighbors must've heard me pleading for help. Thank God someone heard me cry for help. Now, at least I know, we'll be safe.

In the motion it had taken me to turn slightly and look out the window, Brad was able to get his hands under both of Lindsey's underarms and he pulled her up and out of my arms with all of his might. The police were just moments away. Brad couldn't possibly hurt her in that amount of time.

Brad took Lindsey and started for the stairs to the front door. I started, too, because I felt an intense need to run to them. As I put my first foot on the top step, Brad turned around and growled, "Don't you fucking move. You stand right there. Right where you are, and don't you fucking move. You got it? You're not that stupid that you don't understand what I'm telling you, right? Don't. Fucking. Move."

I had a moment of satisfaction thinking that Brad was going to run right into the police. That he would reach the front door and be hit with the shock of his life. The police would be waiting for him.

What I heard instead was laughter. It was Brad who had called the police.

Laughter...

Brad was at the front door, holding Lindsey in his arms and I could hear him talking to the officer. The second officer was walking up behind the first. After every four or five words, Brad gave them a humble chuckle. His voice was jovial, calm, and seeking camaraderie with these older officers of a small town.

"Yeah, man, I'm soooo sorry to have to call you, but my wife is totally out of control and I'm afraid she is going to hurt our daughter. Man, can you believe this? She took a swing at me and then actually clocked me. When she started acting like she was going to hurt Lindsey to get back at me, I figured I better call you and get someone out here to help me.

"Sorry, man, it's kinda embarrassing that I have a wife like this. We've only been married for about a year and a half, and turns out she's crazy. She's just some control freak. Used to be an airline pilot and she must think I'm one of her flight attendants she can boss around (insert laughter here). You know how wives can be, right?"

I was struck with such a wave of nausea that I had to draw in my breath and hold it. My vision narrowed, as I reached out to hold the wall. He called the police and set the scene. He held our daughter in his arms with a smile on his face. He was humbly telling these officers that *I* was abusing *him*. I had never even thought of abusing anyone. I'd never even honked my car horn at anyone, never spoken up if my food was cold or the wrong order, I let people cut in line in front of me — I'd spent a lifetime of trying to please everyone. I had taken shit my entire life to keep the peace, toed the line to do the right thing, so I simply couldn't wrap my head around the surreal situation that I had become.

"Are there any weapons in the home," I heard the officer ask.

"Nah, just my wife!" was Brad's reply.

Both officers found this hysterical. He did a masterful job of being the poor husband, standing at the front door holding his baby girl while his crazy wife must be foaming at the mouth at the back of the house.

I hadn't been able to move. I was still standing where I was told to stand. The officer was startled to see me standing at the top of the stairs. Sure, I did look insane at that moment.

His face went from smirk to taut as his hand reached over the top of his gun. "Ma'am, I need you to back away from the stairs and stand over by the wall."

I silently do exactly what he says.

"Do you have a weapon?"

"I've never held a gun in my life."

"Guns aren't the only weapons around, why do you assume I'm talking about a gun?"

"I'm sorry. I don't know. I don't have a weapon. I don't have anything." I have cotton mouth and I'm having trouble simply getting the words to squeeze out.

"Your husband says you're threatening to hurt him and your daughter. He claims that you hit him. What are you doing? What's going on here?"

"I don't know." That's all my brain could answer to. It truly couldn't accept what was happening. I was ashamed. I had never even gotten a speeding ticket or been called to a principal's office. I had never done anything outside the realm of legal, and suddenly I found myself standing in front of an officer for the first time in my life being accused of something I didn't do—and I can't defend myself. I didn't know I even needed to defend myself.

"Well, what do you mean you don't know? Are you on medication?"

"No."

"Then how can you not know what's going on? Your husband says you're an airline pilot. Says you're some kinda control freak and that maybe you'll hurt your child if you don't get your way about something. Are you an airline pilot?"

"Yes. No. Well, I am, but I'm not flying right now."

"What? You don't even know if you're a pilot?"

"I do know, but it's a long story. I am a pilot. I will always be a pilot, but I'm not flying right now." The officer tips his head slightly and says, "Did you get fired?"

"No, of course not. My husband asked me to quit, so I did."

"Are you mad at him about that?" *Actually, yes, I am.* That question focused my thinking for a moment. It was a new question that had never been asked, and I was surprised at my own internal answer. It distracted me. I was a little mad about that, but I was pretty certain that was not what he wanted to hear right then.

"No, I'm not mad at him about that. I'm still a pilot I'm just not flying right now, but I will again soon."

"You sound awfully confused."

"I am. I am totally confused. I just don't understand what my husband is doing…"

"Well, he seems pretty calm and knows exactly what's happening. Did you hit your husband?"

"No, I didn't hit my husband."

"Did you touch him in any way?" I am from the Midwest. I reflexively tell the truth without giving the rest of the story. I never think for a moment of what the officer is implying or getting at. I simply tell the truth and say, "Yes, I pushed his face away from me when he was yelling at me."

"Okay, I'll make this easy. Who touched who first?"

"Well, I did. I pushed his face away from mine because he was yelling swear words in my face."

"Swearing at someone isn't illegal, but hitting someone is."

"But, I didn't hit him. I just pushed him away from us."

"Us?"

"Yes, he was yelling swear words in front of our daughter, and I got mad about that."

"Your daughter is a baby. She doesn't understand swearing. Why would you get mad about that? Do you get mad easily?"

"NO!" But now I really was getting mad. He wasn't letting me tell him what happened so I skipped the story and just showed him my arms. I thrust my arms out and showed him how they were covered in angry red marks and some had already turned strange colors because blood vessels were popped. I was so embarrassed to be showing this stranger my arms, my shame, my life.

"Feel the back of my head! There is a huge goose egg where he smashed me into the wall." The officer walked up to me and I smelled his underarm deodorant as he reached to the back of my head and started pressing. It took two presses before the third one found its mark. When he pressed on it, the pain sent a wave of nausea through my stomach, and I reflexively sucked in a deep breath of air that mixed in with the smell of his deodorant. The violation to my sinuses caused more pain to my brain.

The officer looked down at his fingers and they were coated in blood. He walked to the sink and washed his hands, but couldn't find the paper towels, so I told him there was a dish rag hanging on the stove handle.

The officer looked at me and said he'd be right back. He turned and went back downstairs to where I could hear my husband laughing and talking with the other officer. All the voices mingled and the rise and fall of questions faded as both officers walked up the stairs.

Both officers approached and stood on either side of me. "Well, the story both of you gave are extremely different, but the one event that you both confirm is that *you*, Mrs. Armstrong, were the one to start the physical contact. Whatever happened after that doesn't matter because you started the aggression. It's a matter of who-touched-who first, so we're arresting *you* for assault, battery, and domestic violence. Since you used your daughter in the argument, this could be a felony charge for you. Do yourself a favor and remove your wedding ring and any necklaces you might have on because they will confiscate it at the jail. Also, go find your driver's license for identification. It makes the booking process go faster."

As they helped me remove my necklace and rings, I saw Brad sneak up onto the lower steps. Just his head was visible and I could see his smirk. He then pressed his lips to his teeth in victory and kissed Lindsey on the cheek while watching an officer fumble with my necklace — the necklace he gave me on our first Christmas together.

Lindsey.

"Please. I am still nursing Lindsey. You can't take me away from my daughter! She needs to be nursed. Do you know what Brad did to me? Doesn't that matter? How can this man push me into a wall and down the stairs and hit me repeatedly, and you're arresting *me*? He doesn't have a single mark on him and I have blood oozing out of my arms and out the back of my head. I never hit him. You can't do this! " The officers looked at each other and for the first time, I saw some hesitation in what they were about to do. The officer who first heard my allegations looked at Brad.

"Mr. Armstrong. Do you think you might have someplace to go tonight? Is it possible for you to leave the residence this evening and let things cool down awhile?"

"No. I don't have any place to go. This is my home. Lindsey doesn't need to be nursed. She's eating oatmeal already, so she can just go without nursing. You can take Erika away. She's just trying to manipulate you."

That was all they needed to hear. Once my rings were removed, they asked me to turn around so they could place a zip tie type of handcuff on me before escorting me out the front door.

At the sight of my departure, Lindsey started to cry at the top of her lungs. The sound sent daggers to my heart and I sobbed so loudly I was startled by the strength and emotion of it.

My neighbors lined the end of their driveways at the sight of two cop cars in my driveway. They watched as I took the walk of shame, handcuffed, from my front door to the back of the squad car. Brad stood in the doorway, bouncing Lindsey while both of her hands reached out to stop me from walking away. Brad allowed her to watch the entire process. As the two men in uniform walked me away while my baby was being held by a monster, I could feel the thread that tied Lindsey and me together being pulled to its limits, and the pain was beyond imaginable. Lindsey had twisted her upper torso so both of her arms were stretched out to bring me back. In agony, she screamed at the top of her lungs. Brad ignored her while holding his smirk as the frantic creature in his arms watched her mom being taken away. Scooting into the back seat of the squad car, I saw Brad look up and acknowledge the neighbors at the side of the road by waving and giving them a thumb's up not to worry. Everything is okay here.

This malfunction is not on any checklist.

16 Rapid Decompression Checklist

1. Checklist – NO! There is no time for checklists
2. Oxygen mask – don before you do anything
3. At flight level 400, you have 15 seconds of useful consciousness
4. Speed brakes – deploy and dive for hell
5. Rapid descent - don't stop until you reach breathable altitude

Passengers have heard the flight attendants give their safety briefing so many times, most tune them out. Since you probably know the safety briefing, do you remember that comment where the flight attendant says you should put your own oxygen mask on first and then your child's? It doesn't matter that the flight attendant says this because in actual emergencies, mothers still put their child's mask on first before they put their own mask on. Fathers, on the other hand, always seem to remember to put their own mask on first. Let's just blame instinct here, okay?

Mothers don't instinctually think of themselves first, it goes against our natural reflexes to take care of everyone else first. However, you must remember that you put your child in danger if you're worthless. If you pass out due to lack of oxygen, then your child will sit there and watch you wither away from brain damage due to the lack of oxygen. You need to stay strong, and taking care of yourself is a priority.

Most decompressions are slow leaks like the one that slowly killed the crew and passengers, including Payne Stewart, on a Lear Jet in 1999. The crew didn't recognize their own hypoxia symptoms (lack of oxygen) which caused them to slowly pass out. You'd think if you started seeing your copilot and passengers fall asleep, you'd wonder why, but no one will ever know what went on in the cockpit. Maybe they got hypoxia and passed out at exactly the same rate? The aircraft eventually ran out of fuel and crashed in a field near Aberdeen, South Dakota.

Rarely is there an actual rapid decompression (instant and complete loss of cabin pressure), but pilots train for it constantly. If it's an explosive decompression at high altitude, even the best trained pilots are still going to die and you can forget about the passengers living after that. Corporate aircraft fly at higher altitudes and at 41,000 feet, you have about twenty seconds of useful consciousness before you pass out, and given the health of most Americans, it might be even less than that.

In a rapid decompression, the outside pressure disappears so all the pressure inside the aircraft wants to go out (okay, folks, don't panic. We're talking about an enormous gaping hole, like an entire cargo door ripping off. It's never happened at that altitude before and this won't happen from something small, like a puncture from a bullet or even a window blowing out). Putting on your oxygen mask will make no difference because you need the pressure to get the oxygen into your body. You'll have an enormous fart and then pass out. The flight attendants won't mention that during their pre-flight briefing. The whole ordeal is rather unlikely, but some things in life are even beyond unlikely and yet, they still happen.

While I was handcuffed with my hands behind my back, I kept squirming to try and find a comfortable position to sit in the back of the SUV squad car on the way to Golden, Colorado's jail. We were idling at a stoplight as a daycare school bus full of raucous kids pulled up next to us. I could feel the stares of all those pure innocent children peering into the backseat to get a look at the perp. I've often been on that side of the view and have always wondered how someone ended up in the back of a police car. I felt my face tingle with the flush of shame, and to this day, that moment still haunts me. I was once innocent like they were, but that person no longer existed. I turned my head away from them and put the side of my face against the back of the seat so the children could not see my face. I gently closed my eyes and silently cried. I was drowning in my ocean of confusion, pity, and growing dismay. All those years of always doing the right thing didn't matter. I had worked so hard my whole life to be a good girl. I had always operated within a circle of acceptable behavior, never brushing anywhere near the edge of the law, and in the end it just didn't matter. All it took was for one person to rise above by stepping on others, and a life of focus blurred away. I can blur the memory in and out of my reality. When I focus, I can remember it all too clearly:

I am checked in and handed over to the Jefferson County Inmate system. I am told I will be placed in the violent offender category, which requires a special colored jumpsuit and different procedures. I am told to strip naked, right now, in front of the two female guards. I pull off my clothes and take off my nursing bra. The two nursing pads I had inserted inside my bra to absorb leaky breast milk are stuck to my breasts. I peel them off and both breasts start dripping. Just the slightest touch and off they go. To add to the humiliation, there is a reflective surface on the near wall in which to see yourself in case you have a moment of vanity. It's not a glass mirror, it's something like steel shined to an unblemished finish so you can see yourself perfectly. My cesarean incision is still bright red and it makes a smiley face as I see the combination of my engorged red nipples and scar looking back at me.

The guard is brisk, efficient, and bored. She's seen it all. I have nothing to compare this to except for what I see on television, so I ask this character if I can make a phone call. She just snickers, shakes her head while speaking to herself, and simply says, "Nope."

The guard notices I have dried blood in thin riverbeds down the back of my head, neck, and arms, and my back is now revealing angry bruises where it was slammed against the wall. After letting me get dressed into my violent orange jumpsuit, the guard tells me she is sending someone in to take care of it. I watch her as I wait and wonder what she sees here in a day. None of the guards wear makeup. Why would they? There is no one that comes before them who needs to be impressed. They all wear their hair pulled back into severe pony tails. Simple and efficient.

I see a woman walk in with a First Aid box moving around in the corner and I assume she is a nurse. Not sure if she is, but a nurse is someone who is caring and can help. That's what I've been taught. I had to go to the nurse once in kindergarten when I threw up my pink frosted Valentine's Day cookie. She was so nice and called my mom, and I got to go home.

The nurse lady walks in with a plastic box of healing supplies, but everything still hurts. "Please. I didn't do anything to be here. My husband hurt me and then lied to the police. He set me up and I didn't know it until it was too late. He's got my daughter and I'm afraid he's going to run away with her. I have to do something. Please. Can I call someone so they can check on her?" I walked to the edge of hysteria once I started talking, but the story sounded so absurd, I could hardly believe it myself. Just saying those words out loud loosened my grip on reality. A pilot fights to stay in the air until the moment metal meets earth, but I feel like I am locked out of the cockpit, knowing that the airplane is going to crash. There is something I can do, but I can't get there.

The nurse lady stops what she is doing and gives an exasperated sigh. She sets down her supplies and puts her hands on both of my shoulders and turns me around so she can look me in the eye, "Honey. You're screwed. I see this every day. Don't you get it? The cops hate domestic calls. It's their most dangerous call outs. People are crazy when it comes to love and hate. People don't care who they kill when they're all fired up with emotions. The cops know who done it, but if they arrest the *woman*, that's the last time they get those kind of calls at that house. The woman will put up with all the hitting and abuse after that. She knows she's got a record now and if they get a call at that house again, they ain't gonna believe her. You're in the system now, and you've gotta put your head down and just go with the system. Do what the guards say. Do what the judge says. Get the hell out of here and then get the hell out of where you're at, and don't look back. I mean it. Otherwise, it might be your husband who I see here next because he killed you.

"It's a twisted world, honey. It's not about right and fair, it's about survival. I should know, I see it in action here every day. The system isn't about punishing the wrongdoer; it's about making it so miserable for everyone in the system that no one wants to use it again."

I hold my breath while taking this in. I blink. I blink again and let that settle into my psyche and open my eyes to the world. Stomach acid begins pouring into my system and I feel the blood drain from my face. This woman holding my shoulders is so smart, how could I be so dumb?

The nurse lady finishes cleaning my superficial wounds. There isn't much she can do about the lump on my head except put a bag of ice on it. She covers the bloody trail of cuts and bruises around my wrists. I look like I've attempted suicide. She tells me I just have to deal with the rest of the bruises with time. She doesn't say anything about the internal damage done to my soul.

The next stop is a holding room with a television. There's a movie playing, and I have to go to the bathroom so badly my gut aches. There's a toilet in the middle of the room that's full of shit and backed up to the surface. Someone tried to cover it up with neat layers of toilet paper, but the evidence shows through.

There are people constantly coming and going in this room. I sit here for two movies—maybe four hours and see about twenty different people. No one speaks to me. No one speaks to each other. Women only in this room, but twenty feet to my right is the holding room for the men, which means they all walk by my room.

From my vantage point, I see every single person getting their mug shot taken. I've already had mine taken—I don't look good in orange. The reason mug shots are consistently scary looking is that they ask you a long list of questions and at some point during this question and answer session, they take your picture. I look drugged as they take my picture in mid-blink. If I saw my mug shot on the news, I'd say she was guilty just by looking at her.

I finally get moved to the violent offender section of the jail where I'm informed that since I was transferred right after dinner, there will be no food on this day. I couldn't eat if they paid me. The benefit of being a violent offender is that you are kept insolation. As soon as the jail door is slammed shut, I pee in the glory of isolation for what seems more than a bladder could ever hold.

It's already dark outside. I know this because there's a horizontal window about four inches high and about two feet long. I've seen these windows from the outside and always thought it was an unusual architectural choice, but in actuality, windows further the punishment. I look out on the world and feel I'm no longer any part of it. Evening rush hour is at its peak and there is a trail of red brake lights leading into Golden. I can see from my fish tank an ocean of normal people going home to normal families, with normal spouses, and normal frustrations of life. Normal is not something I've ever wished for, but now desire with all my heart.

It's the end of December and Colorado is in the middle of the coldest week of the year. The outside air temp is below zero and since no one has to worry about the quality of the accommodations, the temperature inside my cell is about fifty degrees, if I give it the benefit of doubt. There are no bars on the door like the movies. Since I am a violent offender, my jail door it is a solid wall with a slot that opens for food to come in. This also means there is no direct heat, and the only reason my cell is warmer than the outside is because there is heat at the guard's station in the center of the jail...

There is no bed. There is a concrete wall with a concrete ledge that bulges out and is meant to be slept on. There is a half inch plastic mattress similar to a camping mattress you put your sleeping bag on. To cover up, I reach for the one thin wool blanket I was issued. No pillow. The concrete wicks the cold air from the outside and carries its punishment into the cell with me. My shirt is soaked from hours of breast milk dripping on it, and the wetness has now traveled to my pants and underwear. My breasts ache and I am soaked to the bone. The cold burrows into my core. I am laying in the fetal position with the blanket over my head trying to hold some warmth, but I am so far beyond cold that I can't relax my muscles to fall asleep.

The added annoyance is that they never turn the lights off. The flickering of cheap lights guarantees that no one here gets REM sleep. I lay there shivering in the fluorescent glow for the next eight hours; sleep is out of the realm of possibility. I have nothing to do but replay the last eight hours of my life and realize that the one man who I thought was my future has just taken away everything I was and would be. I am now nothing. I, Erika, no longer exist.

By morning, I am sitting on the concrete ledge, rocking like an insane patient. I'm so cold and emotionally exhausted that I now understand how a mind can slip into madness. We all unknowingly walk so close to the line.

Sometime after the sun pokes over the horizon, I hear the slot in the door open and a bowl of unflavored oatmeal, a syrupy orange flavored drink, and a book are silently pushed into my hell. Oh, thank God, a book. A book. I don't care what the book is; I just know those pages will take me out of here.

I have not been able to call anyone or talk to anyone. I'm also realizing that no one has even read me my rights. When are they supposed to do that? They are just words, but words put in a certain order create society's law. There are our words of law versus our reality. The reality is that there are words that can put innocent people in jail. Words are power. Lies are power. Sometimes the truth gets lost in all those words.

I push the food away, but grab the book. It is a small paperback and I read it cover to cover. It's mindless and unmemorable, but it's a chance to move my brain off the task of absorbing what has happened and is still happening, and what's next.

Good God, what's next?

Lunch came and went and still, no one. It's been twenty-four hours since I became Alice in Wonderland. Finally, around midday, my door buzzes open and a voice booms through a speaker in the wall that I didn't know existed in my cell.

"Step out of the cell and face inward at the doorway."

I step to the opening of the door and turn around. I feel strong arms pull my hands behind my body as I'm strapped into handcuffs again. The faceless man with arms walks me to the elevator. I step in, he pushes a button, and I'm sent alone into the bowels of the building. At the bottom of the rabbit hole, the door opens and no one is there. I step out and a voice overhead tells me to turn left and follow the line on the floor. Doors automatically open and close, and I am walking underground from the jail to the courthouse. I follow the line which ends at an elevator. I step in and magically, the elevator carries me up to where there is sunlight. This time, someone is waiting for me. The stone faced guard says nothing, grabs me by the shoulder, and pushes me in the direction that he wants me to go.

As the guard opens up a door, I am greeted with the rise and fall of frustrated voices. The room I end up in has all the violent offenders put together. All men and me. They see the color of my jumpsuit and they all mock my ability to scare them. I have no makeup on and my long blonde hair hasn't been washed for several days, since I hadn't fit in a shower before I was taken away. I also have the added humiliation of breast milk stains making a large circle over each breast.

The purpose of this meeting is for each person to talk to a public defender for about five minutes. I haven't been given an opportunity to call anyone, so I guess there is no need to call a lawyer. There are two public defenders at the table, but only one person does the speaking. My defender asks my name and shuffles through a pile of papers until he finds my checklist of sins. He reads the charges aloud to me:

"Ah, yes. Here you are. You are charged with domestic violence, assault, and battery and you have two choices here today. You can either accept full responsibility and enter a diversion program—which means you get out today—or you plead not guilty and speak to the judge. If you plead not guilty, you will have to remain in jail for the next five days before the judge can even hear your case. You picked the short straw by getting hauled in on a long holiday weekend. New Year's Eve and New Year's Day are both holidays, and then it's the weekend, so you'd have to wait until Monday. Do you have any questions? You have to decide right now what you're going to plead."

"What's a diversion program?"

"It's a program that gets you counseling."

"And I get out of jail today? Just like that?"

"Well, you still have to go before the judge and enter your plea and see if he'll accept it. The victim also has a right to make a statement in court before the judge."

"What do you mean? What victim?" I honestly don't know what he means.

"Your husband. The victim. He gets to come to court today and make a statement to the judge to help the judge decide how to rule. I have his written statement here." He shuffles to the bottom and hands me a disheveled piece of paper and I see the awkward, slanted writing of a lefty.

"He says he wants to file charges. If he files charges, there is a good chance you'll have to serve jail time. We can probably get it down to Misdemeanor Assault in the 3rd degree, but there is still jail time with it. Maybe just a little with extensive community service or some variation of that. Either way, you will have a record."

Below the standard name and address and personal information summary, there is a "victim's statement" which is filled in its entirety. The beginning of the form is fill-in-the-blank, but it allows for freestyle writing at the end. The weight of his statement hangs heavy in my hands:

...I am so ashamed that my wife can't control herself, especially since she is a mom. I don't think she should be left alone with our child.

I hope this trip to jail has helped my wife think about what she did and maybe she has thought about how she is going to apologize to me and make up for this. I don't know if I can trust her ever again. This trip to jail should be able to teach her a lesson, but this doesn't even begin to punish her for what she's done. She needed some time to think things through and this has hopefully given her that chance.

I plan on pressing assault and battery charges and if possible, further criminal charges and believe she should not be allowed to leave jail. She is a violent person and who knows what else she could do?

I want to also mention the excellent work of the Evergreen police officers who helped out in this matter. They are to be commended for their professionalism.

Brad Armstrong

I have not had food for over twenty-four hours, so the bile in my stomach is fierce and demanding. I read those words, in his own childish handwriting, and hate enters my body for the first time in my life. It's as permanent as losing my virginity. There is a before and after, but never again will I have that moment back. It has infused every cell, and I don't know what to do with it.

Hate. Pure. Perfect. Hate. It's accompanied with adrenaline, and my hands start to tremble as I read it again. The moment is so intense that I forget that a whole room of people are staring at me, waiting for an answer.

"But this isn't true. He lied; he made this whole thing up..." The public defender raises his hand to stop what is about to tumble out of my mouth. He's heard it all before, right?

"Look, you got arrested, not him. The judge will at least give the officers the benefit of the doubt. The best thing to do is just tell the judge it was a bad fight and that you're really, really sorry. Be humble. Don't give the judge any attitude or start telling him the cops made a mistake. They hate that. The cops hate it, too. Your best bet is to take the diversion program and go home."

The room is full of voices. There is no privacy, and every single person waiting can hear our conversation. They're next to sit at this table, so they want to hear their choices, too. The other inmates start murmuring, "Just go home, little girl. It ain't worth fighting it 'cause you ain't gonna win anyways. Don't you know that the *cops* are judges, not the judges? The cops decide for the judge who gets judged…" I am eerily calmed by the support of the other inmates. They're laughing and tossing out lighthearted advice; it must not be a big deal.

"Fine, I'll take what's behind door number one," I say, and the public defender smiles.

"Diversion program?"

"I guess. It sounds better than sitting here for the next five days, or longer."

"Do you understand that you are pleading guilty?"

"Oh, wait. No. No way. I am absolutely not pleading guilty. I guess I didn't realize that. Wait. Why do I have to plead guilty to enter the diversion program?" The public defender sees my hesitation, and he just wants to get on with his day, so he reassures me with, "Because that's the only way out today."

"Seriously? God. Okay, whatever, just get me out of here. I just want to see my baby …" With that, I sign on the dotted line. The public defender then says, "Oh, there is a restraining order placed on you automatically, so you might not be able to see your baby when you get out. It depends on a few things…" I wait for him to explain, but the guard has already put the handcuffs back and speaks over the public defender's voice as he commands me to turn around and walk. He walks me to a room behind the walls of the courtroom and there is nothing left to do but cry again while I wait to be judged.

Within thirty minutes of my signature, I am escorted, handcuffed, and walked into the courtroom where I'm placed in a plastic chair against the wall, facing the judge. I lean sideways against the Berber carpeted wall, and can smell the wool and feel the anxiety of the room. When I crane my neck around to the right, I can see the spectators of the courtroom, and there he is. Brad has on a dark blue Polo sweater with a red horse on it. Something his mom bought him so he could look innocent in court. This is the first time he'd ever dressed "preppy." It's disgusting. He wouldn't even put on nice clothes when my family came out to Colorado for Christmas just a few days ago. He had dinner in his tie-dyed t-shirt while the rest of us had on something more presentable. Too bad he didn't put on his true clothes today.

I hear two cases, and then it's my turn. I hear my name, and the bailiff takes off my handcuffs and walks me to the defendant's podium. Simultaneously, Brad walks up to the prosecution podium, and the judge then allows him to read his victim's impact statement. With his voice, his words, his sentiment, I am disgusted to the core. I can't look at him. I have never looked at anyone with hatred before, and I'm afraid of it. The hatred has rushed up from the depths of hell and if I look at him, I might make him burst into flames. So I look at him, but despite this new strength coming from hate, he doesn't burst into flames. After Brad's statement, the judge reads more paperwork and formalities, looks up, takes off his glasses, tilts his head and with exasperation, asks, "Well, *Mrs.* Armstrong, please tell the court why you're here today."

"Because I had a fight with my husband."

"Lots of people fight with their husbands. Tell me why you're here and not at home."

"Because it was a really bad fight?" I don't know what he wants me to say. The public defender said to be humble, but to do this in front of Brad is literally killing me.

"Did you hit your husband?"

"Absolutely not."

"Really? Then why are you here? There are charges here that say you hit him and threatened to harm your daughter. You stand here today and not your husband, so there must be more to your statement. You will end up with jail time if this goes to a hearing and you're found guilty…"

"I pushed him."

"You pushed him?"

"Yes. I pushed him away from my baby, and the officer said because I touched him first that I was the one in trouble." I see the judge pause and pick up more papers. He isn't reading anything and is just paging through them as he questions, "It says here you're willing to go into the Diversion Program. Is that correct?"

"Yes."

"Okay, let us see if Mr. Armstrong thinks that's going to be sufficient." He turns to Brad and softens his voice. "Mr. Armstrong, I have heard and read your victim's impact statement, and you state you want to press charges. If we send your wife to counseling, do you think that would be a satisfactory compromise?"

There was a long pause as Brad acted like being asked this question was too daunting to answer quickly. We all sat in suspense and he took a deep inhale and spat, "Oh, I suppose. How long does she have to go counseling?"

"Thirty six weeks, every single week for two hours each week, she can't leave the state, and she has to pay for it. If she doesn't go or doesn't pay, she goes to jail. It's that simple."

This is the first I've heard about the parameters of my counseling. I didn't even think to ask the PD how long, how much, where, and with whom. Because I am new a mom and growing babies are tracked in weeks, I reflexively realize I could almost grow a baby in the amount of time I will be in this diversion program.

"If she doesn't go or gets arrested again, she goes back to jail?" The smirk in his voice is undeniable.

"Yes. And if she does it again, she stays in jail."

"Then I guess I'd agree to that."

"Okay. Done."

His enormous wooden gavel hits its mark, clips my wings, and the punishment begins.

17 Declare an Emergency

1. **Transponder code** - set to 7700 to let everyone know you're in trouble
2. **State to ATC** - "I am declaring an emergency"
3. **Focus on what is working**, rather than just the failure
4. **Fly the airplane**

Pilots hate to declare emergencies, even if a wing falls off. It's like admitting defeat. Oh really, double engine failure? No problem, I can handle it. The engine fell off the fuselage? Well then, I'll just step harder on the other rudder. It'll just be another great story to talk about back at the hotel bar—that is, if we live. Let's find out.

The number of black boxes recovered from accident investigations that record the calm, cool voice of an in-command pilot when his aircraft is undoubtedly doomed is overwhelming. Women pilots are even worse when it comes to declaring an emergency. It's just that we've worked so damn hard to get where we are (yes, the guys have, too, but we've been plowing the way for the women coming up behind us, as well), that we don't want to tell anyone we can't handle the situation, even if it's not our fault. We don't want help, we want to do it ourselves, and we don't want to draw any more attention to the situation if at all possible.

Once you officially declare an emergency (you have to say the magic words, "I am declaring an emergency" to air traffic control), the whole aviation world stops for you. All other aircraft in your airspace are diverted or put in holding patterns, and airport operations shut down until you're on the ground.

Emergency vehicles will be standing by. Of course, the media will be there, too, and they'll blame you for not seeing that the bolt on the landing gear tire wasn't torqued correctly which caused the tire to fall off on rotation. The bolt went around 72 times instead of 136, but, of course, it's the pilot's fault for not visually knowing the difference. It's always the pilot's fault according to the media.

Pilots shudder when another aircraft declares an emergency. All aircraft in the vicinity (which covers hundreds of miles) are often pulled off their intended paths, sent to holding patterns, and, usually, controlled chaos follows the magic words, "I need to declare an emergency."

We have absolute empathy for the other pilot, so we gladly do whatever we need to do for the aircraft in peril, but it's still a pain in the ass. If it's a long emergency, it can turn into fuel emergencies for the other aircraft. Because we're put into holding patterns, it burns up fuel in our reserves (which is why we carry reserves), but if there is any weather in the way, one aircraft's emergency can send ten others into critical fuel conditions.

Until the end of time, pilots will perpetually be called into the Chief Pilot's office for not declaring an emergency. Their argument will be the pure evidence that they are standing in the office and not dead — so, what was the emergency? We're trained and cajoled that it shows more competence to declare an emergency, even if it's marginal, than to not declare one. Better safe than sorry is what they remind us.

Well, you can't have a pilot without ego. They have to have egos, and they're bigger than most, so pilots will continue to refuse to declare an emergency. That's just the way it is. Let's not forget though, that more than one person can declare an emergency during the situation. Anyone on the flight deck, flight attendant, passenger, control tower, or just a bystander watching airplanes from the ground can declare an emergency for an aircraft in distress, but they have to know it's in trouble.

From the outside, an airplane can look majestic and powerful, while inside all the systems can be failing in sequence. It can start with just one failure, but the failing system can take down the rest of the functioning equipment if the checklist isn't complied with correctly.

I had just had a major malfunction which created an emergency of epic proportions, but I was still not willing to admit it.

After the judge made his ruling, the bailiff wordlessly grabbed my arms and cuffed me in front of Brad and the rest of the spectators in the courtroom. I held my head high, but I was dying inside. It had been thirty hours since the beginning of the end.

The bailiff pointed me down a hall and once again the ghosts in the machine opened and closed doors and elevators for me on my journey back to my jail cell. I was informed that lunch was over, but dinner would be served in two hours. I told the guard that I was going home and didn't need dinner. He just slammed the door in reply.

Dinner was served, and I didn't know why I was still there. When the guard slid the food in, I asked him why I was still here. "How the hell should I know?" was the reply.

The sun set and I could feel the cold racing into the cell again. I just didn't understand why I was still locked up. I had been awake for about thirty nine hours and was trembling from the exhaustion and cold. My shirt was stiff and crunchy from the hours of breast milk leaking on my shirt, and it suddenly hit me like a brick wall that they had stopped leaking and hurt.

This was how my daughter was weaned from me.

All those hours of pumping my breasts in the airplane bathroom during stopovers and filling the freezer full so that I could breast feed for a year was now over in what would be three days away from her. This connection was taken from a mother and daughter, never to be returned to us. Because of what? I just couldn't comprehend what my life had become. How did I let this happen?

By my best guess, at around 8:30 p.m., a tinny voice barked through the speaker in my cell. You can make a phone call. One.

I jumped up and walked to the phone cradle mounted to the wall and stopped dead in my tracks. Who the hell was I going to call? It was late on New Year's Eve. All my friends in Colorado were casual acquaintances, and I couldn't even imagine the humiliation calling one of them to pick me up from *jail*. My friends were all mothers with young children. They were all happily married with respectful husbands. I'd be expelled from every playgroup and get-together for the rest of Lindsey's life. I lived in a small town and I couldn't do that to her. Hell, I couldn't do that to myself. I had no family in Colorado. I had no one. I had no money. I didn't even have money for a cab. No car. No job. No pride. No hope. No future. Nothing. I had nothing except desperation. The only reason I had to live right at that moment was my baby, who was at home with *him*. I was forty minutes from home. Home. I just wanted to be home with Lindsey. I hadn't been away from her for more than an hour or two since I left flying.

Reality hit me like a ton of bricks and I swallowed the bile floating up from the pit of my stomach. My vision tunneled as I dialed my home number to bum a ride home from the very person who had sent me to jail. The irony tasted bitter on my tongue.

"Yeah? Hello."

"Brad, it's me. I need a ride from jail. I'm sorry you have to wake up Lindsey, but I don't know how else to get home."

"Lindsey's not here."

"Where is she?"

"My mom's neighbor's house."

"What?"

"I dropped her off at my mom's house yesterday, but my mom had plans for New Year's Eve, so she dropped her off with another neighbor, but she didn't tell me exactly where. Betsy or Betty or something like that."

"You don't even know where our daughter is?!"

"Do you want a ride or not."

"Yes. I need a ride."

This was the first gut churning moment when I realized I had lost all control. I had stopped flying my aircraft and settled on the idea that I was in an unrecoverable flat spin. Forget declaring an emergency, I was going to have to bail out of my aircraft. I was now just a passenger in my own life at the mercy of a man who had damaged me to the point where I didn't know if I could ever be put back together again.

At 10:30 p.m. on New Year's Eve, I was sent down to the jail's discharge office. I had to holler "hello?" because no one was there, and I wasn't sure what to do. I was still in my jail clothes and wondered if everyone had gone home, until I heard footsteps down the hallway and a male voice ask for my name. A button was pressed and a rack of clothes like the dry cleaners came to life, making the clothing of my former life dance in jubilation at the thought of being returned to my body.

Not only my life, but my body and soul had changed as I put on these old clothes. My breasts were empty and my plan of nursing for the first year was a mere pipedream. Even though these were my clothes, the clothes I put on were of another person. They were on me, but I was no longer me. And then, I waited.

I could hear his pickup truck coming into the parking lot, a big red Dodge Cummins diesel with an unmistakably high-pitched whine that was the signature of a turbo diesel.

There were fees that had to be paid. Checking out of jail is similar to checking out of a hotel. Jail isn't free. They charge you for your stay, but they don't ask how the accommodations were.

If I'd known that I had to pay for this, I would have asked for turn down service and a chocolate. Oh, and maybe a pillow.

Brad rolled his eyes and sighed over and over while reviewing the list of charges. They didn't take credit cards so he had to write a check, which they electronically transfer the money before you can leave. It was my money he was using, but he acted like he had just signed over his last penny.

The cold outside air took my breath away. We didn't say a word as we got in the truck. The clock said 11:23 p.m. on New Year's Eve, the cusp of a new year.

Not a word was said. Nothing. There was no music on the radio; there was just the black clear sky and occasional burst of fireworks being launched off the decks of mountain homes. Happy mountain homes with happy mountain people.

As we approached Elk Meadow Open Space Park, I told Brad to pull over. I needed to tell him it was over. I had the speech in my head, but my thoughts were derailed at his first reaction.

"Pull over? What the fuck for? I'm not pulling over."

"God, Brad. Really? We need to talk."

He took the turn too quickly and we skidded across the gravel and came to a stop before pulling into the trailhead parking lot. He shut off the truck and turned towards me in one simultaneous motion.

"I expect an apology from you." He glared at me and pursed his lips.

"What??"

"I had to get up and come get you out of jail on New Year's Eve, and I expect an apology from you."

I sighed. "Brad, I can't live with you anymore. I'm leaving. What you've done is so beyond horrible, it can never be fixed. I want a divorce. Lindsey and I will stay in town, but we're leaving. There is something wrong with you."

He laughed. He held his belly like it was hurting him to laugh this much. It was the first time I had ever wanted to punch someone in the face. For a split second, I thought it might be worth it. I'd punch him in the nose, get out of the truck and run. But it was freezing cold and he was the only one who knew where my daughter was. I'm a good person, and even though I really, really, really want to punch him in the face, I didn't

"Erika. How stupid can you be? Are you having your period? YOU just got *arrested*. There is nothing wrong with me; it's *you* that has something wrong. If you ever try to leave me, or divorce me, or cheat on me, or do *anything* to me, I will have you arrested again. You'll never, ever see Lindsey again. I'll make sure of it. What judge would *ever* give you custody? You're a violent offender and you just got out of *jail*. You even have a parole officer assigned to you now! Ha! You've got no job, no family, and no friends. Now that you've been arrested, you're not gonna be able to get a job. You got nothin' except me. So you're going to go home and go to bed and get up tomorrow as my wife just like before. God, I thought this time in jail would've taught you a lesson, but I guess you're a slow learner 'cause you just don't get it…"

He was right. I just didn't get it. I absolutely didn't get it. What I internalized was that Brad had just summarized my emergency situation to my own ears, and the situation was dire. I needed to bail out of the airplane, but hadn't thought to pack a parachute.

I think the Chief Pilot's office would have declared this a justifiable emergency.

Yep, you're thinking to yourself, just leave. Just leave. It's easy to say, but definitely out of the realm of possibilities given the mindset I was in. When I look back, I'd give myself that same advice, but I couldn't see through the fog of fear. I couldn't declare an emergency because I'd been broken and couldn't see a way out. There are plenty of books telling women how to leave and when to leave. But the shelves are empty when it comes to telling women how to live in this impossible situation. I *couldn't* get out, and the best I could do was to make it up as I went along.

My life existed only for my child and what was best for her. I couldn't support her at the moment, and I couldn't leave her with him. If I ran, I'd be caught. I had a record. As Brad so happily reminded me, my flight crew included a parole officer. It was now my responsibility to check in with my parole officer and show him I was living a "normal" life. I had to attend domestic violence counseling classes or I'd be arrested. I wasn't allowed to leave the state. I had to prove that my once-extraordinary life was no longer extraordinary. It was just extra, extra ordinary, and that's all I could be from now on. White trash. No. Now I had to strive to live like white trash. I might as well put a wife beater shirt on Brad while I hide in the shadows to complete the scene. My world had once been endless. Now it was confined to this little itty bitty life of fear. I used to put an airplane upside down and in a spin on purpose, and not be afraid. I was now the definition of afraid.

In the weeks and months after my return, I was a walking deprivation chamber. I honestly couldn't feel anything—good or bad. I didn't notice if the sun was shining or if the rain was pouring. Food had no taste; I couldn't smell fresh air, and my thoughts repeated over and over. I couldn't get the nightmare of being attacked out of my mind, and the transition of thought went from the attack, to the scene in the truck in which he told me I needed to apologize to him.

Like the characters of *A Nightmare on Elm Street*, I was even afraid to fall asleep because if I ever reached deep enough peace to achieve REM sleep, I had horrific nightmares about Brad attacking me. My husband. The one person in this world who promised to love and care for me. The same scene would replay in the nightmare, and I would wake up drenched in sweat with my heart racing. It was the beginning of sleep issues starting with insomnia. I was exhausted, but I couldn't get to sleep. My mind would not shut off.

I have never taken sleeping pills because it's not allowed in the aviation industry, and I didn't want to now because I had a little girl I was always listening for. I still can't believe how naïve I was. I refused to medicate myself, even though I was falling apart at the seams. In the reverse of a drug addict, I felt that by not taking pills I was still in charge on my life, which should have made me feel better. In truth, I wasn't in charge of anything in my life, and I should have found a way to at least get some sleep.

I knew the importance of sleep after working the red-eye for two years. I knew and viewed what lack of sleep did to a pilot's motor reflexes and focus. Even though we were fully awake, tired brains still try and shutdown if denied rest. To combat this, to the horror of public opinion, I used to tell my copilot and engineer to sleep once we were established at cruising altitude. I found that even a few minutes would refresh their focus and spirit. I would assign turns and told them to lay their seat back and rest, even if they couldn't fall asleep. But come on, these were men. They were out like a light in less than five minutes. I would let them rest for about twenty minutes and then let the other crewmember sleep. I never slept because I was the captain, but I felt this was safer than denying our circadian dysfunction. My advice: get some sleep. You need your strength and focus for the landing.

Two weeks after court, my orders came in to meet my parole officer and check in with him. I drove to the county offices and waited with the rest of the offenders. I brought a book with me and didn't look anyone in the eye. I had no idea what to expect when I met Sam. He was wearing a cliché social worker gray cardigan sweater and had the grizzled appearance of having seen the dregs of society. I was sure he'd seen it all, and after seeing the waiting room full of offenders, I figured he just wanted to get me in and out without any hassle.

I began the conversation like the game in the courtroom. Just comply and agree and get the hell out of there, but Sam asked me about my life and history. He looked at the court report, and asked, "Okay, now tell me what really happened. This doesn't add up. I ran a background check on you, and you haven't even had so much as a speeding or parking ticket in your life. That kind of person doesn't end up in a parole office without some help."

With that question, I burst out crying. I told him the whole story. Reliving it again made me nauseous, and I was sobbing like a toddler by the time I was done. I was inconsolable.

"Erika. You're not the first woman to sit here. I've seen variations of this story over and over. You now belong to a secret society of battered women who have had the added insult of being tangled in the legal system. You will not find justice here. There is no easy way out, either. Actually, right now, there is no way out except one, and even that will leave you with the burden of having a record. Every time you apply for a job, the question will still be, 'Have you ever been arrested,' and your answer will be 'yes.' You plead guilty to a crime. Most people don't know that when they accept the diversion program.

"I'm going to give you a list of counselors approved by the county for the diversion program you agreed to. I have to remind you that you must adhere to these rules. They're strict, and your failure to follow them will land you in jail. If you don't show up, the counselor will call me, and there will be a warrant issued for your arrest if you don't have a medical reason. You better be in the hospital or in class. It's serious, so don't screw it up. Don't give anyone any reason to put you back in jail. If you even get a speeding ticket or have any type of police contact, you need to call me *immediately*. You also cannot leave the state. Do you understand all of this? You'll need to attend your classes and you'll also have to continue meeting with me for the next year."

I nodded and quietly accepted his list of recommendations, including names of people I would have to meet with for the next thirty-six weeks. I had officially lost all control over my own life.

"Erika, do you have any family here in Colorado? Where are your mom and dad? Siblings?" I hung my head as the feelings of humiliation and loneliness penetrated even further.

"No, I have no one. My dad lives in northern Minnesota and my mom lives in Phoenix. She's sick and can hardly handle day-to-day life. My sister has disconnected from the family. All my other relatives live in Minnesota. I just moved to Colorado and have no close friends. I have a ton of acquaintances, but no one who can help me with this. I love my parents dearly, and I can't drag them into this."

"You mean your parents don't know about this? The abuse?"

"God, no. I don't want *anyone* to know about this. I wish *I* didn't know about this. My parents wouldn't believe it anyway. Anytime my family comes to visit, Brad puts on the best show you can imagine. He helps cook, does the dishes, tells jokes with my dad...they are always saying how lucky I am. Both my parents were against my marrying Brad in the first place, so it would just turn into an 'I-told-you-so fest.' I have to just live with this."

"Yes, you have to live with this punishment, but no, you don't have to live with the person who did this, Erika."

"For now, I do. I have a baby, I have no job, and now with this arrest, I can't get an aviation job, and it's the only thing I know how to do."

My domestic violence/anger management counseling classes were on Tuesday nights. I told Brad that I needed to leave by 5:00 p.m. because my class was an hour away. The two-hour class was the closest class I could get, so I wouldn't get home until 9:00 p.m. He said to make sure that Lindsey was fed and bathed before I left, and that he would get her to bed.

The hour-long drive gave me a chance to work myself up into a frenzy of fear for my first intake meeting with the counselor. I imagined a room full of men smoking cigarettes telling each other how they enjoyed beating their wives and why should anyone tell them to stop? I figured I would be the only woman there, and that getting raped was a good possibility when our session was over each evening.

As it turned out, my fears were unfounded, since it was a women's only group. Gina, the owner and therapist for the diversion program, was not what I expected. She was five feet five inches of understanding and had a pure hatred of mean men. She had been in an abusive relationship herself and kept the passion of pain from those moments with her at all times. She had no tolerance for any woman who defended being abused.

I met with Gina privately and, through my embarrassment and humiliation, we completed my intake session. My face was red when we got done, and I was utterly exhausted. Sitting in an empty classroom for people who got arrested for domestic violence, Gina leaned her chair back and said, "Give it to me. What are you doing here, and what do you want to get out of this? I teach Domestic Violence and Anger Management counseling, but I mostly work with the women in these situations. Rarely do I have a woman who is an actual abuser. Don't get me wrong, I definitely have some women in here who are scary as shit. They'll throw a punch at anyone, and they do extensive damage. But if you listen to 'em long enough though, you'll hear their story, and it ain't pretty. They have a reason to be mad at the world. What they're doing isn't right, but they've got a good excuse. Usually, I have women who have just had enough and tried to defend themselves, and got messed up with the cops. The anger management I teach is how to handle what's been done to you, because if you didn't have anger before, you're going to have it now. I know the state doesn't realize this is how it is, or what I teach. All they know is that I produce results, and my students don't re-offend because I teach them how to stay safe, even though these men will still abuse my clients. Your husband will probably switch from physical to mental abuse now—in every way shape and form—from holding or stealing your money, to isolating you. And the best part is that he'll use your kids to control you. Does that sound about right to you?"

I just sat there with my mouth open and tears clouding my vision.

It dawned on me at that moment that I was already in that world. He had already taken my money, but I had to remind myself that I'd given it to him. He had used my daughter to get me arrested, but the fault was mine for not defending myself better. I was isolated by circumstance. He had his family and familiarity around him, so even though he had no close friends, he had support and strength, and I didn't realize it.

Denial. It stealthily creeps in and, like a mosquito, you don't even know it's in your body until the poison has already been released. As Gina described the symptoms of abuse and the topics we'd be covering in class, I quietly told myself that I was too extraordinary to fit any of these categories. There was no way that I was so stupid to have chosen an abuser as a husband. I loved myself, and I loved my life, so why would I have done that? Nope, there had to be a misunderstanding, and I would learn how to fix this mechanical problem. Now, where did I put that checklist?

My first Anger Management class changed me forever. What started as visions of high school dropout, bar-brawling women picking fights with their men turned out to be eight other highly educated sophisticated women who were in situations so vastly different from mine, yet so identical that we could trade places.

Since everyone in the class has started at different weeks of the year, women were always coming into the program while others were close to leaving. The format of the class required that every new person had to share their story of how they got there before joining the group. Just the thought of telling strangers what happened made my insides turn to liquid. I didn't know where to begin, and since I hadn't heard any of their stories yet, I thought for sure I would be laughed at for sticking to the old prison adage of "I'm innocent."

I methodically explained the fight that landed me in jail. I repeatedly explained how it was my fault, too, and that I shouldn't have pushed him away from me. I took ownership of my role in the fight, thinking that's what I *should* be saying. I explained that as a mother, there was something there that day that made me behave in a way I couldn't explain. When my husband swore at me and called me names in front of our daughter, a new emotion tore through me that told my body to get this predator away from my baby. I told my story looking at the floor. I couldn't bear to look up or into anyone's eyes; I was so ashamed of myself. Once again, I couldn't stop the tears from falling, and when I was done, I took a deep breath and looked up. Reflecting back to me were sixteen sad, concerned eyes, all with tears and an understanding that transferred through the moments of silence following my story.

Gina just let the room be silent and, per protocol, nobody made any comments. The next woman began her story, and I couldn't wait to hear how someone else got here, too. Just by looking at her, it had to be a joke that she was sitting in this class. She was a sophisticated, soft-spoken, silver haired grandmother from Evergreen. At five-foot nothing, Mary's story didn't need height.

Mary and her husband had gone out to the Little Bear (the local watering hole with great music and burgers) with her out-of-town family and some friends for some dancing and dinner. Shortly after dinner, her husband was tired and wanted to leave early. Since there was a large group, Mary decided to stay behind.

When she returned home with her family, her husband of thirty-five years accused her of having an affair. Several of Mary's family members wrestled her husband onto the couch, all while her husband called her a string of obscenities. She admittedly lost her composure and felt the only appropriate response was to bop him on the nose while he was pinned under one of her family members. This should have been the end of her story, but it wasn't.

Two days later, Mary's husband, still beyond angry about his humiliation, went to the doctor because he thought his nose "looked crooked." The nurse asked how it happened, and her husband, knowing that by telling the nurse about what his wife had done would get her arrested, told the nurse every last detail. By law, the nurse turned Mary in. Mary was babysitting her grandchildren when two uniformed officers pulled into her driveway to arrest her for assault and domestic violence at sixty-two years old. Mary, a sophisticated, soft spoken regal woman was placed in the back of a cop car, in front of her grandchildren, and taken away. The arresting officer could have picked her up with one arm and carried her to jail, she was so dainty.

The stories were all similar. One woman had thrown a candle holder and was charged with assault with a weapon. One had pulled the phone out of the wall so her husband couldn't call his girlfriend (interfering with a telephone is illegal, too—I didn't know that). Each story had its own premise, but the end result is that the women were sent to jail.

I walked out of my first anger management class ironically relieved but with a sense of connection with a subversive group of women I never knew existed. After I got in my car, I took a moment to lay my head on the back of the seat, close my eyes, and exhale. I had been holding weeks' worth of stress in my neck and shoulders and for the first time since that first night in jail, I felt a huge rush of release. My eyes flew open as my body came alive with the thrill of letting go of the stress. Surprisingly, this class was the first ray of light, and like a sunflower seeking the sun's path, I wanted to follow it. I was already looking forward to the next class. I never needed anger management classes until now.

Each time a pilot transitions into another type of aircraft, it often feels like learning how to fly all over again. It involves many hours of study, and every aspect of the new airplane affects your thought process. For example, some airplanes have more sophisticated weather equipment, which allows you to fly in some really bad weather. But now that you're flying in really bad weather, the danger can be just as bad as trying to avoid it. The equipment gives you confidence to knowingly go into icing conditions or close to a thunderstorm, but despite the equipment, you're still in a dangerous situation.

Starting a new business required a new thought process, too, and, thankfully, gobs of time. Brad now spent long days away from home, which meant I was with a baby, by myself, day after day after day. Like a robot, I would greet the day without emotion, get through the morning routine as a wife, and waiting until I was alone to be who I wanted to be. As Brad's car backed out of the driveway, I became another person, and found joy in finding new activities to do with Lindsey.

I now had an assigned flight schedule, and had settled into the routine of my domestic violence/anger management classes on Tuesdays and being away from home as much as humanly possible with an infant. I attended every book club, playgroup, and field trip I could find. I went to story time at the library every Monday, and planned one trip into Denver every week. When the local mother's group was looking for a leader, I quickly held my hand up and managed to double membership within a year. We had seventy-five names on the Mothers and More roster, and I could walk into the grocery store on any given day and run into someone I knew. I was fanatically creating a life away from home to divert my attention from the fact that I still had to go "home." I had lost my sense of home—that place and space that you walk into at the end of the day and know that you'll be safe and comfortable. I'd also lost my sense of home within—that connection with yourself when you look in the mirror and know that you are what you see.

Zombies are real. I was one, and that's what I saw when I looked in the mirror. I was a zombie seeking nourishment, but I was looking in all the wrong places. All this time, I know Brad was going crazy trying to figure out how to make a marriage again after what happened. He got what he wanted, he had total control, but he never realized before that you just can't fake a marriage. Oh, you can go through the motions, but it's like trying to tickle yourself. As the cycle goes, he was once again extraordinarily kind. He offered to watch Lindsey so I could go to book club, and kept telling me that he would land a big contract soon so that we could get our financial life turned around.

My inability to respond the way he wanted was propelling his frustration to the explosion level again. We both felt it this time. He honestly felt that if someone is saying and doing nice things, then all other previous grievances should be put in the past. He kept telling me to "…just get over it. *God*. Why are you still moping around? It's done and over with, so just pull your head out of your ass and get on with it. Why can't you move on? You have to have a screw loose if you can't pull your shit together over just one thing that happened. What's the big fucking deal?"

I asked myself these questions daily. The problem was that I had an answer for every question.

I couldn't move on. Every week I went to domestic violence class and learned about domestic *abuse*. It's passé to think that it takes a punch or a hit to be abusive. Abuse comes in all forms, and over 4 million women experience it every single year in the United States alone. You can imagine the world wide numbers. It includes being called bad names, public humiliation, isolation, degradation, controlling your finances, threatening your family, threatening to take away your children, forcing you to have sex without consent, as well as the classic physical abuse and threats.

Ten weeks into taking classes, I told myself that I had to devise a way to get out. I didn't know where to begin, but I knew I had to at least plant the seed of thought. About the same time that I shifted my thinking, Brad announced that we needed to attend marriage counseling to find out what was "wrong with me." I was blown away, along with being impressed that he'd made this decision. He had already found a counselor, and had even secretly met with her. My thoughts were derailed at this announcement, and since I had nothing to lose except more money, I agreed to give it a try. Marriage counselor. What a great example of an oxymoron—emphasis on the moron. There was nothing to do but continue trying to fly the airplane.

18 Approach to Landing Checklist

1. Thirty minutes out – stretch and wake up. Ding FA for coffee
2. ATIS – listen and set up STAR arrival route
3. Pilot voice – turn on and update passengers
4. It gets busy in the cockpit very quickly so plan ahead
5. Be ready for missed approach and alternate airport

Pilots begin the approach phase of flight many miles from the airport. The faster and higher you are flying, the father out that you begin getting information about the upcoming landing environment. At least fifty miles out, most pilots have started dialing in the Automatic Terminal Information Service (ATIS). This is a looped recording that broadcasts essential information about the wind, active runways, precipitation, visibility, altimeter setting and any unusual situations at the airport. If the weather is lousy, pilots must verify if they have enough visibility to legally land, in which case they need to get their Jeppesen or NOAA approach plates (electronic, too) out to shoot an instrument approach or plan on flying to their alternate destination.

ATIS also gives information about the condition of the runway—especially important in the Midwest because it will explain snow conditions on the ground. Don't forget, besides performing the landing, you also have to be able to get the aircraft to a complete stop, preferably on the runway.

Instrument flying is also called "flying blind." It just means that you are completely in the clouds and do not have the horizon to verify your position in space. Instrument flying, and especially landing during low cloud decks and low visibility, requires withdrawing every penny of training sunk into the brain of the captain and crew.

To add to the fun of flying in the clouds, there is a crazy phenomenon in the cockpit called spatial disorientation, or vertigo. Simply put, it means that without a visual reference or horizon to confirm your attitude, your body can send you the sensation that you are turning, but your instruments say you are flying straight-and-level. It can be completely disorientating and requires that every pilot develop a total sense of reliance on the flight instruments, and disregard other indications of motion from within.

Because of this intense reliance on instruments, it's also important to not hone in on just one indication. During flight training, pilots are constantly trained to cross-check all indications and not just rely on one instrument. Many a pilot has focused on an inoperative instrument and loyally followed it into the ground because it said to do so. Pilots must remember to pay attention to the big picture and what all of the instruments are confirming together as a committee. When they are giving the pilot mixed signals, the trick is figuring out which instrument to ignore. You must ask yourself, "Who is giving you the correct information and which one is feeding you bullshit?" Knowing the difference could be the difference between life and death.

The black box of the Air France (Airbus A330) flight from Rio de Janeiro to Paris demonstrates how one instrument, an airspeed sensor, malfunctioned and caused an "error chain" of events that brought all 228 people into the Atlantic Ocean. Just *one* wrong indicator can mess up everything. Mechanically, the aircraft was just fine, but since the pitot tubes iced over, the pilots were told by the onboard computer the incorrect indicated airspeed. The onboard voice responded by calling out "Stall!" followed by a loud and intentionally annoying sound called a "cricket." The pilots reacted over and over without thinking about *all* the possible causes, and within fifteen minutes, all those thousands of hours and flight training disappeared into the depths of the ocean. One wrong indicator.

I had just one wrong indicator, and I followed her guidance into the ground.

Brad said the therapist he was seeing was named Lynn. He thought she'd come from hippie parents because she dressed the part and he thought I'd like her. I liked her just by listening to her description. I had been in my diversion program therapy for about three months and was getting so much out of it that I was looking forward to this next step of healing.

And I was healing, but the marriage was still in ruins, and I had no ambition to try and fix it. Brad knew it and pointed out that it was a flaw in my character that I couldn't learn how to forgive and forget. On many levels, I agreed. What was wrong with me that I couldn't get over this? I had a baby, a marriage, a husband, and it was my responsibility to get my entire flight crew to their destination. Since I was locked in the marriage like being locked in the cockpit, I decided I might as well troubleshoot the problems until I had it figured out. Pilots can't really *fix* anything, they can only put the airplane in a condition to continue flying and wait for the mechanic to fix it once they're safely on the ground.

Lynn's office had warm colors, soothing music, incense, and comfortable chairs. At this point, Brad had met with her about twelve times. Yes, that many. Since he was a "victim" of abuse, he was entitled to a state funded victim's counseling program. He was getting counseling as the *victim*. To complete the image, he greedily lined up for this free service, doing what he needed to do to seal my fate and hide his deceit, but I often wondered if deep down, he knew he needed help.

Lynn wanted me to meet with her alone for the first session, and then she'd bring Brad in with me for couple's counseling.

During my first session, she spent most of our time leaning back in her chair with her mouth open. What I was told her was completely different than what Brad had said, and she kept saying so. Brad had told her his story of my arrest, but the story that Brad gave her was obviously far removed from what I was explaining, and I could tell she was struggling to keep up. She was scribbling furiously on her notebook and kept having me wait while she checked on her notes from Brad's session.

I still could not talk about what happened without crying. I told myself that I would detach myself and just tell the story so that I could set my emotions aside and hear what she had to say. I gave myself the lecture during the drive to her office, but I still cried. Hell, I was crying in the lobby before I even was in her office because I knew I had to retell it again.

Accompanying the tears was a new twist that hadn't been there in my first recalling of the event—anger and resentment. Each time I talked about it, the emotions changed from where they came. Instead of my heart, it was coming from my brain, and all of a sudden my brain rankled and festered each time it had to tell the story. This time when I told Lynn the story, I did sound like I needed anger management classes—and rightly so.

Lynn sat back and said, "Erika. There are so many things wrong here; I honestly don't know where to begin. The first thing we have to do is get you both in the same room so I can hear you explain your story in front of each other. Your explanation is so vastly different than what Brad told me that I think that in itself is the first issue. One of you is not telling me the truth, so we have to start there. Maybe that's a bit harsh. Let me rephrase that and say that one of you is remembering it the way they want to and disregarding the facts."

She also asked if there were any physical issues (weight gain/loss, etc.) I was dealing with, and I admitted to her that I hadn't slept for more than a few hours each night for the last seven months. Actually, I had not had eight hours of sleep in a row for almost a year. It's no wonder why they use sleep deprivation as a form of torture in war. I was too tired to feel anything. In a way, my body and mind had reacted like being in a bad accident. You look at the injury and know it's there, but you really don't feel it, yet. It's only later, when your body and brain is over the initial shock and has begun to get down to the business of healing, that you actually start to feel it, and dang, it hurts like hell.

After dropping Lindsey off with a friend and telling her that I had a work related event, rather than marriage counseling, Brad and I met together with Lynn for the first time. She began by explaining her bewilderment at the striking contrast of explanation as to why our marriage was in shambles. She admitted that since she spent an enormous amount of time with Brad that she had a preconceived notion of who I was all about, but that my short time with her has made the situation more mystifying.

She backed up the situation by starting at the beginning. "Talk about your parents, siblings, extended family. Why did those people get divorced? How was your experience when your own parents got divorced? How did that make you feel...?"

During these sessions, I learned amazing details about Brad I never knew. I heard about the specific behavior problems he had starting from when he was very young. He was always in trouble, and from the stories it sounded like he just couldn't stop himself from acting out in frustration. He admitted he'd have moments of rage in high school so intense that he'd black out or forget what he did. He had punched holes in drywall and threatened his mom with physical violence. He said he had made a motion to punch his mom one time, but didn't actually go through with it. It was more to simply intimidate and threaten—to remind everyone that he was his own person and no one could stop him anymore.

Brad also explained that his parents divorced when he was very young, so he acted out to get attention. First and foremost, he despised being told what to do. All the way through elementary and junior high school, he struggled. He butted heads with teachers and anyone else who might have an opinion that differed from his. He was also picked on by classmates and, in return, he lashed out and misbehaved. He said he despised bullies.

When his family moved, he switched schools upon entering high school. With a new school and fresh start, he vowed to be a different person. It worked. He never got into trouble at school. He was still the victim of bullying on a regular basis, but it didn't land him in the principal's office for anything significant. Simply growing up had a lot to do with it, but he also gave enormous credit to his stepdad, James, who, with his Ph.D in child psychology, was calm and patient. The marriage didn't last, but James left an indelible mark on Brad that helped him grow.

All these little stories put the pieces of the puzzle together for Lynn. She explained how all of these events of our past affect who we are now and how we behave.

The review of my history was actually pretty boring. We talked about my being adopted, a latchkey kid, a child of divorce, my mom's depression, and how that all might affect my marriage. I explained that my only anxiety when I got married was having kids—because I was adopted. I just didn't know what genetics lurked in my DNA, and I didn't want to pass on anything weird besides blue eyes.

Lynn's ultimate summary was that I was detached and that my instinct was to run away and ignore confrontation instead of facing it and working it out. That didn't sound too crazy. I thought, *hey, what the heck? I'm sitting here—isn't that trying to face it?* She said it was passive aggressive behavior. She said when I walked away from Brad on that fateful day that it was passive aggressive. She said I knew that he'd be angry if I called him a "dick" and walked away—yet I chose to walk away. Yep, I'll take ownership of that. In addition, I agreed with her detachment analysis. I'd been working on detaching myself from myself every single day lately, and the thought of standing up to confrontation of any sort made me nauseous. I've never liked confrontation, but then again, there aren't too many people who thrive on it. They are the exception. Besides, when I had gone the confrontation route, it got me tossed down the stairs, or an elbow to a new C-section incision…and falsely arrested. Who wouldn't want to detach from that?

Brad and his mother had confrontations on a daily basis while he was growing up and he was accustomed to it. Lying, threatening, and manipulating were normal to him. Lynn said because I knew that, my behavior of being detached was upsetting Brad, yet I continued to do it. This was also a form of passive aggressive behavior which made me a co-combatant.

My analysis was that I was absolutely ordinary, boring, and still fucked up. There were common mistakes of judgment, but no giant skeletons in my past. Despite this, the shell of a soul I had put in my closet a few months ago was decaying and, as in a Poe story, the heartbeat was getting louder, so I simply kept turning up the noise to block it all out.

At the end of the first session, Lynn asked us both if we wanted to try and save this marriage. My heart and head screamed NO! RUN AWAY! But, my passive aggressive behavior towards myself ignored their combined effort, so I simply said, "Yes, sure…" Of course I said I'd comply. What did the counselor think would happen if I said no? She should have known that I was in an environment where it was not safe to express dissent, frustration, or anger, so I had to find other channels to express it. Passive aggressive behavior was the best I could do, but because I couldn't perform it on someone else, I just turned it inward, which preserved my body, but destroyed my soul.

Since I had said "yes," we began by concentrating on teaching me how to forgive. Sticking with my strict agnostic beliefs, I adored the teachings of Buddha, Confucius, Allah, and Jesus. I wanted to live my life as an elevated person who could do extraordinary things, and forgiving this would give me enlightenment. If I could do this, I could do anything. Right?

Lynn said part of the healing process was that Brad would have to discuss what happened that day, in front of both of us. His story began by explaining how I had triggered him by making him think he was stupid. Since he couldn't figure out the QuickBooks program, he felt stupid, but Lynn pointed out that I hadn't said or done anything to make him feel that way. He was frustrated on his own and just didn't want to look stupid in front of me, so he "balanced" the situation by taking physical control of it.

Once Lynn moved his blame train off the track, we could all feel a shift as Brad's defensive story progressively turned into a confession with gut wrenching tears—from both of us. He apologized to Lynn for lying to her and then turned to me and said he was sorry. He said he was sorry about losing control, making me lose my career, and ruining my trust.

My brain ran through all the emotional checklists available, and I still didn't know how to react or feel about this acknowledgement. Over the last ten months, Brad had never apologized for that day or anything related to it. Just hearing him explain how he snapped and went into a "haze" was both vindicating and horrifying. He remembered everything he did to me that day in vivid detail. Ironically, court records would reveal him stating that he couldn't remember anything because he "blacked out."

Lynn said that it would help Brad to visualize his apology if he wrote me a letter, explaining how he felt about what he'd done. In his letter, Brad admitted that he was the aggressor, and that I should never have been arrested, and that, in fact, it was he who felt out of control and should have been arrested. He called the police because he was scared of his own actions. He signed it "Your husband, friend & Lover. Brad"

Vindication. There it was, in writing, and yet it wasn't as satisfying as I thought it might be. Okay, so he finally admitted it. It's something I'd wanted since it happened. Great. Wonderful. But, oh my God, he still did it. He still did those things. My faith and trust in him had been demolished, and I could only wonder if he'd do it again. I couldn't imagine the first incident, how could I prepare for the next? I'd been so focused on the one "incident," hadn't I been denying everything else he'd done?

Finally, my soul turned its attention to the next exhibits of evidence with a vengeance. It was quick to point out that during our first year of marriage and even while I was pregnant, he'd called me a bitch, a cunt, a dumb shit and a prude, to name a few. Name calling was so minor on my list that I hadn't even brought it up in therapy, but it was still there, passively aggressively hurting me. He'd embarrassed me in front of friends and family every chance he got. There were so many instances that they blur together. Our family home videos showed over and over happy scenes where everyone is smiling and laughing, only to have Brad say something like, "What was that? Erika, did you fart?" It would be so completely untrue and so shocking; it would pull me away from the happy moment to process what he'd said and wonder why in the world he would do this. It wasn't funny, but he thought it was hysterical. To me, it appeared that he was jealous whenever I was happy.

Brad stole so many happy moments because he had to control my emotions and the scene. And I let him do it. My self-worth was so low and I was completely wiped out at the thought of more imperfection. So instead of saying, "Who cares if you thought I farted?" I stopped what I was doing to fix it. I had to fix it.

To complete the loss of control, Brad had convinced me to turn my accounts over to him when I was in the throes of early motherhood. His name was on everything, from my savings accounts to retirement plans. It was minor relinquishing to a husband. It was expected. A signature added here, an additional account member there.

Pieces of me were now scattered around the corners of our lives. I was truly flying blind and all my indicators were sending me wrong signals to the point where I had missed the approach and couldn't land at an alternate airport.

Could I ever put myself back together again?

The next few months were an overindulgence of self-help sessions. I was in my diversion program therapy and attending marriage counseling with Brad and Lynn.

The irony is that my domestic violence class was teaching me the exact opposite of what I was being taught in marriage counseling. Each teacher was adamant that their way was correct and the other was wrong. Gina's emotional, angry in-your-face delivery was her way of getting me to confront the situation. On the other hand, Lynn was gentle and loving and hopeful. Gina was right. Lynn was wrong. My intuition at the time was in a diabetic shock and it craved the sugar, so I drank Lynn's Kool-Aid.

I blindly trusted Lynn because she was a therapist. In a way, Brad even used her against me to justify his behavior.

At a minimum, Lynn should have known abuse, seen it, and done something about the abuse because Brad had admitted all of it to her in our sessions. But instead of teaching Brad how to deal with his hair trigger anger and emotions, she left it up to me to learn how to deal with it, to forgive it, and to behave in such a way so as to not receive it again. I was so broken that I couldn't tune my own compass and hold the heading. Instead, I'd flown straight into a thunderstorm simply because I didn't want to lose my heading.

19 Abnormal Landing Checklist

1. **Abnormal doesn't mean you can't do it**
2. **Focus on what is working, not just the malfunction**
3. **Think through worst case scenario**
4. **Plan on worst case scenario**

Anytime you have a mechanical problem, it is easy to forget that the airplane continues to remain completely flyable. Sometimes a crew can get so focused on an abnormality that their attention draws them even further away from safety.

Although any problem on the Abnormal Landing Checklist is considered serious, it is NOT grounds for hurrying a procedure and possibly missing a step that, if properly executed, would have resulted in correcting the problem. Conduct the procedures systematically as a coordinated crew in combination with assistance received from outside sources, and don't hurry. Be methodical.

Under "challenging" conditions (like trying to land with one landing gear stuck in the up and locked position), the probability of commonplace errors goes up with workload, fatigue, confusion, and stress, which can often give a snowball effect that increases the chance of even more problems and errors, thus creating a vicious cycle. Although infinitively easier said than done, this is the point in your life where you have to stop responding reactively and start thinking proactively. Stop looking at the bad indicator and acknowledge the rest of the functioning systems. The glass is half full. Think about what systems you have working normally and make sure they are ready for landing, as well as paying attention to the malfunction.

Time adds an extra dimension of pressure to the situation. When you first get a bad indication, it inevitably gets all the attention at first. That's fine, give it all you got, but immediately pull yourself back into the entire situation. If you're in a landing situation, you have to immediately decide the level of importance of the problem and decide to pay attention to it, ignore it, or just deal with it.

When I was a new copilot on a Falcon 20, we were coming back into the St. Paul Downtown Airport. While on the downwind leg, we were almost set for the landing. I was the copilot, so when the captain asked for gear down, I dropped the lever and listened as the captain pushed the power up. "Hmm, what's going on?" he asked, which isn't a lot of detail, and for a new copilot, I thought I'd done something wrong.

"What? What do you mean?"

"The power isn't coming up on the right engine." To confirm his conclusion, he pushed the lever up and nothing happened.

"Falcon N123, you are cleared to land on runway one three." Tower interrupted our confusion with instructions. "Roger, N123 cleared to land one three," I replied. The way I saw the situation is that we had plenty of airspeed, still had an engine pushing us forward and, except for the last setting of flaps, we were set to land.

"Don't just accept the landing clearance without talking to me first!" He replied, while still playing with the power lever.

"Why not? Just land!"

"I don't know if this will affect my hydraulics, so maybe we won't have brakes."

"Oh yeah…"

Now our minds were racing through systems training and trying to decide that if it failed completely, was there anything we needed to do about transferring hydraulic systems. We just didn't have time to run a checklist. It would be stupid to depart the pattern and take the time to figure it out if we have an engine failing. We were so close to the safe airport. "Well, if we lose brakes, just plan on using the emergency brakes." We both agreed that would do.

In the meantime, he had turned onto final approach. Now, the anomaly with the STP airport is that there are two runways only ten degrees offset from one another. We were cleared to land on 13, which was shorter and we didn't use as often. So out of routine and chaos, the captain was lined up with 14, but I saw an airport operations truck at the other end of the runway.

My mind was reeling with information processing overload, and I asked myself and the captain out loud, "Oh, dang, I think we're cleared to land 13?" The captain said no, we're landing 14, but he did me the honor of telling me to double check with tower. "Tower, Falcon N123, can you verify which runway we're cleared to land on?"

"Runway One Three."

"Oh shit," was the captain's response. We just didn't have time to explain, or ask, or tell anyone what was going on. He just banked it hard and landed on 13, even though we had engine failure and were set up to land on runway 14.

Our passengers had no idea, but our chief pilot saw the landing. He greeted us on the ramp and looked at me and asked, "What the hell was that?!" Since I was the newbie, he assumed that the circus stunt was me. I shook my head, gave him a warning look to be quiet, and told him to wait until the passengers left. For the passengers, even though they were just a mere few feet away from us, they had no idea the chaos and danger that existed. From further away, and with an experienced eye like the chief pilot, he knew we were having an issue. But, since we were on the ground to talk about, it couldn't have been that bad.

After Brad received his initial counseling with Lynn for being the *victim* of domestic abuse, it was sex, or the lack thereof, that was the driving force behind Brad's desire to take me with him to attend marriage counseling. Brad stated to everyone we knew that I had a mental disorder because I wouldn't have sex with him.

At a friends and family gathering, Brad was blatantly rude to people. His mom informed my neighbor that Brad's bad mood was because I wouldn't have sex with him. My neighbor was so outraged at this breach of privacy, that she took my hand and walked me to the driveway to tell me what had been said. I was horrified that Brad would dare discuss a private matter such as this with his mom, and that she felt it necessary to announce it to my neighbor.

In spite of that, it was true. I wouldn't cuddle or reach out to touch him. It was an admission he described at our first counseling session together with Lynn. The image of his words was that I was an unloving icebox who wouldn't put out, and yep, I readily admit I was completely withholding sex. Brad said I was being controlling and a complete monster for doing this. I was his wife and this was part of being married. He called me cold, frigid, and a bitch because of it. Even though I was a new mother with some pretty solid reasons, my state of mind was such that I absolutely agreed. My new lack of self-esteem allowed me to believe I was now all of those names he called me, but I was so repulsed by the idea of letting Brad touch me that it made my skin crawl. Dozens of times he had simply crawled on top of me and said it was time to let it go. My reaction was pure terror and revulsion. I'd get him off of me and leave the room. I'd spend the rest of the night tramping down the feelings of despair growing into my core. I just didn't like him. I had no respect for him, and I didn't like anything about him. After all, sex begins in the brain, not the body.

On the other hand, I felt that I should love him. I had a responsibility to learn how to love him. Damn it. He had admitted his weaknesses and errors in counseling. He had cried and apologized and told me he loved me. He was experiencing emotion and love, while I had shut down my systems and just wanted to land.

Brad also came to the realization that he couldn't force me to love him. He had gone to such great lengths to control me that I think he was frustrated to discover that giving and receiving love couldn't also be controlled. He believed that being honest and admitting his mistakes meant that all should be forgiven.

I constantly felt it two against one. Lynn, the therapist, and Brad were always trying to get me to play along, and this had me constantly at odds with what I believed in every cell of my being. They felt that as long as Brad acknowledged that his frustration and anger caused him to enter this mysterious "fog" that blocked out rational thought, the battle had been won. Never mind that it happened or would happen again...just pay attention that Brad is aware there's an error in the system. I could never do that as a pilot, so how was I supposed to do this with him?

For me, I was even more frightened. He admitted he'd completely lost control of himself when he was angry. Not knowing the answer to a software question is justification for uncontrollable blackout rage? Really? God, what if I did something really bad? How could I trust him with Lindsey if she didn't know what might set him off? Hell, how could I ever trust him with me? Yes, he finally acknowledged it, *but what were we going to do about it*? Lynn's fallback answer was that the disclosure letter Brad had previously written forgave the possible future behavior. Like a good Catholic, she said he should be forgiven for his sin. Lynn gave me the role of God in forgiving Brad, and believed his penance was complete simply because he had admitted his guilt.

When I resisted in giving him absolution, Lynn rolled her eyes and asked me if I understood how hard it was for Brad to admit his guilt. I said I understood, but I silently wondered if she realized how hard it was for me to even hear it. To live it. To be the woman who received it. He would never have written his confession if Lynn hadn't made him do it. It was a forced confession. I still had to re-live what he'd done to me and how his moment of insanity had cost me my livelihood, everything I thought I was, my self-respect, and pride and peace. She'd had twelve sessions with Brad as *the victim*, and it was obvious to me that he was more or less her client—not me.

Lynn's way of fixing him was proving to me that he understood his actions, and I could see that an enormous burden of guilt was suddenly off his shoulders. His albatross was gone, but it flew immediately onto my shoulders, and Lynn made me feel that it was completely up to me to take on the full responsibility of making this marriage survive. Lynn was more or less telling me that Brad was cured. See? Look what a good boy he can be.

The question I had been asking myself—*am I crazy for not being able to get over this?*—was being answered *for* me, not *from* me. Yes, forgive Brad and move on. He's cured. He's fixed. He recognizes it and apologized, so it won't happen again. Right?

After everything I had been through, I just wanted to believe it so badly for my daughter that I skipped some important items on my abnormal landing checklist. Oh, hell, I pretty much threw away all my checklists. I felt an obligation to make this work, but I also had another internal pressure tugging at my soul. I was thirty-six years old and had an intense requisite in my heart that Lindsey should have a sibling.

As shallow and selfish as the reasoning was, I knew I didn't have the ability to divorce Brad and meet someone new in time to create a family dynamic for Lindsey to grow up with a sibling. I knew in my heart that Brad and I would probably never stay together forever, so for better or worse, I decided to fill the emptiness in my heart by having another child. Not very politically correct, and even a bit conniving, but I'm damn glad I did it. Not one moment or thread of regret attached.

~~~

I couldn't have a child without sex (well, I guess I could've...) so back to the sex issue. Lynn said that sex had become a barrier for me with Brad, and I needed to jump this hurdle. She said I'd lost the ability to feel intimacy with Brad, but if I would just break through that wall one time, I'd remember how much I once loved him, and I could then find it within myself to forgive.

So, I drank too many margaritas and set aside my thin thread of sanity. Ironically, the week Brad got sex, our couple's sessions with Lynn came to an end. His excuse was that we were out of money again, but what he really meant is that after six couples sessions he was cured! Which meant he finally got what he wanted, so he was done with her.

During the ultrasound, I kept praying for another girl. Me, the tomboy who'd spent her whole life around men and feared the feminine mystique, wanted another girl. Brad wanted a boy and he was sure this time he'd get a boy. When the nurse said, "Oh, yep, look right there...you can see her Big Mac, it's a girl!" I gasped in happiness and Brad took my hand in sorrow and said, "Well, that's okay."

We named baby two, Piper. While pregnant with Piper, Brad's anger issues were predictably bubbling to the surface again. The sight of my pregnant belly kept Brad from using me as his anger catcher. However, I told Brad it was time to see what other kinds of help we could find when I saw him pick up a wheel barrow and throw it down the hill. Thankfully, we had health coverage at the moment since I was paying seven hundred dollars per month to have insurance (for the pregnancy). He agreed to meet with another therapist. But this time, I made sure it was a real psychiatrist who wasn't at all like Lynn.

His diagnosis was completely different and Brad was flabbergasted. He came home and scoffed at the idea that he might have bipolar tendencies, or depression. The doctor had prescribed some drugs and wanted Brad to try them for a few weeks. The doctor advised him it wasn't an instant effect, and to give it some time before evaluating how he felt while on them.

I researched the hell out of the definition and held my breath as each symptom matched the behavior. The research results also led to the definition of a sociopath. For the first time, I realized there might be a name for this type of behavior besides being an asshole. I was elated to think that there might be some help for us and a specific cure for the behavior. After two days, Brad said he didn't like the way he was feeling on the medication, but that he'd stick with it.

In the meantime, my dad had invited us for an all-expense paid trip to Cabo San Lucas, Mexico. It was our Christmas present, and since I was under the influence of pregnancy hormones that made me cry at a Hallmark commercial, I relished the idea of spending a week with my dad while reconnecting with the stranger I married. I felt blessed to have been given this opportunity to travel again, too, but I was leery about having Lindsey stay with Bernice for so long. Bernice reminded me that she'd raised two boys and they turned out just fine, so when I was four months pregnant, Brad and I headed to Cabo for a week of sunshine in January.

We had a wonderful week of walking on the beach and eating Mexican food. Having my dad there was a great buffer to dampen the strain of our marriage. We could tease each other in front of my dad about real issues we were having, but Brad couldn't use his anger in response since my dad, who'd paid for this trip, was sitting right next to him. Brad was trapped into smiling and giving me a knowing nod. The result is that we had a wonderful week, which gave me a glimmer of hope and excitement for our future. We also both knew this would be our only break before we had two kids in diapers, so we slept as much as possible and detached from the real world.

We came home to find an exhausted but happy grandma Bernice. We thanked her profusely, and as she was walking out the door, she turned around and said, "Oh, by the way, I cleaned out your medicine cabinet and threw away those crazy pills that had Brad's name of them. He doesn't need that stuff anyway. Just witchcraft…"

I was too shocked to respond. Who in this world would go into someone else's medicine cabinet and throw away prescriptions?

That was the end of it. Brad never went back to the psychiatrist again and the pills were gone. I'll never know if it would've worked or not. Like I said before, accidents wouldn't be accidents if only…

Happiness was now two girls in diapers, and book club was where I retrieved my sanity. From the day Piper was born, she rarely napped. Always happy and self-entertaining, she was a comparatively easy child, and I was blessed to have my second child be so easy to please. But the exchange was that I seldom had a quiet moment. From sunup to sunset it was a conveyer belt of food in a child, food out of a child. It was perfect, but I missed the outside world. I didn't even have time to read a book to somehow escape the loneliness. At least when I was flying I could still escape with a book.

Don't tell anyone, but my pilot seat used to make a great reading chair, too. Once an airplane is set on autopilot and is at cruising altitude, a pilot's job switches from actively participating to actively monitoring the situation. While paying attention, pilots are also trying everything they can to pass the time, just like the passengers, so after a few games of Farkle with the other pilot, I'd push my seat back and open a book. Of course we're not "supposed" to, but pilots need constant input, and books kept me thinking. Since I also had to spend long lonely hours commuting to and from work each month, I had time to read a novel each week.

Now, with two kids in diapers demanding round the clock attention, my reading addiction became a physical craving. I didn't just miss the reading, I missed being in the outside world and, just like millions of stay at home moms, reading was the only way for me to escape my four walls and enter another world. If I couldn't leave my house, I could at least live vicariously through the words of others through my books.

My sanity saver during this mom chaos phase of my life was book club. It was that simple. It was the only time where I could engage my brain, be a grown up, and listen to how other adults processed the same words, but took from it a different meaning. I relished when someone had a completely divergent view from what I did. I wanted to know why and how their brain dehydrated the words to find the origin of meaning. The discussions took us off in different directions as we related everything we read to our own lives.

Listening to the intelligence and thoughtfulness of these book club women made me ashamed that I'd ever thought less of the power of women. I had pulled away from this feminine camaraderie for so long because I thought it would make me weak in a man's world, when, in fact, those bonds are stronger than anything man has ever created.

I reveled in split opinions over a book because I could see how each woman's past experiences shaped their perspectives. Listening to their contrasting viewpoints unintentionally triggered my ability to gain the internal strength I needed to thrive in a situation that held me captive. My psyche accepted that I had to live with my abuser for now, but I learned to view it from a different perspective.

While Brad controlled my external actions (I had to watch everything I did and said so as to not make him angry), I was fully in control of my internal feelings, where I could transcend beyond my prison. Since I was struggling with my shame, each moment of joy that I ever experienced was reflexively blotted out by the tall shadow of my self-reproach. Book club taught me to separate the stories and to view each character through my own perspective. I realized that I could have a happy story in my heart. Even though I was trapped, I could still fly. My story didn't change, but the way I viewed it did.

It took years to write the ending of my story, but with their help, I had configured a storyline to allow me to live while I worked toward getting myself out. I concluded I could be simultaneously my own captain and copilot of my own story. My captain character was the old me. When Brad wasn't around, she allowed me to make the most out of every day and accept that it was okay to experience joy, no matter how small it was. She was the one who knew how to soar, but was trapped in the hangar. Since the captain had the most responsibility, she was also the one who held the most shame for what her life had become.

While Brad was home, my copilot character was in charge of us. She was a quiet warrior who knew what to do to survive. She had honed her skills to keep the beast calm. She did as she was told and held her tongue for fear of offending. She was exhausted from having to tiptoe through her life, but carrying the weight made her strong.

With two grandchildren racing through the world, my parents made regular trips out to visit. I relished the visits because Brad would put on a great show for us all. He would help cook and do laundry and all the "honey-do" lists, and he would make himself useful and busy all day. My parents commented how helpful he was, and wasn't it wonderful that he cooked for us. Good God. If they only knew what my life was like when they weren't around. I had never told them anything. I'd never told a soul about my arrest and ensuing year of parole-directed therapy. I'd never told anyone I'd been hit or called every vulgarity one could think of, or that my entire life savings was gone and I couldn't be a pilot again. No one knew except me, and I was going to keep it that way. I disconnected from myself and I wouldn't admit my failure because I'd worked too hard to admit my stupidity. How could I ever explain my subversive life? I wouldn't declare an emergency, even though I'd had a catastrophic, structural failure. I was going to crash, but I needed time and distance before setting it down.

Still unable to get over my constant nightmares about my husband hurting me or my children, I could hardly walk into our nursery without cringing at the memory of being attacked in that room. I couldn't look past the spot on the carpet where the bleach had removed all the color. It was a caustic reminder of the blood I'd spilled from my C-section incision. Blood spilled because of Brad.

Resigned to the realization I would have to tough it out with Brad, I was adamant that we move to another house. It was a superficial fix, but I needed to get out of the negative energy that fermented within these walls. The business had suddenly done very well and the housing market was booming. Our financial future was glowing like a hot star. Moving to another home was a Hail Mary relationship pass—a new home, a new focus, a new life. I thought maybe a shift of scenery would help press the reset button.

I was still worried about our huge debts and thought I could help by eliminating a part time employee and fill in at the office. Brad had told me that he would never allow me to work in our office. We had an argument about it, and I simply said I was coming into the office whether he liked it or not, since it was my company. His lucid reply was that if I came to the office against his wishes, he'd just call the police and tell them I was "out of control again," and since I had been previously arrested, I'd be sent to jail again. He said it matter-of-factly, without any emotion. I bit back the retort. After all, it wasn't about just me anymore. I had two little girls, so why the hell would I risk *that* to work in the office? I still wanted to be able to contribute to the household income, so I came up with alternative ideas.

We put our home on the market, and I began thinking of a way to make some money at our next destination. I have always loved animals, especially horses, so I was thrilled to find a horse property in Conifer with a four stall barn, electric and water, an arena, and seven flat acres — which is rare in the mountains — and a dirt road that led to miles of trails.

I ran the numbers and realized I could net about eleven hundred dollars per month by boarding horses. It was a work from home dream, and I thought I could take the extra income and use it to pay bills and start a college saving account for the girls. It was a far cry from the six figure income I used to earn, but my pleasure was now in simple things. I schemed that we could also use some of it for vacation and fun money since we hadn't had a vacation since before Piper was born. Finally, maybe we could get ahead of our financial burdens and actually have some fun.

I ran the numbers past Brad and showed him the home. He liked the style of the house; I liked the barn. I showed him how I would make money at this, and with the real estate market booming, it would be a great investment. Brad mentioned that *finally* I'd be contributing to the household income. Brad liked telling people that he was the president of our company, while I, on the other hand, did nothing but "stay at home." He never mentioned threating to have me arrested if I tried to come to the business that *I* bought for him.

We talked the home seller down forty thousand dollars off the list price and shook hands. We'd already received an offer on our other home, so we set a closing date.

Closing on our new home to start a new life was an abnormal landing. We got it on the ground, but it wasn't pretty. The money we'd counted on from the sale of our house never appeared because the buyers never showed up for the closing, so my dad saved the day by writing us a check for our new house—all the while Brad promised we'd pay him back in a few weeks. But the housing market crashed shortly after we bought the house, and the money took a long time to appear before we could think about paying back the loan to my dad.

In the meantime, it didn't take long before Brad began considering my dad's equity in the home as his. He took out a second mortgage on our house to pay for a new salesman, and I lost focus of our finances because I forgot what normal looked like. I was always operating in emergency mode, looking at one indicator at a time instead of the big picture. I just couldn't see the towering cumulonimbus right in my path because I was so focused on one instrument—my attitude indicator. If I had paid closer attention, I would have realized the instrument was completely upside down.

20 After Landing Checklist

1. You're still vulnerable to other aircraft, so be vigilant
2. Electrical load – reduced
3. Flaps - up
4. Pay attention to airport markings, especially hold short
5. You're not done yet

The After Landing Checklist is requested after the flying pilot lands and gets the aircraft safely clear of all runways. The most immediate need is to shed some of the electrical load you'd been demanding of your aircraft. and to bring the flaps up.

In the "Olden Days," flaps were left in the landing (down) configuration if you were being hijacked and unable to communicate your emergency. It was a visual cue to everyone around that you or your aircraft were in trouble. You can just imagine how many false alarms there were because leaving the flaps down is easy to do because after landing, you are focused on being on the ground and getting the cockpit ready and positioned for the next trip or flight crew. You are also relieved to be back on terra firma and that relief can create complacency. It's important to remind yourself that the flight isn't over until you get to the gate, chock the tires, and shut down the engines.

If the copilot had been flying the leg, there is a moment of transition from pilot to pilot. It's a transfer of control, and in those moments, you have to be both captain and copilot. If the copilot performed the landing, many large aircraft are configured so that the captain is required to taxi to the gate. Because of this, there are a few moments where duties are being transferred, and the copilot goes from flying pilot to radio operator again — all the while completing the after landing checklist. This also means that the copilot has to instantly redirect his/her attention from outside the cockpit to the inside of the cockpit in order to review airport diagrams and taxi instructions. 99.9% of these transitions go without a hitch, but nothing is perfect.

There was an "incident" in 2008 when an Air Tran Airways Boeing 737 had landed and was given instructions to hold short of runway 34R at Seattle-Tacoma International Airport after clearing the runway. The copilot performed the landing and exited the runway on a high-speed taxiway. Without realizing it, the copilot had rolled passed the illuminated hold short line for the other runway and actually stopped right on runway 34R and then gave control of the aircraft to the captain. The captain shifted his attention from inside to outside, not realizing they were on the runway, then called for the After Landing Checklist while simultaneously shutting down the right engine to save fuel (common practice but in this instance, he shut down the engine within 45 seconds of landing. This should be done as time permits). At that exact moment, a Northwest Airline's Airbus 330 was given takeoff clearance on runway 34R — exactly where the Boeing was sitting. The Northwest Airbus blasted down the runway, rotated, and flew right over the top of Air Tran. They missed each other by about 425 feet.

"Diverted attention during taxi" was the root cause of the incident. It only takes a moment to get distracted, and the brief transition period from looking outside to looking within can lead to a disaster. Often, the stress of a difficult landing causes the pilots to let down their guard since it is such a relief to be on the ground. This was just an incident, and the "Wreckage and Impact Information" category on the National Transportation Safety Board was thankfully left blank.

The irony is that the departing aircraft never even saw the other aircraft in their way. They were unaware that they were 425 feet away from death until they got to their destination. The problem during takeoff is that forward and downward visibility is partially blocked during rotation as enough lift is created to rotate and pull the nose wheel off the ground, but the rest of the aircraft still needs a little more airspeed and lift before it is ready to fly. The departing aircraft performed a normal takeoff and departure, not realizing there was another aircraft on the runway. Maybe it's best that the crew never saw the aircraft sitting on the runway—who knows how they would've reacted? Maybe they would have yanked back on the yoke and tried to fly before they had enough airspeed which might have resulted in a stall, right into the other aircraft.

Somewhere in my landing, I transferred control. Since I was busy chasing two little girls, I unknowingly, handed over control, assuming I would get it back. When I finally pulled my head out of the cockpit and looked around, I realized it was too late and that I was committed to my forward momentum. I could see the cliff closing in as I careened towards the end of the runway.

Our new little ranch was situated at 8500 feet in Conifer and I could almost touch the airplanes I used to fly. Since the housing market had crashed and the other business was struggling, I quickly filled up my barn and time with other people's horses. I had been around horses most of my life, but this was the first time I was solely responsible for their care. I also had the new dynamic of dealing with horse owners, and they were more of a pain in the ass than the horses were.

The first lesson I learned rather quickly was that each horse produces about fifty pounds of waste every single day. Roughly in a year, with four to six horses, I was moving about 73,000 pounds of manure and pee, by myself. I would strap Piper into the Baby Bjorn on the front of me and put Lindsey in the backpack and we'd all go out and clean the barn. Within weeks, I had developed lower back pain that wouldn't go away and created a constant level of agony that eventually made me nauseous. Never before believing in chiropractic, I was willing to try anything to get some relief. I was grateful that after just two sessions, I was once again pain free.

Instead of doing all this manual labor with two kids strapped to me, I opted to just get up before Brad left for work so he could watch the kids while I cleaned the barn. Seven days a week, fifty two weeks a year, I would head out in all weather and take care of my magnificent beasts. Brad wouldn't let me get my own horse again, so I had people paying me to feed my addiction. I didn't get to ride them, but I was grateful for their presence.

Like a Buddhist monk in training, I found a level of Zen being out in the silence of the barn while I shoveled shit. Brad hated to be out there, so the compromise was that he kept an eye on the girls while I went to work. The fifty feet to the barn was a great commute. I'd get most of my chores done in an hour, walk in the house while simultaneously Brad was walking out. Most days, the girls would still be sleeping so they'd wake up to find me dirty and reeking of manure, but wide awake and ready to start our day.

Horses are notorious fence breakers. The mares kick and squeal and, inevitably, they'd nail a fence with their hoof. At first, Brad would help out with some of the repairs around the barn and paddocks, but after a while, if I needed help, he would charge me.

Since the move to Conifer, the economy had completely collapsed. The housing sector, which was where our business was, had receded to the depths of hell. We barely had enough home closings to pay the mortgage, so the money I earned from boarding horses was now the only thing putting food in the fridge, which made Brad *charging* me for repairs all the more insane. What was once fun money was now feeding and clothing us. The money I earned boarding these horses filled his stomach with food, as well as his children's, yet he charged me for his help. His justification was that he already had a job and that he'd never agreed to two.

The hours spent in the barn alone saved me. It was those serene moments in the wee hours of the morning that drove my spirit to break free from the shackles of someone who wanted to control and give rise from someone else's pain. I knew I needed to prepare quietly, with extreme patience and focus. These hours of contemplation while shoveling shit gave me strength and focus. The Zen saying, *Before Enlightenment; chop wood, carry water. After Enlightenment; chop wood, carry water* looped in my brain. I just changed it to throw hay, shovel poo. It was the drawing in of my focus that changed me.

To Brad's dismay, I applied and was accepted to the University of Denver's continuing education program in the fall of 2008. Brad probably thought my criminal record would be cause for denial of entry to college, but fortunately they don't ask, so I didn't have to tell. They accepted some of my credits from the University of Minnesota, but none of my aviation credits at Embry-Riddle. Even though I had almost four years of college already under my belt, the best case scenario was that if I took classes every single quarter, without a break for three years, I would get my BA degree. So I spent the next few weeks applying for several scholarships and won a Daniels Fund Scholarship that would pay a significant chunk. Landing check complete.

I learned more in three years than I had in my previous forty years combined. Since online classes are heavily reliant on research papers, I excelled. I flourished in the hours of research, interviews, and Turabian style. I reminisced how I'd once been very smart, and I could be smart again. I shoveled shit for my girls, not for me. I inhaled information about globalization, international economics, financial instability hypotheses, and I conjured up visions of grandeur working at the World Trade Organization. The college experience at forty bolstered my confidence that I could once again be a driving force in this world.

The University of Denver is known for its travel abroad requirements to complete your degree. In my Global Studies program, I was required to visit a foreign country. I tried to wiggle my way out of the seven day trip by explaining that I'd been to twenty-two countries and couldn't I just write a research paper on another country's economic structure? The answer was an unequivocal "no," which meant I had to go to Quebec City, Canada. Geez, really, eh? This is not what I considered a foreign experience, but in July of my second year, I was heading to Canada for my "foreign travel" experience.

The trip allowed me to think about myself, and I hadn't done that for years. The person I used to be gasped in the mirror at my reflection. *Hey, I remember you! What happened to that encompassing smile you were born with, that twinkle in your eye, that contentment that comes from knowing who you are and what you want? What happened? Did you remember the basic rule to just fly the airplane? What? No checklist for this particular emergency? So what? You're the manufacturer, make your own...*

I came home from Quebec with a refreshed attitude because I'd found the "old me" again—the Me who knew how to take control of her life. My captain me. I didn't care what Brad thought of me, and I didn't try to hide my disdain of his existence. I stopped pretending. I flat out told him "no" to things I wouldn't do or agree with, and he was taken aback at my change in behavior.

Since I had been gone for a week and my mom-guilt was overwhelming, I decided to plan a day out with the girls the day after I got back. That morning, I had Lindsey on my lap and we were looking online for information on children's activities in the area. We had a new desktop computer, and I was still getting used to the functions. I was Googling "Jump Street" and accidentally clicked on a previous selection of Brad's which turned out to be the furthest thing from a children's activity. Lindsey got an eyeful of completely naked women showing their most prized possessions. Lindsey thought it was hysterical that a grown woman would forget to put her clothes on.

I sent Lindsey to the kitchen for an apple and clicked on "view history." Page after page of pornographic websites appeared. Mostly run of the mill porn, but a few had girls that were dressed like little school girls—pigtails and uniforms, minus the shirt. Some of the sites were truly hardcore and others with sadomasochistic themes. I really didn't give a damn that he was looking at porn, but it wasn't just a little. I had caught him looking at porn many times before, but now it was hundreds of sites, and some of them were chat rooms. Now I knew why Brad was so adamant that we get Skype hooked up to the computer.

Considering our deteriorating lives, I didn't blame Brad for turning to porn. We're human with human desires, and I understood the need for a sexual outlet, but Brad was raising two little girls and his thinking that this was okay didn't sit well with me. Not only did I not want this in my home, it just added to the misogynistic view that Brad had of women—that women were just objects to use and abuse.

That night, I told Brad what I had found. He said his behavior was completely normal and that, once again, I was the one with the problem. "So what if I've been looking at porn since I was sixteen? Get over it. Every guy does." He said he would find a marriage counselor the next day to prove that his behavior was "normal."

My reply: "Please do."

"Actually no, viewing pornography every day is not a normal or healthy activity," explained Bridgette to Brad, marriage counselor number two. She ran through the wide variety of pitfalls that pornography had on a relationship and marriage.

"Pornography all too often crosses the line into addiction. Those people who exhibit a pathological pursuit of rewards can easily become addicted (I liked that term "pathological pursuit of rewards" because it described Brad; he took everything from everybody and moved on). It also desensitizes men who are in a relationship with a woman, which can dehumanize her, and is often the breakdown in a marriage. The woman also feels like she could never live up to the images the man sees. And it's true. She can't. Most of the images are digitally corrected and, of course, most of the bodies have been surgically altered, if you know what I mean."

Bridgette was young with two boys of her own. Her analysis of our situation was blunt, to the point, and emotional because she often gave advice in the context of a mother's point of view. She was teary-eyed when discussing our situation and the effect it was having on our children. I liked her. Brad hated her.

At the end of the first session, after I had laid out my laundry list of concerns and overview of our history, she tilted her head and raised her eyebrows, and asked the one question that changed the course of my life: "Do you actually *want* to make this marriage work? You appear to be disconnected from this relationship..."

I looked her in the eye and without a moment's hesitation, said "No. I am exhausted from trying to keep the peace. I'm not me anymore, and I haven't felt happy for years, except for being with my girls. My insides are bleeding and I've been walking on eggshells for so many years, I don't remember what the ground feels like. I am done trying to make this work. I can't do this anymore."

The air was sucked out of the room, so I took shallow breaths to stay alive. We sat in silence as the terse announcement settled into Brad's psyche. *No.* Not often heard and rarely understood; for Brad, the word "no" hit harder than any fist. I had been emotionally detaching myself for years, and I was good at putting on a happy face to keep the peace. He probably thought I was at least content. For Brad, the announcement came as a reality check. Deep down, he must have known, but he never allowed the thought to burble to the surface. After years of controlling the puppet, I'm sure he was astonished to see Pinocchio come alive and stand on her own two feet.

Immediately, Bridgette told Brad it would be best if he could move out for a while. She knew the potential for violence and abuse, and her concern was legitimate. She said he needed to work on some issues before living under the same roof again, even if he/we knew that a divorce was pending. She asked us to come back and to approach the counseling session as a tool to handle the upcoming divorce, and to work out the new issues that were bound to come up.

We explained that, financially, we needed to share a dwelling for a while. Bridgette nodded and explained she'd seen many marriages languish in the depths of blackness for years because of financial constraints. That alone was an additional reason why we needed to continue talking to her.

We met with Bridgette two more times, and after that, Brad said he wouldn't spend another penny on her. "Why the hell would I give a *marriage* counselor money if she is just helping you plan a divorce?"

The elephant was acknowledged for the first time. I had admitted to Brad that I had no intention of staying married to him. As strange as it sounds, I needed the external confirmation from Bridgette that I wasn't the only crazy one here, and that the issues I had been dealing with all these years were intense. I really didn't have to live like that—even if I had two kids. Actually, Bridgette pointed out the disservice I was doing to the girls. How are they going to know what a healthy relationship looks like if this is their only example? "Do you want your girls to end up in a marriage like this?" Nuh uh. No way.

The elation I had hearing a psychologist tell me I was normal gave me the confidence to tell my two best friends, Marcie and Sandy, about what I had gone through all these years. We'd been friends during that horrible time, and I couldn't even tell them to their face because I knew I couldn't rationally talk about it. Instead, we met for dinner, and I told them through my wringing hands and threats of tears that they'd be receiving an email from me. By telling them the truth, I made my life real again. I was gaining my power. While it hurt like hell, I knew that the healing would soon follow.

The phone rang within ten minutes of my sending the letters. Both my friends were in tears realizing the secrets I'd been holding for seven years. I was ashamed that I'd kept it from them, and they were honestly sad that I felt like I couldn't tell them at some point along the way. My embarrassing admission to these two beautiful souls released years of self-loathing, and allowed me to gather up additional strength to press onward and upward.

Even though Brad and I knew we were getting a divorce, we didn't know where to begin. Without being told, Brad packed up his stuff and moved into the guest room, but it seemed to put even more stress on the situation. I was still finishing up school and Brad was busy with his race car, the economy, and our company. He'd recently bought himself a new mountain bike, so he was off on either four tires or two.

He was even less considerate than a roommate, and went out of his way to make life even more miserable. Anytime I spoke to him, he would act like I didn't exist. I could be at the breakfast table with the girls and ask him a question and he would just ignore me. The girls would watch us like a tennis match to see what would happen next. One morning, Lindsey turned to me and said, "Well, I can hear you, Mommy, even if Dad can't."

Then it happened. For the first time in my life, my body failed me. I was dealing with what I thought was an upset stomach, but while getting ready for bed, the ache turned into severe pain. I couldn't catch my breath and I had to do shallow pants to manage the agonizing pain from inside my core. It was constant and wouldn't let up. I thought I was having a heart attack. It scared Brad, too. He called my friend Aimee, who lived at the end of the road, to come down to stay with the girls while Brad drove me to the hospital.

After checking to make sure my heart wasn't failing me, they performed subsequent tests. Gallstones. Hundreds of them. Personally, I think the culmination of years of constant stress manifested into the poetic diagnosis: all that hurtful bile I couldn't get rid of finally required intervention from an outside source.

I stayed one night after surgery and went home the next morning with instructions to not lift anything for a few days.

Brad had fed the horses while I was in surgery, but the stalls hadn't been cleaned, and it was just getting worse. I woke up the next morning at home and willed myself to go out there, but I just couldn't do it. I asked Brad if he could please feed the horses. I needed this income to buy groceries and pay our bills. He rolled his eyes and headed out the door. I crawled back into bed and tried to force my body to instantly heal. I took some deep breaths—and then grabbed a Percocet.

While walking back from the bathroom, I stopped to watch the horses as they waited for Brad to get them their grain. Just like small children, they poked and bit each other to bridge the boredom of waiting for their food. Naomi, my favorite mare, was obsessed with food. Her restricted diet made her feel like she was on the edge of starvation, even though she was about 200 pounds overweight. Brad laid the bowls of grain out and Naomi took a few bites, but she thought it might be best to steal from the horse next to her, too, just to make sure she got more than anyone else.

I held my incision because I was laughing so hard. Watching her sneak over and push her nose into her neighbor's food dish, take a bite, and then move on to the next horse's dish temporarily made me forget my pain. Silly innocent fun.

However, Brad didn't see it that way. He saw what Naomi was doing and walked up to her and punched her in the nose. She was so startled that she ran into the next paddock, trying to understand what just happened. She probably knew she was being naughty, but the punishment didn't quite fit the crime. But it didn't stop there. Brad followed her as she ran away. As Naomi stopped to turn around and reassess the situation, Brad ran up to her and grabbed a tuft of mane and leapt onto her back sideways. He drove his knee into her side over and over again all the while he was yelling, "You dumb fucking horse. Eat your own fucking food!"

Naomi just stood there, with a grown man on her back, driving his knee into her side. She had always trusted humans and in return, treated those around her with calm and care. She was trying to process this bizarre and hurtful turn of events. We both were.

The scene from my bedroom window had instantly gone from serene to insanity. I struggled with the warped window until it finally lurched open, and I yelled, despite the pain in my abdomen, "What the hell are you doing?" He gave her one last jab and jumped off.

Despite having been in surgery a few hours earlier, I completed the rest of the barn chores. I went slowly and used my arm strength to get it all done. It felt good to move around anyways after laying in a hospital bed, pushing my happy button which released paid medication at my whim. It also helped remind me that my body was still strong and that a little gallbladder removal wasn't going to slow me down. Sometimes, even though it's part of you, a diseased organ needs to be removed. After watching Brad punish the horse for a minor infraction, I knew he was like a mindless cancer latching his own pain and anger on anyone else. I'd watched him do it to me.

When Brad got into the house, I asked him why he did that to Naomi. He looked at me and shrugged, "Do what?"

I am ashamed of myself when I try to explain why it took so goddamn long to get divorced. I can't believe I wasted all of those years putting on a happy face, while inside my pain turned me numb as Novocain. My only solace is that after talking to many divorced women, I found that it's actually very (too) common for women to languish in marriage hell for years due to finances and young children. We're always waiting for the right time or moment to file for divorce, but let's face it, there is never a good time. My excuse was that I wanted to finish my BA degree at DU. I worked with passion and focus, and the 3.9 grade point average proved it.

As my last quarter of school began, I told Brad I was ready to schedule our first mediation session. Yes, I still believed that we could have an amicable divorce for the children's sake. Brad was astonished that I was ready to begin the process and kept saying that he thought I wanted to wait until I was done with my classes.

After several weeks of coordinating everyone's schedules, the mediation was scheduled. It was a full on war. Brad would go out of his way to not help with anything, even the girls. Even if I asked an innocuous question like, "Do you know where Lindsey's backpack is...?" His reply would be silence, like I didn't even speak or exist. The girls couldn't quite grasp what they were seeing, but they knew something was horribly wrong.

I had worked so hard at covering up this bad relationship, and I always wondered how much they actually knew. I'd smile and say everything was fine in a sing-song voice, but I doubt my eyes hid the pain. Kids are so much better at picking up the atmosphere of a room than we give them credit for. It was clarified one night while reading a bedtime story to Lindsey. I closed the book and, out of the blue, Lindsey turned to me with her head tilted and asked, "Mom, I think I am a lot like you, don't you think? If I'm like you, and dad is so mean to you, does that mean that dad will be mean to me and not like me either?"

Out of the mouths of babes.

21 Post-flight Inspection and Reflection

1. Check for damage from your journey
2. Use this as a chance to stretch your legs after a long flight
3. You can now officially log these hours in the logbook

The post-flight inspection is the least utilized checklist. After flying all day, you're exhausted and you just want to go home, so the last thing you want to do is walk around the airplane again. You justify your lack of self–discipline by promising to check the aircraft with more enthusiasm on your next pre-flight inspection. But this is your only opportunity to look at any damage that may have been done along your journey. Once you walk away, if further damage is done, you'll never know if it was done during your flight or after you got on the ground. This is a peace-of-mind checklist. Maybe that little sound you heard on your descent was something important.

When I was a copilot on a Citation II, we were flying at night above a solid layer of clouds, when we felt and heard a subtle and quick twang in the airframe during our descent. Airplanes normally creak and groan as they transition through pressure and temperature changes, so we didn't give it too much thought. The captain and I looked at each when we heard it, but the flight controls were smooth and there were no other unusual sounds or vibration, so we soon forgot about the little noise.

We landed, taxied to the FBO, and got our passengers on their way. Since I was the copilot, it was my responsibility to do a quick post-flight inspection. Honestly, most flight crews don't perform this check, but I was still young and ambitious. It was nighttime, so I was just giving it a cursory inspection to make sure all the major parts were still attached. As I walked around the inboard leading edge of the left wing, I could see something was wrong. There was a dent, only about three inches wide but almost two inches deep. Grey and black Canadian goose feathers were imbedded in the impact mark, and blood and feathers had exploded onto the air intake of the engine and side of the fuselage.

Murphy's Law rules on Sunday nights, so maintenance was closed at the FBO, and there were no other mechanics on the field who could inspect the aircraft. We had to wait until morning to figure out how bad it was and if the aircraft was flyable. Needless to say, we had to charter another jet to get our passengers to their destination while we stayed behind to figure out what to do. We ended up getting a Special Flight Permit from the FAA to get the aircraft home, which meant that we had to stay out of the clouds and all precipitation because our wing's leading edge de-ice equipment was inoperative. It was hard to do since we were flying from South Carolina to Minnesota, but as luck would have it we had blue skies all the way home. The plane was in the shop for three weeks.

On the flight home, all I could think about were the odds that we'd hit a goose at seven thousand feet, at night, above a solid cloud deck. Were the birds stuck above the clouds and couldn't navigate through them? If so, wouldn't it be exhausting and stressful to have to fly and fly with all your might to find a safe landing spot? Clouds are nothing but water droplets. There are no physical barriers to stopping someone or something from going through them, but if you can't see to the other side, or the ground, you don't have anything to reference your position, which is disorientating. It's incredible that something that weighs nothing and has no touch can be the biggest barrier of all.

The majority of our paperwork for the divorce process was the endless financial and physical property statements. This was the first time in years that I had sat down and dug through our financials. Not just our personal bank statements, but the business's as well. This was an epic post-flight financial checklist.

The first mediation session is all about "discovery" and formalities and what to bring to the next meeting. Since Brad had changed all the passwords and had taken my name off of all our joint accounts, I was flying blind when it came to our finances. I had been locked out of my own accounts for almost a year and didn't have any money except for what I took in from horse boarding. This "discovery" meeting required Brad to hand over financial statements. I took the copies home with me and "discovered" two very important problems. First, Brad had a secret bank account, and second, he'd been stealing from our company. He had created a ghost employee who was drawing paychecks, but the apparition was actually Brad.

I also happened to see a bank statement from our company that had several transfers of a few thousand dollars to an account I didn't recognize. This turned out to be a secret account that he'd set up the same week he had taken the girls and me off his insurance policy, and put his mom on, instead. He'd also cancelled my health and car insurance—something that came as a huge shock.

Brad requested at our first mediation session that I continue paying my life insurance premium. He insisted that I maintain a life insurance policy—his passion for this demand was bone chilling because it was one of his top demands. My backbone tingled at the sentiment behind his actions.

I should have known that the moment I told Brad "no" that he would retaliate. In the months preparing for the divorce, I had been working on getting the girls and me emotionally ready for the impending changes. Brad, in the meantime, had been locking me out of my own accounts, taking me off all of our insurance, and stealing what was left of our lives together. He removed my name from our accounts as the listed beneficiary and put his mom's name on. I suspected his mother was copiloting the situation.

During Brad's brother's divorce five years earlier, I'd overhead a discussion Brad's mom was having about custody. She proposed to Brad's brother that he kidnap their child and take her out of state. She thought so little of the bonds of motherhood and her daughter-in-law that she insisted it was his right to take their daughter because she believed he'd be the better parent. When she realized I had heard her conversation, she rolled her eyes and simply said that some people didn't deserve to be a mother. I agreed. It's how I knew she was offering Brad the same advice about me and the kids, and the thought was horrifying. I trembled at what Brad was capable of, and to have his mother backing him had me seeing a red echo on my radar screen. I still didn't have an attorney at this point, but I honestly felt I could deal with it like a checklist, one thing at a time.

I presented the financial theft discovery at the second mediation session, which also made it the last mediation session. Brad said there was nothing *illegal* with what he did, so fuck off. He also told the mediator he could tell he wasn't going to get what he wanted in mediation, so he walked out of the session. Hi ho, hi ho, it's off to court we go.

Our mediation sessions ended right before the holiday season. It had been planned months before that we would be hosting Christmas at our house. Airline tickets had been purchased by out of town relatives, and I had a tradition of inviting friends without family in town to join us, so we already knew we had a houseful of people coming. I wanted this for my kids since I didn't know what their next Christmas would look like.

Given that our plans were already set, I asked Brad if we could have one final, peaceful Christmas in the house and after the holidays were over, we'd go down to the courthouse together to file jointly for divorce. Since I was locked out of my accounts, I didn't think I could even buy Christmas presents, let alone find an attorney who would take me on my word. Agreeing to file for divorce without attorneys sounded like a great idea, since I couldn't afford one anyway.

Right before the snow started flying, I had walked down to the barn to put away some hoses and summer gear. Attached to the barn was a workshop where Brad kept his race car. It was such a part of the barn that when I walked in, I immediately saw the empty space where it was usually parked. Brad was always afraid someone would steal this car, and seeing the empty spot, I feared that it had actually happened. The barn was never locked, and it would have been easy to grab it. I dropped what I was doing to run up to the house and tell Brad the bad news.

I walked into the kitchen and said, "Brad, oh my gosh, your car is gone. The barn door was closed and everything looked okay, but the car is gone!"

Brad just kept stirring the soup in the pot on the stove. He didn't even look up. I realized I misinterpreted the situation, so I asked, "Brad, where's your car?"

"Gone."

"What do you mean, gone? Where is the car?"

"It's gone. I hid it. It's *my* car, and I can do whatever the hell I want with it." (he chose to forget that it was "our" money that sunk thousands of dollars into it). He set down the spoon and snapped his head towards me. "And think about this," he said, with his shark eyes flashing, "if I can make an entire *car* disappear, just think how easy it would be to make *you* disappear…"

I had misread the situation completely, so the threat was a double whammy. I blanched at the realization that my life had just been threatened. I turned on my heel and silently walked back to the barn to collect what was left of my security in the world, which wasn't much.

That night, I sent an email to my friends telling them that if I disappeared or died in some strange way, to look no further than Brad. I implored them to dig deeper, because he did it, even if he made it look like an accident.

I also kept tabs on where my girls were at every second of the day. I had my friends keep an eye on them at school, and made sure they were put on the bus. I made sure to be there as they stepped off the bus. I spent my days looking over my shoulder, waiting for the knife to plunge into my back while I was looking forward. I knew that if I ran with the kids, I'd lose them permanently. The state frowns on parental kidnapping, and Brad would make the most of it, so I knew I had to just secure what I could and brace for impact.

Behind my back, on December 4th, Brad had snuck down to the Golden courthouse and secretly filed for divorce—even though he had agreed to go with me after Christmas and file jointly. He wanted to be the one to say *he* filed for divorce. He wanted to control even this. He arranged to have me served divorce papers on Christmas Eve, in front of the children and twenty four other friends and family. To this day, those divorce papers remain the best present I've ever received.

Every year for Christmas, my dad sent Brad airline tickets so we could all join him at his timeshare condominium in Cabo San Lucas, Mexico. When Brad found out he wasn't invited this year, he raised his chin in the air and told me that if he couldn't go, neither could the girls. I rarely got see my dad, and we were excited to get away. But two days after Christmas, Brad told me that if I took the girls on vacation, he'd wait until I got to the airport, then he'd call the police and immigration and tell them I was kidnapping my children to Mexico. He said he would never give permission for me to take this annual trip with my dad.

This announcement turned into an argument. I rarely engaged in an argument when the girls were in the house (it was winter break), but I told him what I thought of him, and he was flabbergasted that I was actually talking back to him and standing up for the rights of my two girls to go see their grandfather. Not to be outdone in showing he still had control over me, he stood at the top of the stairs, narrowed his eyes as he sneered at me, "You're out of control. I'm taking the girls, and I don't know when, or if, you'll ever see them again." He turned and yelled down to the girls in front of me, "Girls, pack your bags. We're leaving. Right now. Say good-bye to your mother…"

The blood drained from my face, and I instantly flashed back on my mother-in-law telling Brad's brother to take his daughter and run, and I believed there was a very real threat that if he took the girls, I'd never see them again.

"You are not taking the girls anywhere," I said, shaking. "I'll call the police if you try." I was willing to die, get arrested again, or take a beating, but Brad was not taking the girls.

His face twisted as he laughed, "Yeah, right. Ha. You know as well as I do what will happen. You will be arrested again, just like last time. I'll make sure of it. I know damn well you're not calling the police. God, you're so lame. Just shut the fuck up. I'm taking the girls…"

I walked to the phone and dialed 911.

The police arrived as Brad was still downstairs trying to get the girls packed. I told the officer what was happening. Brad came up and tried doing what he'd done seven years earlier. This time, these officers were from a different generation, a different town with a different agenda. This time, I was the one who called and, for better or worse, the one who calls gets the initial benefit of the doubt.

"Oh hi, officers. I'm so glad you're here. This woman is a whack job and totally out of control. She's done this kind of thing before. She has been arrested for assault and domestic violence. You can go look it up. She is probably just in need of a tune up. Got room in the back of the squad car today?" Hahaha.

The officers said that no, actually, what *he* was doing was wrong.

Brad just stood there, miffed that these two uniformed officers didn't back him up. His ploy wasn't working and he was a bit confused. He tried talking man to man.

"No, you don't get it. She's done this kind of thing before. I just filed for divorce against her, so she's all pissed off and out of control."

The officer looked at me and said, "Well, actually, she looks like she's pretty much in control, and she has a legitimate reason to be upset. Brad, do you have someplace you can go for the next few days?"

"What?! No, way, I'm not going anywhere," was his indignant response.

"Ma'am, do you have someplace where you can take your children and be safe for at least tonight."

Brad's head snapped around and he said, "You're not taking the girls anywhere!"

"Sir, I am asking that your children's mother make sure your children are safe. Ma'am, do you have a friend or someplace safe you can take yourself and the children?"

I said yes, I had friends who could help me out. Brad's eyebrows rose, and I could see his anger flash. Maybe because seven years had passed and police were trained differently to handle domestic abuse calls, but, thankfully, these officers saw the situation clearly. With that clarity, I also knew this loss of control over me and the situation would cause Brad's anger to escalate.

I brought the girls to Marcie's house and asked if they could stay with her. Marcie was strong for me, as always, and I asked her if it was okay if I stayed at my neighbor's house. I was housesitting for my neighbor while she was in Texas, and I needed to gather my thoughts and keep the girls away from me in case Brad tried to harm me. I didn't want them exposed to any more of this. I knew this police interaction was a pivotal moment and that I had to prepare for battle. Marcie knew exactly what I meant and she said that after all these years, she would do anything to help set me free.

I was thankful for my neighbor's empty house. The television wasn't even working so I had absolute, terrifying silence. My pilot training of remaining calm in the wake of an emergency abandoned me, and I freaked out at first in the absolute nothingness. But life knew better than I did. It was silence that I needed. All I knew was this was it. Something bad was going to happen, and I needed to protect my girls and myself. I needed a checklist, but what kind of a checklist? I was in a relationship with someone who did things so out of the normal range of behavior, I couldn't guess what his next move would be. His manufacturer did not provide guidance for others trying to operate this particular machine.

I knew I had to return to the barn in the morning to feed the horses and complete all the barn chores, so I sent a text informing Brad that I would be arriving at the barn at 9:00 a.m., and that my friend and neighbor, Leigh Ann, would be meeting me there to make sure I stayed safe. I asked for him to be gone from the property so I could complete my chores.

At 8:59 a.m., I drove down to the barn. Arriving one minute early unknowingly turned my life around for the better. I knew I needed to wait until Leigh Ann got there before I got out of the car and went to work, so I turned off the ignition and looked to the top of the driveway waiting for her car. As I looked down to check my phone for messages, I heard my back driver's side car door open. I turned to see Brad grabbing the children's car seats. "You fucking cunt," he yelled, "I'm going to get my girls, and you're not going to see them ever again!" In his anger, he yanked so hard that the back of Lindsey's car seat fell off. As he walked to his car, I got out and bent over to pick up the seatback off the ground. Brad ran up behind me and as I stepped back, he was on me. I turned around and he was standing with a tape recorder in his hand. He started yelling into the tape recorder "Ouch! Damn it, stop hitting me!" while I just stood there holding the car seat, dumbfounded.

He smirked, turned around and walked away while yelling into the tape recorder, "Damn it, stop it, stop hitting me, get away from me...I'm calling the police!"

He did call the police. He was standing by the front door, telling the police that I was "out of control and she's hitting me. She hit me in the chest..." while I was about thirty yards away by the barn.

What Brad didn't know was that Leigh Ann was in the driveway and had witnessed the entire scene play out. She watched as Brad ran up behind me while talking into the tape recorder. She watched him stand at the front door, talking to the police on the phone while telling them I'd been hitting him when, in fact, I'd been standing next to my car with a broken car seat, crying, because I thought the nightmare was going to happen all over again.

Leigh Ann, who is a drop dead gorgeous blonde from Texas, walked up to Brad and in her best pissed off mom voice yelled, "Brad, what the hell do you think you're doing. Are you fucking insane? What kind of man does this? No, what kind of FATHER does this? Shame on you. *SHAME ON YOU!* You stop this right now. Enough is enough."

It was all over for Brad and he knew it. Brad was getting into his car as the police drove in and blocked the driveway. No one was getting away this time.

Brad told them his version about my hitting him and said he had a tape recording to prove it. With this apparent proof in hand, the officer motioned for me to come over and listen to the supposed evidence.

"Where did she hit you?"

"She punched me in the chest."

"Lift your shirt please."

I could see Brad hesitate and press hard on the front of his chest as he raked his shirt up, but there was nothing there. "Well, I have a recording! Just listen!" We all listened to Brad's robotic claim he was being hit.

In the meantime, Leigh Ann spoke to the other police officer and told him what she'd seen. The officer kept shaking his head as he heard what Brad was attempting to do. This same officer came over to me and wanted the whole story, from the beginning. I gave him the highlights and explained he threatened to take the kids. I explained what happened seven years earlier and that his pattern of behavior wasn't changing, but his anger was rising as his plans to have me arrested fell apart.

I also mentioned he'd threatened to make me disappear, and the officer's face melted with concern. I couldn't believe that finally a police officer believed me. If I hadn't lived it, I would have thought it all a complete fallacy. What kind of man manipulates his wife by repeatedly lying to the police in order to have them control and abuse her for him and through him? The officer said that it happens all the time, but it is usually the woman who sets up the man.

The officer clenched his teeth in anger at Brad. "Look, this situation is volatile. If you remain here with him, you're going to end up dead. I'm not a lawyer, but if it was me, I'd go get a restraining order. Today. Right now. After we leave. I'm not giving legal advice, but I'm just saying what I would do."

For once in my life, I was one step ahead. I told the officer that I had already met with my attorney after Brad threatened to take the girls the day before and that we'd gone to the courthouse and received a temporary restraining order. It had been approved and filed, but we hadn't received the order and paperwork, yet. It was probably waiting for me in my email. The officer said that was enough verification for him.

The officer walked up to Brad and, this time, it was Brad who had to leave. By force. Right now. But it wasn't enough for Brad to pack up his things and get out. He stole the children's school pictures, clipped the ignition wires for the furnace, and took all my personal files, as well as the financial records from the file cabinet.

He never lived there again.

He moved into his mom's house and gained a collaborator to scheme how to take even more from me. After all, they knew they'd stolen my heart and soul.

The judge approved the temporary restraining order. I would learn later that even though it's just a piece of paper, its strength is giving the victim confidence that the offender needs to go away and stay away. It's a bit like thinking that if you close the hangar door, the tornado won't harm the aircraft inside. In reality, the hangar door now has a chance to crush what it is protecting.

It took six months and three court dates to wade through the temporary divorce orders. During this time in limbo, Brad lashed out whenever I was within striking distance. The first time I dropped the girls off in an exchange of parenting time, Brad yanked off and stole the trailer hitch off my car. And that was just the first day. It was a constant barrage of minor cuts while waiting for the next court date.

On the first day of court during temporary orders, it was finally time to appear before a judge to let her begin the arduous task of untwining two lives. We were told in the very beginning that the judge would not decide custody issues. For now, I was primary caregiver and Brad had visitation every Wednesday and every other weekend, which is the standard formula. Brad had already stated he no plans of paying child support, and he expected 50/50 custody. Now that the children were older and easier to care for, he wanted them back. His view of women was so distorted, how could I ever trust this man to care for two growing girls? His anger always on the edge, and I constantly feared for their safety—emotionally and physically. He already admitted he suffered from disassociated amnesia, even though he called it blacking out from anger. What was going to happen when these girls became teenagers and started sassing back? They were already trying out their talk-back skills with me, so I could only shudder what he'd do to them.

I presented my case first, and drew upon my flight engineer skills to explain the mechanical failures. It took most of the day to lay out the years of abuse (physical, verbal, mental) along with the slow, grinding theft of all my financial assets over the years. The dysfunction in the marriage was relevant to the dissolution of the marriage, and it all had to be presented.

Brad's attorney had already asserted that I should not have the children because of my arrest for assault and domestic violence. However, the letter that Brad had written to me and our therapist, Lynn, became his downfall and set the stage for my ability to disprove all of his lies. His own words worked against him, and treated the court to the truth of how he had lied to the police to have me wrongfully arrested. It was his own words that explained the extent of his abuse. He hadn't bothered to tell his attorney about the confession because he'd taken my folder that contained a copy of the letter when he was forced to leave our home. What he didn't know was I had the original letter in my fire box behind my dresser. Even his attorney was stopped short when I read his letter in open court.

When Brad got up on the stand after lunch, determined not to be outdone by the truth, he told lie after lie. He ended his performance on the stand by testifying that I routinely got drunk at the book club I ran, then drove home. Hearing this outrageous lie was the final straw. The truth was that it was a rare moment that I ever had more than a glass of wine. But behavior and emotional intelligence were the character traits the judge was basing custody on. If I couldn't prove him wrong, I ran the risk of losing custody of my children.

Brad's blunder was that there were over forty women in my book club who had known me for years, and they don't take shit from anyone. It had been painfully easy to threaten his wife, but he had no comprehension what it meant to threaten a woman of the pack and the children she was raising. Like pilots who band together to fight off an FAA representative doing a surprise ramp check, these gentle and benign women of my book club became a force to be reckoned with.

I asked if one or two of them could appear as a character witness for me. They shrugged and said they'd figure something out for me. I really wasn't expecting anyone to show up.

On a cold Valentine's Day morning, unbeknownst to me, twenty-two women quietly changed the course of my life. These women got up before dawn, sent their kids to school, then drove down, or sent their affidavit, to the courthouse to refute Brad's statements, and to be character witnesses for my life.

These book club warriors had known me for years, but many weren't close friends, and some I only saw at book club. They didn't know the details of my situation, they didn't have to. They understood that I was being judged by strangers and that the outcome would decide custody of my children. The same children I used to bring to book club when they were babies.

Most importantly, after hundreds of hours spent discussing our lives through the books we read, they knew my intimate philosophy on life. Through our books, they knew my morals and values. None of them knew of my abuse or my arrest, but these strong, proud women simply knew what it meant to be kind and to devote everything to their children. Like me, they had adventures and careers before children. We all quietly gave ourselves up without having to explain that to each other, because we all understood. They simply knew that someone was trying to take my children from me — the nightmare of many women — and by showing their support for me in court, they were able to show the world.

I sat alone on the stiff wooden bench outside the courtroom, sick with fear and anxiety. My attorney was late, so I was listening intently for the *ding!* of the elevator announcing a new victim. I heard the elevator door open and the determined click-click of high heels across the tile floor. I looked at the face approaching me. It took a moment to comprehend that a member of my book club was here. It felt out of place until I realized they had always been a part of my story. Suddenly, the elevator began to continually chirp a happy *ding!* followed by muffled voices that raised when they saw me sitting there. "Hi Erika! We're here! Tell us what to do." As captain, I was suddenly extraordinarily proud of my crew.

By the time the tenth woman turned the corner, I was in tears, overwhelmed by their quiet support. For the first time in years, I felt a sense of pride. I had been raising my children alongside these women, and none of us asked for or received recognition for the sacrifice and devotion. We just did it, and here they were, doing it again.

The judge was a bit miffed, as well as Brad and his attorney, when we all walked into the courtroom. Brad looked at all those faces, and I could see the disgust in his rolling eyes. Every woman there was ready to get up and testify that I was a good mom and that I didn't go to book club to get drunk. I went to book club to share my life, my ups and downs, frustrations and victories, with a group of women who were as diverse as the books we read. We came from all backgrounds, socio-economic living conditions, and geographic location, but we all had one theme in common: we are women and mothers. Sometimes the common denominator is so simple, it's overlooked.

None of the women had to testify. The case was done just by having them show up. Brad's attorney rested his case, and we let the judge decide our fate. The result of temporary orders was that Brad was going to have to pay dearly. Since he had shut me out of all our joint finances for almost a year, he had to pay back maintenance (formally called alimony) and child support. All that time spent changing passwords and account numbers ended up costing Brad money.

Temporary orders maintenance was double what I'd been trying to negotiate with Brad at mediation. The restraining order against Brad would stay in place, and we were allowed to be in the same room as long as it was for a children's activity. These were just temporary orders, and the most important decision — custody — was put off until the trial. Between now and the trial, a court-appointed family investigator (CFI) was going to crawl through our lives with a microscope and determine what would be best for our children. It is a strange society that we live in.

The FAA can reexamine an airman at any time if the FAA has reasonable grounds—usually an accident or regulation violation can trigger a pilot to be grounded. It can take months and even years to go through the case and an appeal. In the meantime, the pilot is unable to earn money as a pilot, and even if innocent, the process will cost the pilot a lifetime of effort.

For my marital accident, it took six months just to get a court date for a permanent divorce orders trial. It was scheduled for two days. I think the philosophy behind that is after all that time, most people start moving forward with their new lives so that by the time the court hearing arrives, most couples have reached a point where they can divvy up the assets and call it quits. Then again, I said *most* people.

During those dreary months of purgatory, a new person entered our lives by force: our Court Appointed Family Investigator—or CFI for short. Craig could have passed for Santa Claus's brother, complete with a round belly and full white beard. But his less-than-jovial outlook on life was influenced by having seen it all and heard every lie imaginable. He'd been doing this for thirty years and after being around the worst of humanity, he was now a curmudgeon who had forgotten why he'd entered this profession. However, every once in a while, he would let down his guard and you could see that he'd been passionate about his job, and that at one time it hadn't been about the money.

I often wondered what sent him down this path of having more power than God. He held my children's fate in his hands, and whatever he decided, the court would usually order accordingly. Sure, the judge had final authority, but the reality is that they all listen to the CFI, because if it goes badly, the judge can go back and blame the CFI. The CFI was the captain of my airplane, and the court sat in the control tower.

By court order, Craig was allowed full access to our innermost personal lives. It was Craig's due diligence to call teachers, pediatricians, doctors, psychologists, marriage counselors, friends, and family. He interviewed all of us individually as well as together. He even came to our homes to watch us and to make sure our home environment was up to par. I felt like I was part of the cast of a bizarre sitcom called, "This is Your Life, Now Defend It!" Every parenting mistake or raised voice was under question. In an email, I had once said that the most physical contact I had doled out for punishment was a swat on the butt. Now, even that had to be defended. "So, you stated that you once struck your daughter..."

I had to dig back into my parenting past and track down every teacher, parent, or activity director I'd ever dealt with, or had interaction with my children. It was humiliating to have to explain that I was in a custody battle and I needed them to send in a report on my parenting ability, good or bad, for a court trial. The embarrassment was well worth the effort. In the end, I had twenty-eight people take the time to fill out an affidavit, have it notarized and sent to Craig. It was this overwhelming outside proof that made the difference, because Brad was all too happy to tell anyone and everyone that I was the worst mother ever to roam the planet. It wasn't a trickle of Karma coming back to me; it was a tsunami—the perfect parenting storm with a blinding rainbow at the end.

Legalities bind me to keep the contents of the CFI report confidential, but I can summarize the outcome as this: The pattern of abuse and Brad's long history of lies and deceit were clinically itemized and condensed into a forty page report. He only had two people give an affidavit, besides his relatives. This report was the bible that the judge was going to use to determine the structure of child custody. The two-day trial was set, so all I could do was sit back, put my tray table up, and leave my seatbelt unbuckled.

With four hours of sleep, I walked into the courtroom to debate and hear my fate. It began with four hours of volleying back and forth in court over terms. Brad stated he'd never pay alimony or child support. He wanted the business, the rental house, the kids, and for me to take all of his debts. In return, he generously allowed that I could stay in my home (valued less than what was owed on the mortgage, due to the real estate market), and I could keep my six year old car. We managed to haggle out most of the terms, but we came back to the judge still deadlocked on the business.

The judge went off the record, sat us all down again, and took a deep breath. Pulling his glasses down the bridge of his nose, he turned his attention to me.

"Erika, this probably isn't going to feel like it right now, but I am going to give you the highest compliment that you can find in this courtroom. I am just letting you know that if you were to ask me to decide right now, I would probably rule to have Brad take the business. You have a strong resume and education, and you have a better chance of going out into this world and making something for yourself than he does. Brad can hardly take care of himself, let alone support a family. I believe the only way he will be able to carry his load is if you leave him with something he's already doing.

"Erika, you once made a lot of money, and I'm confident you can do it again. Your attorney said you would approve to receive this as maintenance, which means Brad gets a tax deduction and you pay tax on the income, but at least the state will monitor the payments. You won't get any maintenance (alimony), but you'll get back a portion of what you put into the business. Does that make sense?"

Actually, it made no sense, but God was asking me a question, and I didn't want to appear flustered at his absurd conclusion. I could see on my radar scope that he was flying me into the center of an F5 tornado and yet, I calmly said, "Yes, I suppose it makes sense."

My inner flight crew was having a conniption fit: "What?!!
Holy shit. Does he have any idea that I can't get back into
aviation after an eight year absence? It's currently the worst
economy in the United States' history, and unemployment is
over 9%. He's got to be joking. I found and started this business
with my money! Brad would still be a wrench monkey at the
airport at two in the morning in the snow if it wasn't for me. Are
you fucking nuts? *I'm* a mom who needs a flexible schedule and
to set my own hours so *I* can be there for the girls. That's why I
started my business. Now I have to get an office job down in
Denver? Three hours of every day will be spent commuting
while my kids are in daycare...how is giving Brad my business
fair to me or my girls?"

Even after this agreement, Brad reiterated to the court that
he would not pay maintenance. While on the stand, his attorney
asked why he felt he shouldn't have to pay maintenance. He
sneered at me and the courtroom, and said, "Because she should
get off her ass and get a job..."

Our business had brought in about $2.5 million dollars in
the last four years, but he was trying to prove it was worth about
$30k (the franchise fee alone was $40k). Since my attorney
agreed to have Brad pay me back my half of the business in
"maintenance" payments (he should have been required to buy
out my partnership as a business transaction, not a divorce
proceeding), Brad would only agree to pay a total of just $40,000
with payments spread out over two and a half years. He also
agreed to pay $50 per week, per child, if I took over his home
equity line of credit debt for $50,000. Fine. Sure, even though
that would take nineteen years to make it equal. Whatever, I'll
take it. To summarize, this left me with no alimony and
$50/week per child in child support while he was earning about
$85,000 from *my* business.

Post flight inspection complete. Yes, major damage found,
but can't do anything about it now except to get in for repairs.
Check. Now, get him the hell out of my life.

Worth every penny lost.

The most important question was left until the end, custody. Craig's CFI report summarized the dysfunction of the marriage and Brad's neurosis, but it was what was listed below the sum line that counted. In the end, there was no doubt Brad loved his girls, but it was determined that I should remain primary caregiver. That also meant that for the rest of my children's lives, I had to break my connection with them and hand them over to Brad every Wednesday and every other weekend. Holidays, vacations, and special occasions had an assigned caveat for each year, which we still fight over on a regular basis because it's as murky as mud. I wanted my children to have their dad in their lives. After everything I'd been through, I still thought it was important, and it wasn't my place to take that from them. He was the other half of my daughters, and I completely understood the bond should remain, no matter how dysfunctional. But I still had a primordial fear based on fact: Brad could be dangerous.

After cowering through the financial division in court, I was loud and outspoken during the custody negotiations. I said the only way I would agree to this custody arrangement was if Brad agreed to attend consistent and regular psychological counseling. I didn't want Brad out of their lives, I wanted him in their lives in a healthy, positive way, but I knew he needed help getting there. At a minimum, I wanted him to be monitored, even if counseling wasn't helping. I didn't put a lot of hope into psychological counseling, but a counselor is required to call the authorities if they feel something bad might happen. Monitoring him was the best I could do in this era of equal parenting rights.

This simple request that Brad receive counseling was the biggest point of contention during the proceedings. Brad absolutely refused to go. I explained to the court my reasons, and the judge agreed. However, he said he couldn't make Brad go to counseling, but if he didn't go, he would make visitation more restrictive. It was Brad's choice. Brad then said he'd go if I was required to go, too. I said sure, I'd go. I'd do anything I had to do to keep my girls safe and happy.

I did go to counseling, again, as agreed to in court. I even started a support group called the Divorce Club Warriors. Predictably, Brad didn't. He said he considered the *one time* he went the following year as "consistent" counseling. Sadly, the judge never said what his definition of "consistent" was. However, I still managed to regain some power, thanks to the divorce decree which said, "If parents are unable to reach agreement, Mother will have final decision authority." When I had signed on the dotted line in the courtroom that day, I turned to my attorney and asked, "Okay, am I divorced? Is it all over?" The judge had overheard the question and with a firm, loud, and congratulatory voice laughed, "Yes, young lady. You are now divorced. Best of luck to you…"

Since I had just been disemboweled and left for dead, I envisioned myself as Mel Gibson in *Braveheart*. I wanted to open the courtroom doors and yell "FREEDOM!"

22 Closing the Flight Plan

1. As you drive away from the airport, that nagging feeling you forgot something is closing your flight plan
2. If you are on an IFR flight plan, it is closed for you
3. If you haven't filed a flight plan and you have an accident off airport, it could be years before they find you...if ever

It can't be stressed enough that having others know where you are along your flight route is crucial, especially if you should be required to make an off-airport emergency landing. For flights with paying customers, there will always be a flight plan filed with air traffic control, but the pilots who need monitoring the most, novice fair-weather pilots, often don't take advantage of this key tracking system.

Filing a VFR (visual flight rules) flight plan with a local Flight Service Station tracks your aircraft on the radar screen, and if you don't close your flight plan after you land, emergency services will assume you need help and will begin tracing your flight to the point you disappeared. With that said, quite often these same pilots forget to close the flight plan, which triggers a search and rescue.

The FAA realizes that focus is one of the main strengths of pilots—focusing on the task at hand, completing it, and moving on. The FAA recommends that pilots interrupt their focus to remember to close their flight plans. Try putting your wallet or car keys in a different pocket to remind you to close your flight plan. Set the alarm on your cell phone or watch. Put a note on your car's ignition. Whatever you need to do is fine, but find a way to interrupt the start of the next task with a reminder to close the flight plan at 1-800-WX-BRIEF.

So what happens when you don't show up where and when you're supposed to? If you're more than thirty minutes past your estimated time of arrival, a search is initiated via telephone. Someone will call the airport where you were supposed to arrive. More often than not, they'll find you blushing while explaining that you forgot to close the flight plan.

If they still can't find you, air traffic control will start at your destination and track you any way they can. For those pilots and aircraft that are truly in trouble, pilots who filed flight plans are located an average of four hours sooner than those who did not file a flight plan. If you've made an emergency landing in someplace like the backcountry of Colorado, those four hours are the difference between life and death.

The simple act of filing the flight plan requires the pilot to review all aspects of the flight, so it's also a backup preflight checklist. It doesn't matter if there are crystal blue skies and not a whisper of wind when you leave your destination; the world and weather can change faster than a toddler's mood, so it's best to always err on the side of safety and have someone ready to find you if you lose your way.

Wouldn't it be nice if someone came to help you automatically if you lost your way? If your flight plan states that you'll arrive safely in a marriage with two children by forty and you don't arrive at that destination, wouldn't it be lovely if someone looked for you to find out what happened? Sometimes you have to crash land and wait for help. If you know help is on the way, the mere knowledge that someone is looking for you will give you hope. If you forgot or chose to not file a flight plan and you have crash landed, the very knowledge that no one is looking for you will perpetuate your despair.

File a flight plan.

I'd filed a flight plan, but it was so long ago that I forgot it was there.

~~~

During the six months between temporary orders and permanent orders, I had glimpses of the person I used to be. Still without any income except from what I made from horse boarding, dog and babysitting, I told my attorney I had to find someplace to work. Before the sentence was even out of my mouth she said, "Absolutely not! If you show any kind of income, you will be hard pressed to convince the court to give you child support and maintenance, and chances are you wouldn't start out by getting a high paying job. As a matter of fact, in this economy, you'll be lucky to get a job at McDonalds. You'll also forfeit your effort to get your business back. If you're working elsewhere, Brad will simply point out that he should get the business because you're already working somewhere else. Just use this time to get ready for court…"

It was easy for her to say since I was slowly sinking into debt for her. On top of the debt Brad had created, the lawyer bills were rolling in at $4,000 per month. Brad also did creative, fun things like claim I earned money from the business, put my name on the income (while he hid it in secret accounts), and then left me with the IRS tax bill.

For once in my life, I thought *screw it.* I decided to do what I could to earn money during those months and to enjoy my time with my kids and the horses in the barn. If I had to, I'd file bankruptcy just like everyone else. Once I gave myself that permission to fail, my conscience pushed back and said, *damn it, you can do better than that!* Instead, I started doing more daycare and taking in the neighbor dogs when their owners were on vacation. I did odd jobs, and even though I was still sinking, I felt that I was at least slowing myself on the slippery slope. I hustled what I could, but it was the Book Club Warriors that kept me afloat – financially and spiritually—and without them, I'm afraid my flight plan would have slid me right into hell.

My quiet heroes ignited my recovery by organizing meals delivered to my house every other night for an entire month. I actually had a web-based calendar that my friends filled out and sent to me so I knew what I was eating and when. My freezer was bursting at the seams, but that was just the beginning.

They also dropped off chords of firewood, clothes for my girls, and suits for me to use for interviews. My email inbox was full of support, kind words, and offers of free babysitting. My daughter's piano teacher wouldn't let me pay her, and the art teacher at school let my girls take her art class after school for free. I didn't even know her, but she heard we were dealing with a divorce and her motive was purely to help my girls get through it. The tears I had been shedding changed from sorrow to tears of gratitude.

And it didn't stop there.

About two weeks after everyone showed up at the courthouse, I got a call from Candace, a quintessential happy-to-be-a-mom and our jokester at book club. She quipped over the phone, "Hey, it's really weird, but I was handed an envelope with your name on it. Do you mind if I swing by and drop it off for you?" I barraged her with questions because I didn't know what she was talking about. I didn't know why someone had given her an envelope with my name on it. Did I drop something? Shoot, these days an anonymous envelope was bad news.

She came by later that day and handed me a thick, white envelope that was stuffed with cash—over $400 in small denominations. I could hardly speak as the rush of gratitude flooded my emotions, and all I could do was stand there and tremble. It was all anonymous, so I didn't even know whom to thank. She said she didn't want me thanking anyone, that's why no one wrote a check. She also figured I wouldn't cash it if they did.

Candace, who is always smiling and poised, knew I was struggling with my emotions, so she hugged me and told me to just take it and have a great day. I kept my composure as her Mom SUV oscillated out of my dirt driveway. With the dust still rising in the air, I turned and sat down on my front porch steps and cried tears of gratitude. The essence of how I saw the world changed forever. That subtle moment of intense honor, not for the money, but for the thoughts and well wishes behind it— uncovered something within me that has maintained a level of undiminished happiness. I realized I was richer than I could have ever imagined. Since then, I have never wanted for anything more other than to be safe and have just enough to live on, and keep my girls physically and spiritually healthy. Thankfully, all those years of material wishes vanished in an instant by being fulfilled in a different way. I didn't have to be afraid, and I was happy again. I had everything by having nothing, and if I just trusted that everything would be okay, then I would be okay.

I had filed a flight plan with these beautiful women over the years, and during the darkest moment when I thought no one would find my wreckage, they tracked me down and reminded me to pull the hidden phoenix out of the ashes with me.

Look out from your cockpit window and you can see it all around you. You can see the lost flight plans and quiet unhappiness in all those people who literally have everything, yet they are so unhappy and live each day in a void. They are wallowing in the wreckage of the relentless and mindless pursuit of dissolvable "things" and power that I used to chase and thought was part of the formula for happiness. I still work for those "things," but my happiness is not dependent on it. It's just a bonus if I get it now. I couldn't see it before because I hadn't been pushed to my spiritual limit. I hadn't been pushed over the edge to find that the drop is short and the view is wonderful.

As ironic as it sounds, if it had not been for Brad's neurosis, I would never have found this level of joy and contentment with uncertainty. I would never have known the sheer gratitude for just being here, being me as I am, and thankful for all that I had done with my life, no matter how screwed up it was at the moment—and I can't think of a better revenge as having found this contentment within my core.

This passion still wakes me up every morning, and I want to jump out of bed to feel it and share it with my friends and neighbors. I want to share my flight plan. Because of this, I have learned to fly with my feet planted firmly in the ground.

23 Contrails

1. Contrails are evidence that you were there
2. They form because the exhaust of the aircraft is both gas and sold particles
3. They are made of water and the suspension of billions of liquid droplets
4. They can also form by intense air pressure and lift from a wing, but these are only visible for a few seconds or minutes
5. Contrails are simply what you leave behind

The contrails of my past still cast a shadow, even though I have moved forward and reached my destination. They are simply proof that I was there.

Over the next year, I endured having Brad file another seven frivolous court actions so he could continue the abuse. Six months after the property settlement, he decided he wanted my twelve-year-old refrigerator, a swing, my kitchen table and chairs, and one of the dogs. My divorce decree stated that all further disagreements would go to mediation, which meant I had to spend another $300/hour to negotiate items that hardly added up to $300. It should have been a loser-pays scenario.

Brad also called the police on three occasions over the first winter when a typical mountain snowstorm made it impossible for me to get my kids to his house. The police would arrive at my house and I'd explain the situation, which flabbergasted them, so they got on the phone in front of me and the children and scolded Brad for his behavior. "Sir, why in the world would you insist on putting your children in danger? The children will be staying with their mother until she feels the roads are safe enough for travel...Yes, when *she* decides they're safe."

Brad also continued to file lawsuits. He filed to try and make me sell my home, he filed contempt of court because I took my kids on a vacation—even though he was informed and it was during my parenting time, he filed again because I took them horse backing riding in Estes Park, he filed another because he wanted me to pay for items in the rental home—items he broke while he was living in our rental home, which I'd paid for before we were married. He filed to have me cover the costs of painting the bathroom walls. It just didn't stop. He was still in control of my life by filing these frivolous lawsuits. To make matters worse, he didn't have to have an attorney to do this. He'd just walk into the courthouse and file a contempt of court motion for $25, but it cost me thousands to have an attorney prepare a response. The contrails he was leaving across our sky blotted out the sun.

I put up with this shit for one more year and said enough was enough.

The only "demand" I'd had during the divorce negotiations was that Brad attend counseling. He attended one session in a year and stated this was "consistent counseling." I filed my own contempt of court motion and instead of being rejected like Brad's motions had been, the judge said she wanted to hear this one.

This was the fifth time in front of this judge, and she'd had enough of seeing us. She understood that Brad was using the legal system to abuse me. She called it his "abusive and continual need to control..."

I wanted to see if the judge thought complying with the decree meant once per year. Apparently she didn't, because she ordered Brad to attend psychological counseling and was placed on a six month suspended jail sentence for contempt of court. He was also ordered to pay my legal expenses for the motion—almost $6,000 worth of legal bills. It was a drop in the bucket compared to the $75k I had already spent, but it stopped Brad's legal abuse in its tracks and the peripheral reward was gigantic. I had won. Brad never did attend counseling, even though it was ordered during the suspended jail sentence, but it changed his perception of the situation. Sometimes, that's all it takes.

Winning the motion released a floodgate of freedom within my mindset. I had been dating a man in the next town for a year and a half, but I'd kept him at arm's length because I didn't want him dragged into my past. Over the year leading up to the final court order, Dave had asked me to take our relationship to a higher altitude, but my basic reply was "maybe someday." I know he didn't mind the contrails of my past and was more than willing to battle Brad, but *I* minded. I didn't want Brad as a third party in my relationship with Dave. Winning the court order allowed me to turn around and shut the jail door on Brad.

Despite winning, the past still creeps into my cockpit sometimes and I am aghast to realize a ghost is flying my airplane. In a remarriage or re-relationship scenario, your new role now includes having a ghost as your copilot or check airman. Occasionally, Dave and I have to perform past relationship exorcisms because ghosts can get through my security checkpoints. We simply grab the ghosts, put them in our luggage and check them in. We still have to carry them with us, but they can't do harm when they're locked away.

24 At the Gate

Ding!

Ladies and gentleman, this is the end of our journey together. I hope you enjoyed the flight. My story has come full circle and I am once again on solid ground here with you. I am turning off the fasten seatbelt sign so you are free to move about your own life.

If you look out the window, you'll notice mechanics coming to work on this airplane. It is now going in for maintenance to have its oil filters changed. People have these filters, too, except they're "thought filters," and they need to be changed as often as oil filters. We create them with our own perceptions and, just like oil filters, they get clogged with larger chunks of junk, which only allow certain ideas to flow through. After a while, it can get so clogged with debris that your engine has to work harder and eventually, it will just seize up and leave you stranded. It all depends on the size of the screen you put on your filter. Too easily filtered, or too finely filtered thoughts, presents different problems, so it's up to you to find the right size.

Aircraft mechanics change oil filters, but you, friends, or family can change thought filters. Every once in a while, dump it out and see which fragments of life your screen is holding onto. My screen too often held big ideas that I wouldn't allow to pass through. And then, one giant piece of crap got clogged into my screen which blocked the passageway for all other thoughts. When you feel like you're not running at peak performance, it's time to change your thought filters.

As you exit and walk past the cockpit, you now know a little more about those pilots who, for a few hours at a time, are in charge of your life. The pilots sitting up there have spent years and countless hours of unflinching determination to learn how to keep you safe. And, if you see a chick up there, she's not there because of (or despite of) being born a women. She's there because she is a pilot. She doesn't do anything differently than a man because she doesn't have to.

As you exit the jet bridge, if you need help, ask for help. Don't worry about the taboo of asking for help, because it takes all the strength you have to admit you need it. It's out there and if you're not receiving help, you should be giving it.

Once you reach baggage claim, check your tags. If you have packed a dysfunctional relationship, go ahead and leave it on the carousel. Eventually, someone else will pick it up. It might take them a while to figure out that they grabbed the wrong bag, but as soon as they open it up, they'll figure it out.

As you wait for your bags, you might as well take this time to look around at all the people who are brought together by aviation. All those women with their children are more than women with their children. They are book club warriors, business owners, oil field workers, engineers, astronauts, race car drivers…gender benders. They have their own unique vision and they've taught themselves to lead with values, situational awareness, ethics, and passion. They are leading like it's never been done before. They are being compared to the status quo, but our world is begging for a new style of transformational leadership. They are the new leaders, breaking the mold, and raising children with purpose to keep the world in balance. It's time. Their impact on our world is deep, quiet, and revolutionary. Never doubt the quiet power of women.

No End, just new beginnings.

E pilogue

Three years after my arrest, I trudged through the legal system again to try and get my record sealed and prove my false arrest. I filed a petition requesting that my record be sealed with the District Court in the county where I live. During the process, I was thrilled to learn that if I was able to seal my records, I would not have to disclose any information contained in those records to any employer, educational institution, state or local government agency, or on an application or interview. The only exception is federal level law enforcement/background checks, which is what the Federal Aviation Administration is and does. I could not seal my record from them. Most federal investigative powers have been broadened since the passage of the Patriot Act in 2001, so the FAA and TSA are considered federal law enforcement agencies. They have access to my records.

Ironically, with Brad's help, the judge reviewing the case acknowledged that I should never have been arrested. I was vindicated, but all my pilot currency requirements had expired by the time of the judgment. If I wanted to fly again, I would have to pay a significant chunk of time and money to get back into the pilot's seat. I would have to start from the bottom, again. I just didn't have the resources, and as each year passed the tether to the pilot's seat frayed a little more. After the divorce, I reentered aviation by landing a dispatching job at an international jet company. The hours were horrible (of course, it's aviation), but I got to work from home, so I could be with my kids, and it put me back into the aviation world, even though I flew a desk. After flying a desk and loving it, I began my career as a professional pilot analyst and columnist for several aviation magazines.

I will someday sit in the captain's seat again, but in the meantime I will look to the heavens with a longing in my heart and enough memories to last a lifetime.

What about Dave? As I write this, I can hear his deep laughter that I know will cause our dogs to tilt their head and perk up their ears to see what is so funny. My kids are thriving. They are upstairs making guacamole with Dave and they are inserting weird ingredients like meatballs and pineapple. I bet it will be good because it's not perfect. It will be the odd contrast in flavor that will be enjoyable as well as memorable.

We are perched at 8500 feet above sea level in the foothills, and it is pure coincidence that our house is directly on the arrival flight path into Denver International Airport. I never intended for that to happen. We have two skylights over our bed and when we see an airplane flying overhead, Dave takes my hand and quietly kisses it. It reminds me that my hands used to control those iron beasts, but now my hands are embraced and held in love.

My quiet heroes, the Book Club Warriors, still gather to laugh, talk, and analyze our society's issues through other people's stories. We have watched our babies grow together and the wrinkles on our faces grow deeper. These women are even more beautiful now because they have their stories, and no matter how different our stories are, we all share the common theme of motherhood and life as a woman.

The Divorce Club Warriors grow stronger every day. We all need to help revive our society, so this group helps women going through divorce to help themselves which, in turn, helps others. The structure of family has been bleeding so profusely from the tragedy of divorce that parents are too weak to parent. Divorce consumes a childhood and creates children that don't understand what a healthy relationship looks like. It's a vicious cycle. So we are resuscitating our pride and joining together to show our kids how to live and laugh—and give them back their childhoods.

Erika Armstrong

Brad? He continues the abuse any way he can, but he doesn't deserve more than a sentence in an epilogue. He'll see this as getting the last word.

Acknowledgments

All too often we forget that there is a giant, anonymous crew who work their asses off behind the scenes to get an airplane to its destination safely. The list of people who have helped me soar are long, but pilots are brief. Thank you to my original flight crew: my mom, the first single mother I ever met, Mom 2 for making the tough choice, Richard Anderson (or any variable of that spelling), because I exist, and my dad who gets the Nobel Prize for delayed parenting. You saved me and my girls when it mattered the most.

A Top Gun thumbs up to my agent, Roger Williams, who actually liked that my story didn't fit into just one category at the book store and Lynn Price, my editor and Acquisitions Director of Behler Publications, for sifting through my wreckage and pulling out a phoenix.

To all my flight instructors who had the crap scared out of them during my flight training, I salute you. Joe Mavencamp, John Fleishhacker, and Pete, thank you for your extra efforts that got me into the captain's seat. I honor all my flight crews throughout the years who cringed when I walked in the cockpit, but learned to accept that I wasn't just a chick; I was just a pilot. I realize it was harder for you than it was for me because I was used to the ratio. To the misogynists with whom I flew, thank you. You helped me grow a thick skin and inspired my sarcasm and sense of humor to guide me through dark skies. My bird salutes you, too.

Continued thanks to my life-long instructors: my girls — I love you to infinity and back, and back again. Dave — a rolling happy tear for the pure happiness you helped me find. And, screw it; I'm not supposed to waste space mentioning my pets, but I give an extra ear scratch to all the dogs that have landed at my home and spent thousands of hours in my office watching me work.

A high five to all the current and future pilots out there who have read my articles and followed me through the years as I simultaneously embrace and scold the aviation industry for its behavior. I'm just being a good mother.

Last, but not least, thank you to my friends and Book Club Warrior women in Conifer and Evergreen, CO. You showed up in court on Valentine's Day, never knowing the full story. You had no idea the impact you would have, but the result is what you now hold in your hand.

About Erika Armstrong

Erika Armstrong is currently an award winning staff writer for *Colorado Serenity Magazine*, and her professional aviation articles can be found in *Disciples of Flight*, *NYC Aviation*, *General Aviation*, *Contrails*, and *Business Insider*. Most uniquely, Erika was an international corporate, airline, Red Cross, and 24-hour air ambulance pilot. Even though she isn't currently flying the heavy iron, she is entrenched in aviation, where she owns Leading Edge Aviation Consulting, is a flight dispatcher and pilot recruiter.

Adopted in Seattle but raised in Minnesota, Erika's early membership in the Minnesota 99s (International Women Pilots Association) jump-started her career. After meeting several women pilots who spent their lives complaining about discrimination, Erika decided to handle every challenge with humor and perspective. This attitude and obsessive focus landed her in the captain's seat of a commercial airliner by the age of thirty. She also holds a type rating in Boeing 727 and CE-500 series aircraft and has extensive pilot training from Flight Safety, SimuFlite, NATCO, CAE, Pan Am, and has flown 28 different types of aircraft.

To back experience with education, Erika attended the University of Minnesota's Journalism program as an undergraduate before being lured into the world of aviation. To round out her education, she attended Embry- Riddle Aeronautical University and has a B.A. degree in International Business, Economics and Culture with National Honor Society recognition from the University of Denver.

Living at 8,700 feet in the Rocky Mountains of Colorado, Erika can almost touch the airplanes she used to fly. She shares her house on the hill with her family, friends, three dogs, rabbits, horses, guinea pigs and any other strays she finds along the way.

She always has a spare room for guests so just bring some good stories and a smile.

More information about Erika can be found at her website: www.achickinthecockpit.com

A Chick in the Cockpit
Discussion Questions

1. Could this story have happened fifty years ago? What is your view on feminism and how has it changed through each of your own life phases?

2. Is the title, *A Chick in the Cockpit*, sexist or offensive to you? Why? Can you separate your own beliefs from what society has taught you?

3. There are certain industries that simply cannot be conducive to raising children/having family life. What other careers take parents away from home and what solutions are there to an absent parent?

4. Are you afraid to fly? Why or why not? What is your worst/best aviation experience?

5. Have you ever wanted to be a pilot? If you didn't follow through, what held you back?

6. Have your views or thoughts on aviation changed after reading this story?

7. Do you use checklists at work, at home, anywhere in your life?

8. Have you ever experienced sexual harassment or discrimination? How is it different from the last generation?

9. Erika uses an example of swearing in the cockpit to "talk like a man." Do women swear more now to fit into the man's world? Are we desensitized to it?

10. Erika loses one of her mentors and several friends in aviation accidents, but because of her mentor, she continues training. Have you ever had a mentor? How have mentors changed your life and why aren't there more?

11. Have women changed to blend into corporate America or has corporate America changed to allow women in? Do women lead or still just strive to blend in?

12. In *A Chick in the Cockpit,* Erika mentions being adopted and her belief that core character is set at birth. How does your character affect life choices and do you believe it is set at birth? How do life choices affect character and vice versa?

13. Like most of us, Erika had to spend some time working terrible jobs. What's the worst job you've had and what did you learn from it?

14. Erika never considers that her new female boss would ban her from the cockpit for being a woman. Have you ever been discriminated against based on gender by someone of the same gender?

15. How well do you think you know the opposite sex, and how did you gather that knowledge?

16. How have the roles of men and women changed during the last fifty years and is it a natural change or does it feel forced? Who or what is forcing it?

17. Why is there more divorce in our society now than the last generation? Are couples/families more or less "happy" that the last generation? What do you attribute that to?

18. Did Erika fit your image of an abused woman? Have you or someone you know been involved in a domestic abuse situation? Give examples of abuse, besides obvious physical damage. What would you have done differently to get out?

19. Faced with the probability of divorce while approaching the end of her childbearing years, Erika conceived a child on purpose. Do you agree or disagree with this choice?

20. Do you know your local laws on domestic abuse and what actions warrant arrest?

21. What can we do, as a culture, to strengthen marriage and curb abuse?

22. What past influences are shaping Erika's actions in the story?

23. What gives you serenity and can you find it even though you are alone? Are you only happy when in a relationship? What does our society teach us about happiness?

24. Now that an entire generation has lived through the post Gloria Steinem era, are we better or worse off now as an individual, a family, a child, an employee, a nation. How much of that status is based on the changing roles of women? How can we do better?

25. If you are in a book club, why? Would you have been willing to help Erika like the Book Club Warriors were willing to help her?

26. Has our society created a collaborative environment for women to work together, or compete against each other, and how does that affect our society as a whole?

27. Were there any moments where you agreed or disagreed with Erika's choices? What would you have done differently?

28. What would you do for your children?

29. Did your opinion of the book change as you read it? How did you experience the book?